DEATH AND BURIAL IN
MEDIEVAL ENGLAND

DEATH AND BURIAL IN MEDIEVAL ENGLAND

1066–1550

Christopher Daniell

London and New York

To my parents, David and Dorothy, and my brother
Andy – who all live life to the full.

First published 1997
by Routledge
11 New Fetter Lane, London EC4P 4EE

Simultaneously published in the USA and Canada
by Routledge
29 West 35th Street, New York, NY 10001

First published in paperback 1998

Transferred to Digital Printing 2003

Routledge is an imprint of the Taylor & Francis Group

© 1997 Christopher Daniell

Phototypeset in Baskerville by Intype London Ltd
Printed in Great Britain by Biddles Short Run Books, King's Lynn

British Library Cataloguing in Publication Data
A catalogue record for this book is available from the British Library ·

Library of Congress Cataloguing in Publication Data
Daniell, Christopher.
Death and burial in medieval England, 1066–1550/Christopher Daniell
p. cm.
Includes bibliographical references and index.
1. Funeral rites and ceremonies–England. 2. Human remains
(Archaeology)–England. 3. England–Social life and
customs–1066–1485. 4. England–Antiquities. I. Title.
GT3243.D36 1996
393'.0942'0902–dc20
96–7552

ISBN 0–415–11629–5 (hbk)
ISBN 0–415–18550–5 (pbk)

CONTENTS

PLATES

PREFACE

This book developed out of the need for a general work about death and burial in England within the Middle Ages. (The Middle Ages are defined in this work as 1066–1550.) There are excellent studies on individual aspects – religious beliefs, cemeteries, literature – but they often have little correspondence with other areas of study. Death and burial are, uniquely, not only interdisciplinary, but also applicable and relevant to the entire medieval population. Whilst it is true that the best documentary records survive for the richest and most powerful; the ordinary, undocumented people are discovered in archaeological excavations. It is through interdisciplinary study that new strands become evident, especially when archaeological discoveries are supported by explanatory historical texts.

As well as a description of the processes involved, a theoretical framework is here suggested. This is based on the idea that beliefs in the afterlife are the predominant force in the rituals connected with death and burial. As beliefs change, so do the practices. This is, of course, contentious. Even in well-documented periods, the aspects which are religiously inspired, and those which are socially important, are often difficult to disentangle. A funeral procession with torches and pall-bearers may be a social statement of the deceased's power to some; and to others a way of helping the soul through Purgatory. Similarly it can be difficult to determine the impact of different themes upon death and burial rituals, whether the teaching of the Church, urbanisation, or pre-Christian beliefs.

The uniqueness of the Middle Ages is that for the first time historical, archaeological and literary sources are all abundant, although the ratio of importance changes during the course of the 500 years. At the beginning of the period, in the eleventh century, most information comes from archaeological excavations, although excellent accounts of individual burials and funerals are given by some chroniclers. (William of Malmesbury has been predominantly used in this work, though Gerald of Wales and Reginald of Durham are two of many other chroniclers who could have been cited.) The chroniclers were, however, a small group of men, whereas the archaeologically excavated bodies run into thousands of men, women and children. By the end of the Middle Ages the ratio is reversed. By the mid-thirteenth century the distinctive archaeological practices of charcoal burials and pillow stones had been abandoned, and burials were almost entirely uniform in appearance. Skeletons still give important evidence about disease, but reveal less about funerals, burial practices and beliefs. Whereas archaeology decreases in importance, historical documents detailing funerals rapidly increase. Surviving wills are the most numerous historical source for individual beliefs and practices concerning death and burial. Tens of thousands of wills survive from the fifteenth and sixteenth centuries, which give the viewpoint and beliefs of individual people or communities. For the first time a large-scale view of individual piety and beliefs can be analysed. For 500 years we have a combination of excellent historical, archaeological and literary evidence for the religious views of the time. This combination allows theories to be tested in a way undreamt of for earlier periods.

Three themes have not been explored in detail. First is the continental development of death and burial practices. There is excellent material from individual countries, especially France and Italy (Ariès 1974, 1987; Volvelle 1976, 1983; Banker 1988; Strocchia 1992), but examples show that local customs could be very different to English practice: cadaver tombs, very popular in the rest of Europe, were rare in England. Similarly, charcoal burials were an essentially English method of burial. The second theme is anthropology. Third is monumental brass and tomb development. These have been excellently researched and written up (Coales 1987; Colvin 1991; Binski 1996), and any assessment would have expanded the book beyond its means.

Finally, it is my great pleasure to express my gratitude to all those people who have helped in the making of this book. Thanks are due to Richard Briggs, Jef Maytom and Dominic Tweddle for their patience while work was in progress, and to the numerous readers of chapters: Don Brothwell, Clive Burgess, David Crouch, David J. F. Crouch, Vanessa Harding, Charles Kightly, Terry and Sonia O'Connor, Philip Rahtz, Ann Rycraft, Danae Tankard, Victoria Thompson and Lorna Watts. I am especially indebted to my father, David Daniell, who lovingly read and commented in detail on every chapter, and to Dorothy and Andy, my mother and brother, and Marilyn Campbell for all their constant help and support.

Chris Daniell
York Archaeological Trust

1

DEATH IN THE MIDDLE AGES

The key to medieval religion is the fate of the individual's soul
after death. Death was defined as the moment when the immortal
soul left the mortal body and joined with an incorruptible, sexless,
immortal body, often depicted in art as a small naked person.
The soul itself could never die and its 'life' was 'independent of
the body'. During the soul's time on earth it was bonded to the
mortal body. The soul was unaffected by any bodily illness or
abnormality, and even if the disease led to death the 'soul suffers
no harm' (Hitchcock 1921: 116, 110). The body, however, could
be at the mercy of the soul. Corruption of the soul could result
in physical disease: leprosy was thought to be an indication of
sexual sin (see Appendix 1) and the fifteenth-century priest John
Mirk quoted St Augustine – 'corruption of sin maketh mankind
to turn into corruption of carrion' (Erbe 1905: 225). If the soul
deviated into sin there was also a real danger that it would suffer
the torments of Hell for eternity. The Church therefore had to
correct sins by confession, repentance and penance – the latter
achieved by using the three most effective ways: devout praying,
alms-giving and mass-singing (Erbe 1905: 269). In the worst cases
of heresy or witchcraft burning was used to help save the individual (fire was a cleansing agent for souls) and stop the infection
spreading to other souls. Medieval people could help their souls
in a large number of ways: from spiritual prayers to the physical
actions of pilgrimage or alms-giving.
  The time on earth was transitory and infinitesimal compared
to the life of the soul after death, but the eternal fate of the soul
was determined by its actions whilst in a mortal body. To save the
soul from sin the Church consistently reminded people about
sin, death and the eternal afterlife by encouraging meditation

1

upon death. An important objective was to instill a sense of fear and humility (see Wenzel below), which in turn would lead to repentance. Sermons, literature, stained glass, wall-paintings and devotional texts all deliberately depicted aspects of death, especially the graphic tortures of saints and martyrs. Ill people were encouraged to meditate on their impending death, and scenes of martyrdom and St Michael weighing souls were often painted on hospital walls: examples of hospital wall-paintings showing disembowelling, Becket's martyrdom and St Michael weighing souls survive in a former medieval hospital at The Commandery, Worcester. Plagues were also a regular feature of medieval life after 1350, and the presence of the body in the home, and the funeral processions and services, meant that living with death was a common experience for all.

Meditations on death also led to literary genres (see Chapter 3), and artwork of skulls, skeletons and corpses. On a cadaver tomb a rotting corpse was depicted under a perfect body (see Chapter 7); small paintings or jewellery could be carried around as *memento mori*. Humility – the opposite to the first of the deadly sins, Pride – was an important objective of meditation. With this humility came an awareness of the transitory nature of life:

> Let us therefore keep in mind how brief time is, how certain death, and how unstable our friends, and let us always be prepared . . . for man is taken from our midst like a shadow when it fades . . . Since thus death is common to all, it is said that one and the same captivity will come to all.
>
> (Wenzel 1989: 99)

A funeral was an especially appropriate time to remind the living of the transitory nature of life. Mirk started his burial sermon 'Good men, as yee all see, here is a mirror to us all: a corpse brought to the church' (Erbe 1905: 294), and it was a popular theme for sermons that people should visit tombs and graveyards (Woolf 1968: 88).

Religion, and ultimately the fate of one's soul, influenced all aspects of life, both public and private. In the public sphere were the church services and the great church festivals – Easter, Christmas and the feast of Corpus Christi – for which everyone understood the symbolism and the importance. Instruction came from the open air sermons or guild plays (see Chapter 3) or the iconography of stained glass, sculpture and wall-paintings. These symbols were not confined to the public areas. Houses could have just as many religious objects as churches, and on occasions a licence was granted for a private chapel or altar within the home. In 1439 John Prye and his wife Alice were given a licence to celebrate 'divine service in his presence in any suitable place within their house in the parish of Colbroke' (Dunstan 1966: 146). The furnishings were also often covered with religious symbolism, the romantic and legendary images of knights and heroes side by side with the romantic and legendary depictions of saints, or their symbols, the Holy Trinity and the Virgin Mary. Few furnishings have survived, but the religious nature of many is shown by the household inventories of the time. The inventory of Lord Darcy's goods, compiled in 1520, included hangings showing scenes from the 'Life of St George' and one hanging of King David. In the 1541 inventory for Monttisfort, which belonged to Lord Sandys, there were hangings of King David and Solomon in the great chamber and the adjacent rooms (Howard 1987: 115). Further down the social scale, hangings were also popular. In 1463, John Baret left in his long will 'the stained cloth of the Coronation of our lady' (Tymms 1850: 23). In York there were examples of painted cloths: two common themes were the Seven Works of Mercy and the Last Judgement, one of which was described as 'hanging over a bed' (pers. comm. C. Kightly). Agas Herte of Bury, in 1522, also had numerous religious depictions around her house, both as alabaster objects, such as 'a Saint John's head of alabaster with Saint Peter and Saint Thomas and the figure of Christ' and 'stained cloths' of St Katherine and the Crucifix (Tymms 1850: 115–16). These may have been free-standing, or hung on the wall (St John Hope 1890, pers. comm. C. Kightly). Such images could be locally produced, but also could be valuable and traded widely. The Household Book of Henry VIII recorded that five pieces of Arras cloth showing the passion of Christ, wrought in silver and gold were given to Harman Hullesman who was a merchant with the Hanseatic League (Collier 1857: 136).

Sometimes a house specialised in a particular saint particularly if a person had been named after the saint or a chantry had been dedicated. In the chantry house at Nettlecomb, which belonged to the Trevelyan family, St John the Baptist figured prominently (Collier 1857: 124–8). In the 'chief chamber' was 'a painted cloth of Saint John' (beside a 'cloth of King Henry'), in the closet was a St John's head (probably painted), and the third picture of St John was in the inner chamber.

Many devotional texts were read in the home, for example the very popular lives of the saints called *The Golden Legend.* The best known were the Books of Hours. Thousands of copies survive, and it is a standard item within inventories. To the medieval mind an 'Hour' was a part of the day set aside for religious devotion. The most formal 'Hours' were the monastic Divine Office, or Canonical Hours, which gave a rigid framework to the monastic day. There were seven services: the night hours of Matins and Lauds (usually taken together), followed at three-hourly intervals by Prime at daybreak, Tierce, Sext and None and then the evening services of Vespers and Compline. Originally used in a monastic setting, the Divine Office became an increasingly important part of lay piety. In the transformation from monastic to lay use the emphasis changed from Christ to the Virgin Mary and the 'Little Office of Our Lady' formed the heart of the Books of Hours. The majority of the office was the recitation of psalms, but other contents included a calendar of feasts and saints' days, as well as sections of biblical texts, prayers and the Office of the Dead, which, like the rest of the 'Hours' would have been read daily. This inclusion of the Office of the Dead once again emphasised that the individual must be prepared for death by being conscious of his or her own sin, which would lead to a state of grace after suitable confession, repentance and penance (Littlehales 1895, Harthan 1978: 11–18, Bossy 1991: 140–1).

In exceptionally pious cases, instead of private reading only, the entire household might follow a daily round of prayers. Cecily, the Duchess of York, virtually lived the life of a nun without going into a nunnery: it is possible that she took the vows of a Benedictine nun. She would rise at 7 and then with her chaplain say the Matins of the day and then Matins of Our Lady, followed by a Mass in her chamber. Then she 'eats something, then to chapel for divine service and two low masses, then dinner and reads holy matter: the Golden Legend, St Katherine of Sienna, Revelations of St Bridget ...'. In the late afternoon and evening she

> prays until first peal of evensong, then drinks wine or ale at her pleasure. Chaplain says with her both evensongs;

Lady Day = New Year (25 mar) / Michaelmas = mid year

after the last peal goes to chapel and hears evensong by note; thence to supper, and recites reading as heard at dinner. After supper – with gentlewomen, one hour before bed, a cup of wine, then into private closet, and takes leave of God for all night, making end of her prayers for that day; and by eight o'clock she is in bed.

(Myers 1969: no. 498)

The numerous Christian festivals which marked the turning of the year affected the workings of the household. The most obvious were Christmas and Easter. Two other festivals – Lady Day (25 March, the feast of the Annunciation) and Michaelmas (29 September, the feast of St Michael the Archangel) – divided the year in half and were often used as dates on which to pay rents or to repay loans. Lady Day was also the start of the new calendar year, rather than the present 1 January. Throughout the year, the festivals ushered in seasonal observances which affected everyone. In the forty days of Lent no meat was to be eaten nor marriages take place: marriages were also banned during the four weeks of Advent.

Religion therefore permeated society at all times and at every level. At its heart was the Mass. This was the ultimate proof that Christ had died and that souls could be saved by His sacrifice. The seven services of the Divine Office formed a structure for the monastic day, but it was the Mass which was the most significant service. The reason for its importance was that Christ was spiritually and bodily present within the bread and wine during the Mass. Parts of the Mass changed seasonally, but the central core, called the canon of the Mass, remained more or less constant. A priest was expected to say Mass once a day, except on Good Friday when no Mass was said because of the Agony of the Crucifixion. Two Masses could be said on Easter Day and for special occasions such as marriages or funerals. The only day in the year on which three Masses could be said was Christmas Day.

Within a single church many Masses could be celebrated during the day by different priests. The Masses varied in time and number, and to differentiate between them they had different names. The Morrow Mass was usually held at daylight or very early in the morning, such as 4, 5 or 6 o'clock, and was popular with travellers. The High Mass was usually around 9 or 10 o'clock in the morning. There could also be other Masses said, for example, the Requiem Mass for the Dead. Masses often followed one another. At Lichfield Cathedral the first morning Mass was said at 5 o'clock. Others then followed immediately upon one another every hour until the sung High Mass at 10 o'clock, after which the last Mass of the day was held (Gasquet 1907: 140). Generally, the number increased over time. In 1306, Beverley Minster recorded that it held twenty-five Masses each week and recited the Psalter ten times each month (Leach 1898: 165). The number of Masses rose with the introduction and increasing popularity of chantries. In the Statutes of the Chantry at Sibthorpe parish church, dated 4 February 1342–3, Thomas de Sibthorpe specified that after Matins each day there should be a Mass, followed by psalms, which in turn were to be followed by another Mass (Thompson 1966: 258). Including the obligatory Mass said by the parish priest, at least three Masses a day would have been said in the church – almost the number said at Beverley Minster forty-three years earlier. At Lichfield in the fifteenth century six Masses were said per day: forty-two Masses a week (Gasquet 1907: 141). The increase in the number and types of Masses was mocked by Reformers in the sixteenth century: Erasmus wrote of the 'Mass of the crown of thorns, of the three nails, the Mass of the foreskin of Christ, Masses for those who travel by land and sea, for barren women, for persons sick of . . . fevers' (Every 1978: 108).

This inflation of Masses could reach enormous proportions, and it was a sign of honour to have as many Masses said as possible immediately after death. William Courtney, Archbishop of Canterbury, who died in 1396, requested 15,000 Masses (Dahmus 1966: 229) and Henry VII requested 10,000 Masses to be said for his soul (Colvin 1991: 174). At the extreme, Bokeland in 1436 requested that after his 'wretched body' was buried in the Pardon Churchyard of St Paul's in London, one million masses might be said for his soul, though as this number is so exceptional it is possible it is a scribal error (Furnivall 1882: 104). Several hundred or thousand Masses for an individual soul were, however, by no means uncommon for the richest in society.

The Mass lay at the core of Medieval religion, and in the late fourteenth century *The Lay Folk's Mass Book* described the Mass as the 'worthiest thing, most of goodness in all this world' (Simmons 1879: 2). At the heart of the Mass was the idea of 'transubstantiation' – a mystical process which turned the bread

6

and wine into the literal and physical body and blood of Christ, without changing their appearance. This change occurred during the prayer of consecration. The priest had his back to the congregation and said the prayer in a very low voice. Any noise from the congregation stopped and the church became quiet and still. What was happening had deep theological importance and was the supreme act of worship. At that moment bread and wine did not change their appearance, they physically became the body and blood of Christ.

The prayer of consecration was said as the priest held the bread aloft, which was known as the elevation of the host (Rubin 1992: 57). ('Host' comes from the Latin word *hostia* meaning 'victim'.) This was followed by the elevation of the chalice containing wine, although by this stage the change of wine into blood had already taken place (Rubin 1992: 54–7). As well as being the most important action theologically, the elevation was also the most visually impressive part of the Mass for the congregation and was thought to benefit those who saw it. In 1375 Bishop Brinton of Exeter taught that after seeing God's body no need for food would be felt, oaths would be forgiven, eyesight would not fade, sudden death would not strike one, nor would one age, and one would be protected at every step by angels (Rubin 1992: 63). Many people left immediately after the elevation and it became good luck to race around the churches to see as many elevations as possible. Given this power of the holy on earth it is not surprising that artistically the elevation is often depicted as shafts of heavenly light coming down to earth, or Christ being physically present in the hands of the priest, instead of the host.

There were of course doubters who found it hard to believe that this real physical change happened, and there were many stories relating how the doubters were converted by real body parts or blood appearing on the altar. One of the most famous stories, which first appeared in Northumbria between 704 and 714 in the earliest account of Pope Gregory the Great's life, was very well known throughout medieval England. A woman, who had baked the bread used for the Mass, had doubted that it had really become the body of Christ, whereupon Gregory showed the woman the bread which had turned into a bleeding finger (Colgrave 1985b: 107, Rubin 1992: 116–29, 135–9).

The parishioners were encouraged to attend important

7

Where did this ritual start?

services, but a congregation was an extra, for the priest performed the Mass every day and might well have done so to an
empty church. The only time when the parishioners were
expected to take communion was at Easter. The congregation
normally only took the host, and not the wine, and the power of
the sacred vessels was so great that they could only touch them
with their hands covered.

At every Mass Christ was sacrificed, and the Mass came to be
seen as a distinct sacrifice in itself. Christ, who had received a
human body, literally gave His body and blood back to people in
Holy Communion. In this way Christ, as the head of the Church,
remained ever present amongst the faithful. Daily, in every one
of the tens of thousands of churches in medieval Christendom,
Christ was literally thought to be sacrificed again on earth.
Christ's own sacrifice and death, as well as the afterlife, were
reinforced at every Mass. Christ's death was therefore, at the
heart of the medieval religious experience (Plate 1).

The religious symbolism of Christ's sacrifice was also emphasised by the depiction of the Passion on the rood-screen that
physically separated the chancel from the nave. On the screen
was a painting or sculpture of Christ's crucifixion. (The word
'rood' is Old English for 'cross'). When the host was elevated by
the priest, the congregation's sight would not only be on the
host, but also drawn towards the Cross on the rood-screen at
the most important part of the Mass.

The Mass was the most important of the daily services, but
once a year at Easter the nature and intensity of the Mass reached
its peak. The heart of the Easter celebrations was Christ's death,
and His return from death at the Resurrection, events which
were acted out in church (see Chapter 3). By His Resurrection
He proved not only the afterlife, but also that death could be
conquered and sins could be forgiven. The Easter message is that
physical death is not final, but a stage in the journey of the soul.

The Easter preparations and ceremonies were elaborate and
detailed and lasted from Maundy Thursday to Easter Sunday
(Duffy 1992: 28–32). On Maundy Thursday the priest would con-
secrate three hosts, one for his communion at that Mass, one for
his communion at Good Friday and one for the celebrations
centred on the Easter Sepulchre. Then the altars were stripped
bare, water and wine poured on to them and they were washed
with a broom made of twigs. Christ's humiliation was thus re-

enacted: the stripping of the altar was the stripping of Christ, the water and wine were the blood and water from Christ's side, and the broom twig represented the scourge used on Christ.

The following day, Good Friday, was one of deep mourning and the Passion (Christ's crucifixion) was read from St John's Gospel. The priest took his communion using the host from the previous day. As part of the liturgy a covered cross was brought into the church and then uncovered in three stages. This was then venerated by the priest and people who often 'creeped' towards it in bare feet to kiss it. The 'burial' of the third host and the cross then took place within the Easter Sepulchre to signify the burial of Christ. Christ's tomb, symbolised by the Easter Sepulchre, was the centre of the ceremonies between Good Friday and Easter Sunday. Candles continuously burned around it and a watch was kept until Easter morning. On Easter morning the clergy gathered and processed into the church and censed the Easter Sepulchre. The host was removed and placed in its normal position above the altar. The Cross was venerated and 'raised', and then processed around the church, while the bells were rung and the choir sang 'Christus Resurgans'.

> Christ, rising from the dead, dieth now no more. Death hath no more dominion over him. For in that he liveth, he liveth unto God. Now let the Jews declare how the soldiers who guarded the sepulchre lost the king when the stone was placed, wherefore they kept not the rock of righteousness. Let them either produce him buried, or adore him rising, saying with us Alleluia, Alleluia.
>
> (Duffy 1992: 30)

Once again the Cross was venerated by people 'creeping' towards it and Matins and Mass were then sung.

For the congregation there was still an active part to play, for before or after the Easter Mass was the annual communion of adults, which could only be taken after confession and penance. This was often described as 'taking one's rights' and it was only withheld for serious offences. In larger parishes extra priests were brought in. It was very exceptional, and considered exceptionally devout, for laity to take communion more than once a year – as in the case of Lady Margaret Beaufort who received communion monthly. At the communion the laity – for the only time in the year – literally ate the body of Christ. Christ had not only died and been resurrected, He was also taken into the individuals of the congregation. The veneration of the Cross and the following communion were a communal event which emphasised Christ's death and Resurrection. For the Easter ceremonies life and death were the central themes.

Even after Easter Sunday the sepulchre, now empty, was the focus of devotion with candles burning before it during services, and it was censed at Vespers each evening. If the sepulchre was wooden and movable – and most were – it was removed before Mass on the Friday of Easter week. There was also a tradition of building permanent stone sepulchres. However, the early fourteenth-century examples, such as Patrington in Humberside, were probably built as an aumbry (a secure and lockable cupboard) in which to keep the consecrated sacrament: the sepulchres which doubled as aumbries would therefore have been in use all the year round (Sekules 1986).

Christ's Resurrection was the ultimate proof of an afterlife for the soul and by the fifteenth century the afterlife was basically divided into three: Heaven, Hell and Purgatory. There were a few minor alternatives. Abraham's bosom occurred occasionally in art as it had biblical authority (Luke 16: 23) and two types of Limbo were also possible. The Limbo of the Patriarchs had been for the holy souls of the Old Testament, but was now empty as Christ had released them. The second Limbo was that for children who had not committed any personal sins but whose souls were weighed down only by original sin (Le Goff, 1984: 220–1). These areas were insignificant compared to the all-pervading dominance of the afterlife trinity of Heaven, Hell and Purgatory.

The most important aim for the soul was to arrive eventually with God in Heaven. By the fifteenth century the Last Judgement was no longer as prominent as it had been in previous centuries, and the iconography and beliefs had given way to a belief in Purgatory. Both Heaven and Hell would be for eternity, but Purgatory was for a previously undefined period which could be shortened. In the purgatorial fires and torments the sinful soul would be cleansed of its venial sins and therefore be able to reach Heaven. The alternative to Heaven was Hell, a scene which was much more open to artistic and literary licence. Hell was depicted in the most graphic terms – very similar to the pains of Purgatory – but forever. One often-quoted authority was Lazarus

10

who had spent three days in Hell before Christ had raised him back to life. The punishments given in Hell were appropriate to the crime: usurers were branded with, or boiled in, gold, and the proud were wracked on giant wheels that continually moved to show that they will 'evermore be lift up above these others' (Duffy, 1992: 340) and also possibly to show that the wheel of fortune, which had made them proud, might turn full circle so that they could become the lowest of the low.

If Heaven was the ultimate destination and Hell the ultimate horror, in the fifteenth century Purgatory dominated the theology, teaching, pastoral practice and the beliefs of ordinary people. Since its 'birth' in the twelfth century (see Chapter 7), and official recognition by the Pope in 1254, any lingering opposition to the notion of Purgatory had collapsed by 1300 (Le Goff, 1984: 289), although late in the fourteenth century opposition reappeared in England through the teachings of Wyclif and the Lollards. Whereas before the twelfth century the journey of the soul after death had been unclear, the doctrine of Purgatory gave souls a progression from life to the Last Judgement.

However, Purgatory could, and did, differ in its description between writers. English writers tended to see it as nearer to Hell whereas the Italian, Dante, portrayed it as being nearer to Heaven where souls were healed and their chains loosened. In England the terminology was much more prison-like: indeed many writers described it as a 'prison' or incarceration. Mirk described it as 'God's prison' (Erbe 1905: 269) and a fourteenth-century preachers' manual (Wenzel 1989: 412–13) retold the account of a friend praying for another in the prison of Purgatory (*carcere purgatorii*). The prison was not solitary confinement, rather group torture. Souls were tortured according to their sins. Many writers graphically portrayed the trials and purgation processes inflicted by demons upon the souls. Souls were branded, torn and spiked, thrown from fiery furnaces into ice-cold water, weighed down with rocks or had their tongues cut out.

The supposed truthfulness of these accounts was attested by visions, ghosts or journeys into Purgatory itself. The most famous entrance to Purgatory from this world was St Patrick's Purgatory in Ireland of which several accounts exist (Easting 1991). The ghosts or visions from Purgatory were fundamentally different to modern ghosts in that they were revealed to individuals, rather than being located in one place (Bossy 1985: 29). The ghosts or

ghosts from Purgatory

visions would normally visit at night and reveal to a close kin or friends that they were suffering torments in Purgatory. Normal reasons for suffering could be either because of something not yet completed (such as Masses left unsaid or wills not executed) or because of their sinful life. However, despite the number of apparition stories, it was orthodox teaching that the living could not hold direct converse with the dead (Duffy 1992: 328). Even so, the presence of ghost stories formed a powerful incentive to remember the souls in Purgatory, for a ghostly visitation to remind someone to be more prayerful was the last thing an ordinary citizen wanted. Purgatory was horrific and filled with the most horrible sights, sounds and smells which the medieval mind could imagine: but it was not Hell. Hell was forever; Purgatory was for a limited duration. By definition the souls in Purgatory were certain of their eventual salvation (Duffy, 1992: 344–5).

The belief that souls would be eventually released was a central part of medieval religion. Increasing amounts of energy, money and effort were devoted by the living to shorten the time their own souls, and those of others, spent in Purgatory. The living and the dead were therefore bonded together. Each day the priest prayed for the souls that awaited the mercy of God whilst in Purgatory, and individuals prayed for their kin and friends, or left instructions for their kin to be prayed for in their wills. It was not sentimentality that meant that testators asked for prayers to be said for their parents or kin. Those souls would be suffering torments in Purgatory.

the poor in Purgatory

To be forgotten in the pains of Purgatory was a terrible fate, and to be avoided if possible by buying prayers with money or offering gifts to individuals or the church, such as a new chalice or cope. This process inevitably meant that there were a large number of the poor and socially insignificant who, because they could not pay, would be forgotten and so would suffer in Purgatory without any relief. Fortunately the Church devised methods to help these souls. At every Mass general prayers for souls were said and a third of the consecrated host was dedicated to souls in Purgatory. A special day, All Souls Day, was also reserved on 2 November of each year, when a Requiem Mass was held for all souls in Purgatory.

Whilst it was thought that these general prayers helped many souls, of much greater benefit were the prayers for individuals.

Prayers for specific souls were thought to be the most effective way of lessening their agony. It therefore became very important that a soul should be remembered. For the richest of society, daily Masses were said by chantry priests, whilst others were remembered yearly on the anniversary of the death or burial.

The concentration upon the soul and the anniversary of death or burial meant that remembrance of the dead became a key element in the celebrations of a church. The prayers for the dead gave a structure to the Christian year, whether by the death of Christ, saints, or worthy individuals. As anniversaries were celebrated it was immaterial in which year the person died, and it is very rare for the actual year of death – or even century – to be recorded in the obit rolls of prayers for the dead. (The word 'obit' comes from the Latin *obitus* meaning 'death', or 'the day of death'.) The whole of the Christian era was celebrated in a single year. This mystic time-scale meant that anniversaries of donors to the church were fitted into the major Christian festivals, resulting in a seamless progression of prayers. The remembrance and anniversaries of the dead therefore became a pattern in their own right, forming a framework not only for the year, but also for God's plan for earth, which incorporated all of history and the future.

An alternative to prayers in one place only were reciprocal prayers or obits, which were popular in some groups of monasteries or religious institutions. At the time of an important death, such as that of a prior or abbot, a monk or messenger would journey around the specified monastic houses with a request for prayers for the soul. These journeys could be extensive: 139 monasteries were visited after the death of Thomas Hatfield, Bishop of Durham, in 1381; 292 monasteries after Walter Skirlaw's death in 1416; and 407 monasteries for the Prior of Durham also in 1416. It is unfortunate that only in a few instances can the route be determined for short distances (Raine 1856), unlike the famous French example of the nameless traveller who carried news of the death of Count Wifred and requests for prayers. His travels in southern France in 1051 to over one hundred monasteries can be mapped in detail (Southern 1954: 21–2). Sometimes two individual places had a reciprocal agreement, such as Barnwell Priory and Colchester Priory (Rubin 1987: 186). Hospitals too sometimes prayed for each other's dead, and the hospital of St John, Cambridge, prayed for its own members and for the dead of other religious houses, notably the dead of the hospital at Ely (Rubin 1987: 186). These services were normally for the religious, but occasionally such services could take place for important laity. In 1539 Thomas Boyes wrote to Lord Lisle about a reciprocal service for the Holy Roman Empress which took place in London:

> And on the viii day of June the goodliest solemnity is done for the Empress at [St] Paul's by the King's commandment, and so in every church in all London, that ever was seen. All Paul's was hanged about with black cloth with the arms of the Emperor and also of the Empress. And there was also made in the said church of Paul's a goodly rich hearse, garnished about with arms appertaining to the Empire. It is voiced here to be as rich a thing and as honourably done as ever was seen. My Lord Chancellor [re]presented there the King's person, the Duke of Norfolk and the Duke of Suffolk, with ix earls, were mourners, and there was x bishops with their mitres. The Bishop of London sang the mass: there was no preaching, but the bells ringing through all the parish church from Saturday at noon until Sunday at night.
>
> (Byrne, 1981, Letter 1445)

Other religious institutions also offered up prayers for their founders or benefactors. Monasteries and friaries responded by prayers for patronage, and theirs were the prayers of the ordained or holy, living a pure and righteous life. At the other extreme, hospitals could offer up the prayers of the poor, humble, afflicted and grateful.

Alternative systems were developed at parish level to pray for the individual soul in Purgatory. A common method, but potentially a very expensive one, was the foundation of a chantry. A chantry was literally a Mass recited at an altar for the soul of the founder, although prayers for family members could be included. Within this definition there was a wide range of possibilities. The cheapest was a Mass at an established altar by an existing priest. Further options became progressively more expensive as the amount of construction work and numbers of chantry priests increased. At the lower end of the scale was a new altar for one or more priests within the church, and more expensive was a new chantry chapel (which was a building attached to the parish church for one or more chantry priests) (Plate 2). The most expensive option was to found a 'college of priests', where special accommodation was built for the priests, who would then pray for the founder's soul in their chantries. The founder also had to endow the chantry and its priests with the necessary items needed for the Mass: vestments, chalice, paten, altar clothes and candles.

The chantry was often started in the founder's lifetime, but it was more important for his soul after death. The lifespan of the chantry could range from a few years to 'perpetually', or until the money ran out. Short-term chantries could be endowed with money, but for longer-term chantries lands, rents, tenements or other possessions were given. The revenue from these assets would pay for the priest and any helpers he may have had to sing Masses for the founder. In at least one case detailed accounts between 1453 and 1460 have survived for the house in Bridport of two chantry priests. The everyday expenses included the buying of furniture, a scythe for cutting the weeds in the orchard, and the penny paid for mending the wheel-barrow (Wood-Legh 1956: xxii).

The fundamental responsibility of the chantry and its priest(s) was to offer up an unceasing round of Masses and prayers for the founder. Most often the chantries were staffed by only one or two priests, but in some areas so many chantry priests were together that a college was founded. One such college, St William's College, York, was built in 1465–7 in the shadow of York Minster for the chantry priests of the Minster. As well as new foundations, colleges could be imposed upon existing churches, as at Howden and Hemingbrough in the East Riding of Yorkshire. Parish churches too could have a college of priests attached, as at St Michael, Paternoster Royal. The college was founded in 1410 by the famous Lord Mayor of London, Richard Whittington and was served by five priests.

There were various levels at which memory and prayer operated. The most specific tended to be family-related. Chantries, set up for prayers for the individual, also accommodated family members and ancestors. The living (or 'quick') were linked to their ancestors and could actively help them by prayers and good works. The foundation of a chantry was meant to provide an unceasing round of prayers and Masses for the founder.

There was, however, some confusion between chantry Masses

for the dead and the daily High Mass which mentioned the dead as part of the liturgy. There was a theological difficulty as well, for a single Mass was thought to be of infinite value for all, so technically one Mass for a single soul was no more beneficial than one Mass for one thousand souls. In practice, however, the Mass was thought of as a unit of merit, which increased as the number of Masses increased (Tanner 1984: 105). One attempt to explain the difference between the benefits of a daily Mass and a Mass for one soul was written in a fourteenth-century preacher's manual.

> Sometimes the question is raised whether one Mass is more useful to the dead than another, since every Mass is for the dead, but not every Mass is 'of the dead'. The first is the case, because when the Host is broken into three parts, one part symbolises our thanksgiving for the saints, the second part for those living on earth, and the third part our sacrificial gift for the souls afflicted in purgatory . . . [However] only that Mass is 'of the dead' in which throughout all its parts mention is made of the dead, as, for instance, in the introit, when we say 'Give them eternal rest, O lord,' and so forth; and similarly in the readings of the Epistle and the Gospel. But as they say, the offering of the blessed Body of Christ is of equal value for all, and yet the particular intention a priest has when he offers the Eucharist up to God may bring greater benefit to one person than to another. From this it is clear that when a priest promises someone to celebrate a Mass for the soul of a friend, he does not make good his promise unless he does all that belongs to a Mass established for this purpose. If, however, he simply promises to say a Mass for someone's soul, the promise can be fulfilled by whatever Mass he says.
>
> (Wenzel 1989: 411–13)

It is therefore clear that there was a practical distinction between the general Mass, and a Mass in which a person was specifically named, a position summed up by the 'so-called' Council of Lambeth in 1281: 'Let no man think that one mass said with pure intention for a thousand men might be considered equal to a thousand masses [for one man] also said with pure intention' (Powicke and Cheney 1964: 895–6, Menache 1990: 91).

16

If the expense of a chantry was beyond a person's means, then the alternative was to have a yearly 'anniversary' service, which could be funded by endowments of property, rent or possessions. One such use of property was consented to by the Bishop of Hereford, who agreed that Canon David ap Jake should rebuild five shops attached to his house so that the extra rent could be devoted to the obit services for Blanche, Duchess of Lancaster (Capes 1916: 17). On a more personal level the prebendary of St Stephens in Beverley Minster gave a property in Beverley to the vicars 'for maintenance of an anniversary on his Obit, with service and mass for the dead with music' and that if the vicars should default the punishment would be 'suspension and excommunication by the Chapter' (Leach 1898: 369–71). These anniversary services could be as large, or larger, than the original burial obsequies:

> Bartholomew the archdeacon, for his obit of a common simple mass. There were present Colles, Suetesham, Druell, Stevenys, Lywer, Morton, Brownyng, Odelond and Marton. Also 18 vicars. Also 18 annuellars [chantry priests]. Also 10 secondaries. Also 14 choristers. Also servants of the Exchequer $8^{1}/_{2}$d. Also to 4 poor men, 4d. Also to the sacristers for a peal, 4d. Total 6s 7d.
>
> (Myers 1969: no. 457).

The anniversary also acted as a communal statement of memory, both of the person's soul, and also of the power and social standing of the living relatives.

The communal remembrance of the soul, as opposed to the individual remembrance by the chantry priest, was reinforced by the use of the bederoll. The bederoll was a list of names of souls to pray for which was read out in church. The reading was therefore a deliberately public occasion and formed a dual purpose: not only were prayers given up for the souls of those named, but the reading also acted as an encouragement to the living to try and get on the bederoll themselves. It could also be seen that the bederoll was socially cohesive, binding past generations into the present, though, by constant reminders, it could also have caused friction amongst people with grudges to bear.

There were two main types of bederoll, the general and the particular. The general included all Christian people including the 'spiritualitie' (pope, bishop, parish priests) and the 'temporal-

17

itie' (king, queen, royal family, lords). The second type named individuals who had 'honoured the church with light, lamp, vestment, or bell, or any ornaments . . .'. Who was included in practice could vary from place to place. In the fourteenth-century poem 'St Erkenwald' many of the poor seem to have been included:

> Yet plenty of poor people are put in graves here
> Whose memory is immortally marked in our death-lists
> (Stone 1977: 34)

By the fifteenth century new names could be added for a price. Such a record has survived in the Salisbury accounts for the year 1499–1500 when Robert Southe, Gent, paid 40s. for himself, his wife, and their fathers and mothers to be put on the bederoll so that Christian people would pray for their souls every Sunday. In the same year Stephyn Walwyn and his wife Kateryne gave a vestment of crimson velvet to the priest in exchange for placing their names on the bederoll. In the accounts for 1500–1 the stark statement appears under the names registered for the bederoll 'Nothing, because no-one desired it this year'. Curiously, 40s. was paid 'for registration' of Robert Southe and his wife again in 1510–11 (there is a gap in the accounts between 1501 and 1510) under the heading 'Names placed in the Bederoll this year'. This implies a 'registration' fee of some sort (after ten years) but it is not clear what this was.

For each reading of the bederoll the priest was often paid extra. At St Mary at Hill, London (Littlehales 1905), the parish priest was given 16d. for a year's 'rehearsing' the bederoll of the founders of the chantries in the church yearly between 1490–1 and 1492–3. (The records are ambiguous as to whether there was a separate bederoll for the church, as opposed to the chantries.) The payment was raised to 2s. in 1494–5 and continued at that rate until 1529–30 when it was raised to 2s. 4d. and continued at that rate until the Reformation. In Ashburton (Hanham 1970) the rates for reading the bederoll rose steadily until the 1530s, from 8d. in 1482–3, to 2s. 8d. (1509–10), to 3s. 4d. in 1511–12 (which included an anniversary reading of names), but in 1534–5 only 4d. was paid for reading the bederoll – which might be payment for a single reading. What these amounts are based on is unclear: they are probably based on the number of times read and the length of the roll. The bederoll was also likely to be rewritten. In 1492–3 the bederoll, and other documents, of St Mary at Hill, London, were rewritten by a scrivener for 3s. 4d., but in 1497–8 the bederoll was written out by the parish priest for 2s. and two years later (1499–1500) it was written out again, this time for 4d. The rewriting of the roll allowed great flexibility in adding or deleting names and meant that the roll could be kept to a manageable size. The parish priest usually recited the bederoll at specific occasions, although sometimes it might also be read by a clerk or sexton.

A shortened bederoll, sometimes known as the Dominical Roll, was normally read on Sundays and particular holy days or anniversaries. In the early sixteenth century the parish priest was paid 12d. at St Edmund and St Thomas in Salisbury for reading the bederoll on Christmas day, and the same amount at Michaelmas. (Gasquet 1907: 61) A further amount of 12d. was paid to him for reading the bederoll, possibly for the whole year. The bederoll was read in public and usually from the pulpit. In 1509–10 at Ashburton in Devon 2s. 8d. was paid to the vicar for various anniversaries and for reading the bederoll 'of all the benefactors of the church naming them from the pulpit and praying for them' (Hanham 1970: 39).

Religious Guilds

Whereas chantries were expensive, and buying a place on the bederoll was for individuals, the religious guilds were a communal way of saying prayers for the dead (especially guild members) and ensuring a proper funeral and burial. Medieval religious guilds have been described as 'burial clubs', and whilst they occasionally had other benefits, such as sickness or poverty payments, their principal reason for existence was to offer up prayers and attend the funeral of departed members. The Guild of St George in Norwich met annually on the feast day of St George to hear evensong and Mass and to offer up a candle, and returned the following day to hear a Requiem Mass. 'When a member of the fraternity died, the organisation contributed to two candles at the funeral services and required all other members to attend and make an offering for the soul of their deceased colleague' (McRee 1992). In a study of more than 500 chantry and guild returns from 1389 the core activities mentioned most often were the participation of member's funerals (70 per cent), provision of altar candles (70 per cent), and participation and payment of feast day Masses (50 per cent). It was only the wealthier – and usually urban – guilds which could pay for priests to say daily

Charity, penance and pilgrimage

Masses for guild members, processions and guild liveries (McRee 1992). In Cambridgeshire at the same date, of sixty guilds thirty-nine undertook some service for their dead (65 per cent) and attendance was compulsory in twenty-one guilds (35 per cent). The commemorative rites ranged from the funeral (thirty-two guilds, or 53 per cent), to commemoration services at another time, often the guild's saint's day (thirty-four, 57 per cent) (Bainbridge 1994: 192–3).

All these methods and institutions – Masses, prayers, chantries, obits, colleges, guilds and hospitals – had the aim of a continual flow of prayers upwards to Heaven to help souls in Purgatory. The amount of money and physical and spiritual effort that was expended upon the souls in Purgatory was an indication of the power and the acceptance of the idea.

Despite this continual stream of prayers it was still prudent to prepare for the afterlife whilst living and there were many actions that one could take before the moment of death. Services and prayers were an obvious way of helping one's own soul, and the souls of others, after death. Physical actions also helped, and included charitable giving, offerings to the priest and to the church, penance and pilgrimage.

The key to charitable giving was the seven Corporal Works of Mercy which added burial to the six other works mentioned by Christ (Matthew 25: 34–9): feeding the hungry, giving drink to the thirsty, clothing the naked, receiving the stranger, visiting the sick and helping those in prison. In a study of fifteenth-century wills from York, these works of mercy played a significant role in about a quarter of wills. Even so the giving during life may have been much higher as 'deathbed charity was considered to be of very little value' (Cullum and Goldberg 1993).

The least mentioned of the seven works within wills was burial of other people. One rare example was that of James Lounesdale, who in 1495 provided for 'poor maid's dowries and those without means that they might be buried'. Normally the only mention of burial in a will is of the testator's own body. Occasional references in other sources reveal payments for the burial of the dead. Royal accounts record several instances of such payments, although whether they were technically works of mercy was suspect as many were members of the Royal Family. Edward I often made grants towards the funeral expenses of those close to him, ranging from minor members of his household to his cousin Edmund of

20

Cornwall (Prestwich 1985). Henry VII paid £3 1s. 2d. for the burial of Owen Tudor, who was then a monk at Westminster Abbey, and the third son of Owen Tudor and Queen Katherine, and a further 6d. for the bells. The burial costs of Henry VII's youngest son, Lord Edmund, came to £242 11s. 8d. The costs of Lord Stanley and the Earl of Warwick – who were both beheaded for treason – may have been charitable, or alternatively a mark of honour. More obvious charitable payments were: the 6d. paid by Henry VII 'for the burying of a man that was slain in my Lady Grey's chamber'; in 1502 Elizabeth of York paid 8 shillings to the Friary Clerk of Saint John's for the 'burying of the men that were hanged' at Wapping Mill, and in March of 1503 Elizabeth paid for the burying of Griffith, 'late yeoman of the Queen's chamber' (Nicolas 1972: 181–2, 14, 97). The Works of Mercy were treated as actions that one could perform during the normal course of living. The opposite of this was the deliberate dislocation of life by a pilgrimage to a famous shrine. By the very act of the journey the pilgrim was forced to abandon normal relatively stable experiences of home and became a transitory figure. The nature of the journey was in itself part of the pilgrimage, as was the symbolism of one's life on earth when compared to the journey of the soul.

Pilgrimage was an important method of gaining the help of a saint whilst on earth for the ensuing time in Purgatory. The power of saints and shrines was very well known, and around the shrines would hang the evidence of the miracles wrought, often in the form of wax models. In the St William window of York Minster there are several depictions of the shrine with wax models of the previously afflicted arms, legs and feet hung up around it. This was the case with all shrines and John Paston was one of many well-to-do persons who sent wax models to Our Lady of Walsingham in the fifteenth century (Sumption 1975: 157). At Hereford in the thirteenth century the shrine of Thomas Cantilupe had round it at least 170 silver ships and about 2,000 images in wax or metal of various parts of the human body (Clanchy 1985: 7). A hoard of such votive offerings was discovered at Exeter Cathedral in 1943 and included wax arms, legs and one whole body of a person (Orme 1986: 58). The offerings could range from the expected to the bizarre. Edward I presented a wax image of one of his gerfalcons when it was ill to the shrine of Saint Thomas Becket (Prestwich 1985: 124); a wax anchor was given by some sailors to the St Edmund shrine in Norwich

Cathedral; Henry of Maldon presented his real tapeworm to St Thomas Becket after he had been cured (Sumption 1975: 157); and in the Exeter hoard were the heads and hooves of horses.

These offerings accumulated in every shrine, and between 1535 and 1538 the commissioners for the Dissolution of the monasteries constantly refer to the models and offerings (Sumption 1975: 157). In some cases a dispute could erupt when an expected item was not given after a miracle, as in the case of the archdeacon who insisted on taking the cherry-stone – which had been miraculously removed from his nostril by St Thomas of Canterbury – home with him, much to the dismay of the guardian of the shrine (Sumption 1975: 157).

Pilgrimage remained popular in the fifteenth century even though the journeys were often shorter and less adventurous than in earlier centuries. The pilgrims in Chaucer's *Canterbury Tales* were making their way to Canterbury, whereas in the twelfth or thirteenth century they could equally have gone to St James's shrine at Santiago de Compostela. Medieval authors were well aware that not all pilgrims went on pilgrimages purely for the sake of their souls; many went for the social life. The French authoress Christine de Pisan wrote 'Neither should she use pilgrimages as an excuse to get away from town in order to go somewhere to play about or kick up her heels in some merry company. This is merely sin and wickedness . . . "Pilgrimages" like that are not worthy of the name . . .' (Lawson 1985: 152–4).

By the fifteenth century the nature of pilgrimages had changed. Paying a professional pilgrim to go on a journey became more popular and professional pilgrims were not uncommon. Groups of pilgrims also formed fraternities; one at Worcester was originally for pilgrims who had journeyed to Santiago de Compostela (Lubin 1990: 28). A further development was the pilgrimage for those who could not, or would not, physically travel from home to go to Rome for the Roman Jubilee of 1423. A guide was written, probably at Oxford, which allowed a pilgrim to make the pilgrimage in his or her own home. Ten 'Our Fathers' a day represented ten leagues of the journey, and when the person had notionally arrived at Rome they could distribute alms in their local church which would have been made at Rome. 'And it is my belief that by doing all this he will gain as much or more than he would have done by going physically to Rome' (Sumption 1975: 301).

A further method of lessening the time in Purgatory was that of buying or acquiring indulgences or 'pardons'. These became a common and powerful way not only of reinforcing the terrible pain and torments of Purgatory, but also of frightening people into buying indulgences and so acquiring money for the church. The normal length of time stated on a pardon was forty days. Other lengths of time could also be given, for example, the memorial brass of Roger Legh (who died in 1506) in Macclesfield Church urges prayers for his soul, and the return for 'saying 5 Paternosters and 5 Aves and a Creed is 26,000 years and 26 days pardon' (Colvin 1991: 255). Full remission of sins could be given for a particularly spectacular event, such as at the various Jubilees at Rome, or the displaying of a powerful relic. To be effective the pardon had to be received by a Christian who had truly confessed, repented, and been absolved of sin – in other words was in a state of grace. Indulgences could be given for a variety of reasons, such as 'praying for the soul of Maud Talbot late prioress of Polsloe' in 1439 (Dunstan 1966: 146) or praying for the souls of the three husbands of Constance Coffyn and her parents as she had newly built the aisle of St Thomas the Martyr in Tavistock Church (Dunstan 1966: 347). An early example of this trend was the forty days' indulgence for those who 'say at least a Lord's Prayer and Salutation of the Blessed Virgin' for the soul of Edward I who died in 1307 (Leach 1898: 249). As well as prayers for the dead, other actions could gain one an indulgence: forty days' indulgence was granted in April 1448 to 'contributors to the repair and upkeep of the new bridge called Hatherlegh Brigg' (Dunstan 1967: 1), and in February 1367 an indulgence was granted to all those who took part in the processions, every Wednesday and Friday, for the King, Prince and the army (Wood 1956).

Pardons could be bought from travelling sellers of pardons, or 'pardoners', who normally preached emotively before selling. In the thirteenth century the hospital of St Mary Rounceval, and in particular Brother Lupus, was so notorious that it became a medieval by-word for corruptly selling pardons. All hospitals used such financial expedients, but the 'activities of the Charing hospital in this field earned its immortality in the creation of Chaucer's archetypal pardoner' (Rosser 1989: 311). John Kirkby, the Bishop of Carlisle, like many other bishops, attempted to regulate the trade to prevent 'getting money from the simple'. He desired to prevent feigned pardoners from taking money from the simple by their preaching ... pardoners should not be allowed to publish indulgences and seek alms unless they have papal letters which the bishop has examined and found to be authentic. He has learnt of pardoners with fabricated letters, and declares them to be void ...

(Ross 1993: 134).

There might even have been a trade in smuggled papal bulls to put on pardons or falsified documents: in 1384 an order required Robert de Rellington and William Carter to make a search for illegal gold and papal bulls entering into the country through Scarborough (Calendar of Patent Rolls 1384, page 494). Not surprisingly the pardons were a prime target for the sixteenth-century reformers. Although abuse of the system did occur, many people embraced the idea of pardons, and John Baret of Bury in his will of 1463 asked for the 'pardon ... which I purchased' to be placed at his grave so that 'it may be read and know to exhort the people rather to pray for me' (Tymms 1850: 19). It was also possible to buy a pardon in Rome, and Robert Gardener wanted his priest to travel to Rome to buy a bull – so long as it could be purchased for less than £5 – which would give 300 days' pardon to those who prayed for his soul and those of his two wives (Tanner 1984: 102). The selling of pardons might have led to, or at least increased, spiritual inflation as people were encouraged to increase their payments and the number of pardons they obtained. The whole process was further enlarged from 1457 onwards when the living could acquire indulgences not only for themselves, but also for the dead (Colvin 1991: 255).

There were therefore many prescribed ways of helping the soul or the souls of ancestors, from active physical involvement, such as pilgrimage, works of charity or buying pardons, to spiritual prayers. These actions were encouraged, but there was a darker, proscribed, side to helping one's soul, which could spill over into magic or heresy to which the Church reacted violently for two reasons. The first was that both directly challenged its power and authority. Severe damage had been done to the Church in southern France by the Cathar heresy in the thirteenth century which had needed a crusade to crush it. In England in the fourteenth and fifteenth centuries the Lollards had posed a threat, albeit not so great (Lambert 1992: 243–83). The Church had crushed

24

such heresies by use of the Inquisition and burnings. Power was important, but there was a more fundamental reason: the soul. The Church believed that the individual's soul was the most important thing a person possessed, and that to condemn it to Hell – because of heretical or magical beliefs – was a failing of the Church's duty. The church therefore acted to save souls and stop such beliefs spreading, and handed people over to the secular authorities to be burnt. Cruel and heartless as the burnings and deaths seem now, they were one way that the Church could save souls and stop more being corrupted.

Heresy was normally containable because the heretical believers had a system of beliefs which were consistent and likely to raise suspicions in the local communities. Much more difficult to root out were the instances of magic. The basic difference between religion and magic was that religion was dependent upon God's action. A person could request certain actions, but it was for God to decide. Magic attempted either to force God's hand, or to bypass God and cause the action to happen anyway (Scribner 1993: 476). Magic was practised by witches and wizards. The decision, however, as to whether someone had petitioned or forced a request was a difficult one. Prayers could be offered to God or a saint not only for health and happiness, but also to recover or find property once again; St Anthony being particularly popular for recovering lost goods.

The Church was often tolerant of people on the edge who practised 'good' or 'white' magic, but was fearful and persecuting of those who practised black magic with the intention to harm. Of particular concern was any magic attacking the established hierarchy. In 1441 a case came to court over Roger Bolingbroke and Thomas Southwell, a canon of St Stephen's chapel, Westminster, who had conspired to kill the king by necromancy. Thomas was alleged to have said Masses 'in forbidden and unsuitable places' and to have used 'his craft of necromancy against faith and good belief'. It also came to light that Dame Eleanor Cobham had used sorcery and witchcraft as learnt from a witch; 'and by such medicines and drinks as the said witch made, the said Eleanor compelled the aforesaid Duke of Gloucester to love her and wed her. Wherefore, and also because of the relapse, the same witch was burnt in Smithfield [27 October]' (Myers 1969: no. 514).

The ultimate penalty for heretics and witches was to be burnt, although this punishment was rare before the Reformation. For lesser deviations from orthodoxy the Church had at its disposal excommunication (Logan 1968). There were two levels of excommunication, but at its worst it involved a complete segregation of the excommunicate from all Christian society. This included any dealing whatsoever with any other Christian. It was designed to be a terrible punishment in a society which relied on community and the Church. In such cases the excommunicate's soul was almost certainly condemned to Hell, although many theologians were careful to note that only God could decide. If the excommunicate repented, the excommunication could be rescinded.

Occasionally, orthodox beliefs and magic became intertwined, as in the case from York in 1509–10 when a group of men, which included a wizard and two priests, conjured up a spirit to advise them on where to find a chest of gold hidden in Halifax (Palliser 1979: 233). (Unfortunately it is unknown whether they found it.) Although such cases were not common, the Church was diligent in discovering every detail and correcting the perceived problem. Another grey area was that of surgery and medicine, which could be closely connected with witchcraft. Before the introduction of modern scientific techniques, the role of charms or incantations was just as important as caring for the body. The Church was concerned about the use of charms for healing and during a visitation by the Dean and Chapter of York it was discovered that 'At Handsworth John Parkyn uses incantations and at Little Driffield Agnes Marshall not only uses incantations but is an unlicensed and unqualified midwife' (Myers 1969: no. 450). It could also be difficult for the person concerned to tell whether they were dealing with God or the Devil. The 'unlearned' warlock Richard Perkin of Rotherham confessed that he used charms and prayers upon the clothes of sick people and rehearsed their names whereby a spirit appeared and told him the disease of the sick person 'and in him believed, supposing and demeaning [demying] he had been a good Angel' but after instruction knew him to be 'my ghostly enemy and a wicked spirit' (Barker 1976: no. 1539). In the 'Act for appointing Physicians and Surgeons' of 1511 an attempt was made to distance the professional surgeons from the 'witches':

> Forasmuch as the Science and Cunning of Physic and Surgery (to the perfect knowledge whereof be requisite both

great Learning and ripe experience) is daily within this Realm exercised by a great Multitude of ignorant persons ... that common Artificers, as Smiths, Weavers, and Women, boldly and accustomably take upon them great Cures, and things of great difficulty, in which they partly use Sorcery and Witchcraft ... to the high Displeasure of God, great Infamy to the Faculty, and the grievous Hurt, Damage and Destruction of many of the King's liege people ...

(Frith 1990: 5)

This division was especially difficult to distinguish, for the surgeons had for centuries past used a combination of physical skills and quasi-religious ideas. In 1376 John of Arderne in his *Treatise of Fistula in Ano* had, citing the most authoritative sources of the time, linked surgery and astronomy. He stated that the 'twelve signs of the Zodiac rule the twelve parts of the human body' such as Aries, which governs the head with its contents. When the moon is in Aries 'beware of operating upon the head or face and do not open one of the head veins' (Myers 1969: no. 697).

God was not powerless in the healing process, not the world in general, and He could influence events by the use of miracles. The normal course of events was shown by nature, but as God had created nature He could equally change it if it was deemed that a miracle was needed. It was therefore through miracles that God's plan could be discerned. It was hoped, by recording miracles, that the will of God would become explicable (Sumption 1975: 66). This led to the slightly contradictory position by which the Church was rooting out witchcraft, especially concerning the devil, whilst religious works, such as *The Golden Legend*, revealed that even demons were part of God's plan:

God does miracles by his own authority, angels because they are superior to matter, demons through natural forces inherent in things, magicians through secret contracts with demons, good Christians by justice publicly recognised, bad Christians by such justice simulated.

(Ryan 1993a: 303)

Miracles were one part of God's scheme of creation and the universe. It was a scheme which was carefully mapped out by the medieval theologians and had a direct impact on the expectations of the soul in the afterlife.

Within this structure was the earth. The difference in thought between a medieval person and a modern one was pointed out by C. S. Lewis (Lewis 1964: 98–100). He described a modern person looking out to the night sky as seeing a vast black emptiness with impossibly distant stars. Medieval people looking out to the stars understood the universe in a very different way. They knew that the reaches of space were vast. One estimate was that from the centre of the earth to the seventh heaven ('the vault of the heaven of Saturn') it would take 7,700 days to walk, walking each of the 365 days 40 miles, each mile being 2,000 paces (Ryan 1993a: 293). But even so the earth was contained in a structure and Lewis likened it to the earth being a tiny speck of dust floating in a cathedral.

Furthermore, the earth was not suspended in a black nothingness. Even though out of sight, the earth was in fact in the middle of a vast battleground between the forces of good and evil. The earth, sky and heavens were filled with these forces. The different elements of these forces are too numerous to mention, but the most righteous powerful were the Holy Trinity, the Blessed Virgin Mary and the nine orders of angels (seraphim, cherubim, thrones, dominations, virtues, powers, principalities, archangels and finally angels). Mary was particularly powerful: not only was she Queen of Heaven and Lady of All the World, but also Empress of Hell, which gave her power over all the fiends and devils (Erbe 1905: 297). On the other side were demons and the Devil himself. Each side was engaged in an eternal battle until the Last Judgement striving for individual souls. It was rare that mankind should actually see anyone of these forces in reality, although it was common for saints to see an angel or demon at some point in their lives. The most famous visitation by angelic forces to ordinary humans were the biblical examples of the Archangel Gabriel appearing to Mary at the Annunciation, and the angelic host proclaiming the news of Christ's birth to the watching shepherds.

Man was therefore caught between the forces of evil below in Hell and the forces of good in Heaven. The earth and the skies above were a battle ground, where angels and devils fought for each individual soul. Almost every element of the ecclesiastical ritual and teachings focused, either directly or indirectly, on the soul. A wide variety of ways were used both to save the soul from the clutches of the ever-present demons waiting to tempt it into sin or drag it to Hell, and to limit its time in Purgatory. The combination of spiritual prayers and physical actions was a powerful force against devils, but individuals had to be constantly vigilant and conform with the Church's views. If the right outcome was achieved, a perfect world and the perfect love of God awaited the soul. The cost of righteousness during the soul's brief and transitory time on earth was well worth paying for eternal future bliss.

2

FROM DEATH-BED TO REMEMBRANCE

The death-bed scenes and burial of the body followed definite procedures, though these changed over time and some parts are much better understood and documented than others. Ultimately the liturgy and procedures concerning Christian death and burial were derived from late Roman practice (P. Brown 1981) and were then further developed in France by the Frankish kings between 750 and 850 (Paxton 1990). The monastic movement of the eleventh and twelfth centuries then spread a more standardised burial liturgy across Europe. Following Rowell's account, the liturgy of the Cluniac order can be described in detail (Rowell 1977: 64–5). When a monk felt the moment of death approaching, he would summon the abbot or prior to hear his confession and to receive extreme unction. The dying monk was brought into the presence of the whole chapter to confess publicly his sins, whereupon he would be absolved. He was then taken back to bed where he received extreme unction. This was given by the priest for that week, who came to the bedside in procession with servers, holy water, cross, candles, and the rest of the community. Whilst the dying man received communion, psalms were recited, after which the staff of the infirmary watched over him and a cross and lighted candles were placed at the head of the bed. At the moment of death the man was laid on sack-cloth and ashes, the ashes being in the shape of a cross (pers. comm. D. Crouch) and signifying penitence. The cloister door was beaten to assemble the community to the bedside and then the creed, litanies and prayers were recited. At the time of death the prior commended the departing soul with prayers. This procedure also was followed by other monastic communities besides the Cluniacs. When Archbishop Anselm was on the 'point of death, . . . he was lifted from his bed onto sackcloth and ashes' (Southern 1979: 143).

After death the Cluniac community went to the Lady Chapel and sang Vespers for the dead followed by Matins, followed by the collect *Omnipotens sempiterne Deus.* Bells were then rung, and a second cross, holy water, lights and incense were carried to the body. The body was washed and then clothed in a hair-shirt and hooded habit, and placed on a bier by those of equal standing in the community. The hands of the dead person were joined across the breast, presumably as if in prayer. Between the preparation of the body and the burial the body lay in the church on a bier and there was a continual recitation of psalmody until burial, only interrupted by the offices and the Mass. The night was divided into three watches, assigned to the two sides of the choir. The next morning Mass was offered for the dead, and the deacon censed the body after the censing of the altar. When Mass ended, the body was carried to a place of burial whilst the community in procession chanted psalms. At the grave the body was censed by the priest and sprinkled with holy water. It was then buried and earth was cast upon it. The procession returned after the burial to the tolling of bells (Rowell 1977: 64–5).

If the person was particularly holy, balsam might be applied to the face. The preparation of Anselm's corpse illustrates that the anointing could be a vehicle for a miracle. Initially it was decided just to cover Anselm's face so that it should 'be saved from corruption' but this was extended to Anselm's right hand – because he had written so many good and heavenly things – but in the end there was so much that Anselm's entire body was covered two or three times over (Southern 1979: 143–5). If persons were accorded burial in their clothes, such as high-ranking churchmen, royalty, or, at least in one case, a pilgrim, then they were dressed and taken into the chapel.

Evidence for burial practice within monastic communities is substantial, which contrasts sharply with the paucity of documentary evidence for lay burial practices in the eleventh, twelfth and thirteenth centuries. Some evidence has survived that the more holy and penitent laity did at least lie down on sack-cloth and ashes. Durandus stated, 'some penitents, and dying men, put on sackcloth and lay themselves down on ashes', which he ties into the biblical quotations of sprinkling ashes on the blessed and penitent (Neale and Webb 1843: 180). At the time of death St

Louis of France was also laid onto sack-cloth and ashes (Shaw 1984: 394). In Germany, Caesarius of Heisterbach recounts many deaths where sack-cloth was commonly used, but without the accompanying ashes. One feature mentioned by Caesarius many times was the beating of 'the board of the dead', which presumably equated with the cloister door being beaten (Scott and Bland 1929: 240). At some point, probably during the late twelfth and thirteenth century, the customs began to change and the use of sack-cloth and ashes was abandoned.

Normally the immediate signs of a person's death could be distinguished, either through infirmity or illness, before death occurred. This allowed time for the necessary preparations to take place. A sudden death was feared. Two popular beliefs to prevent sudden death on a particular day included looking at St Christopher (hence the saint was often painted on the wall opposite the church door so a person could see him whilst walking past) and seeing the raised host, which resulted in people running from church to church to see as many elevations as possible. These precautions afforded protection only on the day that they were seen.

The dying person was responsible for leaving both the material and spiritual estates in good order by the writing of a will. In the case of the Vicars Choral in York wills were normally written a week to ten days before death occurred (Harrison 1952: 308), whereas 50 per cent of fifteenth-century Norfolk testators made their wills between three months and two years before death (Maddern 1995: 162), and noble family members often wrote their wills years in advance (Rosenthal 1972: 23). In many artistic depictions of the death-bed scene the will is being written as the person lies dying: this may have been common in practice for there was only 'a narrow gap' (unfortunately undefined) between the writing of wills and the granting of probate from Bury St Edmund's (Dinn 1995: 154). The will and testament allowed the deceased to gain spiritual benefits for the soul and control the distribution of funds to family and friends. The will, however, can be a deceptively difficult document to evaluate. It is often silent about many aspects of the person's life, including long-term religious provision for the soul, for example already established chantries or alms-houses. One finding is that wills from Bristol were only 'used for the detailed prescription of funerary services and little else' (Burgess 1987b: 858). This view seems to be contradicted by an analysis of wills from Bury St Edmunds in 1304 where only 18 per cent (235) made any mention of the funeral at all. The largest percentage of wills mentioning funerals were those of secular priests (seventy testators, of which thirty-three – or 47 per cent – mentioned funerals). This high percentage may be a combination of the increasing amount of detail in wills over time and because of the lack of children to arrange a funeral (Dinn 1995: 153). Funeral arrangements only occurred in a minority of wills from Bury St Edmunds, which probably indicates that the ceremonies were so well known that they did not need to be specified, or that arrangements were made orally. However, it has been suggested that the primary function of a will may have been to pass on property (Burgess 1987b: 858). The will itself was not given much spiritual efficacy, but acted as a sign of the testator's willingness to pass on property and goods, and sever links with the material world. Through wills younger generations were provided for and the family inheritance maintained (Maddern 1995), although the will also kept alive the memory of the testator's soul.

The alternatives to a written will were for the dying person to give a nuncupative, or verbal, will or to die intestate. In such cases the disposal of the deceased's money rested largely on trust. Honesty, however, was not universal and occasionally fraud was discovered concerning wills. A common fraud was when executors kept back money destined elsewhere. At Lyminge, between 1292 and 1294, Thomas Carlisle, the son and executor of his father's will, was reported to have kept back money supposedly destined for the hospital of St Thomas at Canterbury, and the hospital of poor priests (Woodruff 1917: 160). Similarly a brother and sister were charged with keeping 8d. left in a will which was meant for the chapel of Well (Woodruff 1918: 74).

The dying were well aware of the temptation of executors to keep the money or not fulfil their duties. In the description of St Patrick's purgatory one of the groups of people punished were the executors who for a 'long time . . . they delay and not fulfil death's will' (Easting 1991: 92). In the fifteenth century, William Ormesheade, an Alderman of York, included in his will a section about the executors:

> And this I pray, that if the said executors shall be negligent [in selling property and praying for souls] then they shall

answer to me . . . before the most high Judge, and shall fall under the penalty of excommunication which is appointed by Holy Church, and put forth against those who impede the last will of the deceased.

(Cook 1918: 15)

In extreme cases testaments were sometimes forged: in 1383 William Clopton organised the writing of a false will two weeks after the deceased had died so that he could acquire the manor of Newland in Essex (Leadman and Baldwin 1918: 73). This act weighed so heavily on one of the participants that he eventually confessed and the case was brought before the King's Council.

When death approached, it was the duty of the family, doctor or friends to call the priest, who would come with the sacrament whatever time of day or night. Normally if the sickness was not urgent the priest would be informed and he would say Mass in the parish church. It was extremely rare for a Mass to be said in the house of the sick person, although in the case of monks or nuns the Mass was sometimes said in the 'house' to which they belonged. If the case was so urgent that there was no time for a Mass the reserved sacrament, which had been consecrated at a previous Mass, could be taken to the sick. After Mass the priest would then carry the consecrated host in solemn procession through the streets to the sick person's house. At this point the consecrated Eucharist was exposed to the natural elements and rules were laid down about its transportation through the streets. In 1200 the Council of Westminster ordered that when carried to the sick the Eucharist was to be carried in 'a clean and decent pyx . . . with a clean cloth over it, with a lamp and cross preceding it' (Rubin 1992: 78). The pyx was a small closable box, often made of ivory or precious metal, for carrying the host. Many parish churches, for example Willesden in Middlesex, had a pyx specifically for the journey to the sick (Rubin 1992: 80). Archbishop Pecham laid out the rules for the visitation of the sick. The parish priest was to be vested in surplice and stole, and accompanied by another priest, or at least by a clerk. The priest was to carry the Blessed Sacrament covered by a veil in both hands before his breast, and was to be preceded by a server carrying a lit lantern. The server rang a handbell to give notice to the people that 'the King of Glory under the veil of bread' was being borne through their midst, in order that they might kneel or otherwise adore him (Gasquet 1907: 203–4). Margery Kempe described how the Sacrament was taken to the dying in King's Lynn 'with light [*lyte*] and reverence, the people kneeling on their knees' (Meech and Allen 1961: 172). An alternative to the lamp might be lit candles, for in 1364–5 John Belle, the chaplain at Alne, was accused of carrying the Eucharist through the parish to sick people without lighted candles before him (Myers 1969: no. 450).

Lyndwood, the fifteenth-century author of sermons, adds that people should be told to follow the sacrament with 'bowed heads, devotion of heart, and uplifted hands'. They were to be taught also to use a set form of prayer as the priest passed, for example: 'Hail! Light of the world, Word of the Father, true Victim, Living Flesh, true God and true Man. Hail! flesh of Christ, which has suffered for me! Oh, flesh of Christ, let Thy blood wash my soul!' (Gasquet 1907: 205–6). On the return journey, should the sacrament have been consumed, the light was to be extinguished. In this case there was no need for the people to kneel. The visitation of the sick (or lack of it) was occasionally mentioned in visitation returns. In the 1290s the chaplain at Deal was accused of not visiting the sick, and when asked 'said bad words to them' (Woodruff 1918: 85). This was a rare occurrence, however, and visitation of the sick and the last rites were seen as very important duties which were carried out conscientiously.

Sometimes a priest was not present, as at an accidental death, in which case the Church taught that a dying person could make confession to a lay-person if no priest was available. Although a lay-person did not have the power to absolve sins, it was taught that God would grant absolution by special dispensation of His grace. If death was so sudden that there had been no opportunity to confess to anyone at all, it was assumed that a person had made peace with God before death. Some leniency of thought was also shown to suicides (see Chapter 4) even if they were not mad. Some theologians still argued that if there was any sign at all that suicides had repented before death, they could still be prayed for, even if they were considered to have been damned by self-slaughter. Excommunicates could also be prayed for and reconciled by a priest if they were in danger of death. With these safe-guards and potential for leniency it was exceptional for the Church to refuse Christian burial to a baptised member.

In the vast majority of cases a priest would have been present at the death. On arrival the priest started the *Ordo Visitandi*, which began with the gesture of holding the crucifix before the dying person. This had two results. The first was to comfort the person and show that Christ hung there 'with arms extended to embrace, with head bowed to kiss the sinner, his pierced side exposing his heart of boundless love' (Duffy 1992: 314). The second result was to drive away demons which lay in wait for the soul. This was well attested, as in the case of a Franciscan friar from Shrewsbury who, as he lay dying, was surrounded by devils. They came in through the windows and doors and asked him questions he could not answer. It was only when the dying friar was given a cross that the demons rushed away (Wenzel 1989: 233).

The priest was then to ask a series of seven questions, known as the 'seven interrogations': 1) if the dying person believed in the articles of faith and the Holy Scriptures, and rejected heresy; 2) whether he recognised that he had offended God; 3) whether he was sorry for his sins; 4) whether he desired to amend, and, if God gave him more time, by His grace he would do so; 5) whether he forgave all his enemies; 6) whether he would make all satisfaction; and lastly 'Believest thou fully that Christ dyed for thee, and that thou may never be saved but by the merit of Christ's passion, and then thank ... God with thine heart as much as thou mayest?' (Peacock 1902: 69–71, Gasquet 1907: 206). The questioning was intended to be rigorous, as there was not only the belief that the Devil could take advantage of any sins or incorrect beliefs, but also that any sins unconfessed at death would be made public at the Last Judgement before the whole assembled universe (Owst 1926: 339).

After these questions, the extreme unction and the sacrament (called the *viaticum*) were given. The dying person was then thought to be in a shadow world between life and death until bodily death occurred (Dinn 1995: 153–4). The anointing of the extreme unction was considered 'health giving to both body and soul'. It also saved the corpse from being used by the Devil: Mirk described how the Devil took an unanointed corpse and rode it around a town to the astonishment of the population. Even a pious hermit was not safe – even though his soul was saved, the Devil gained power over his anointed corpse (Erbe 1905: 295). Durandus described the anointing, and the rules that applied to it: it could be administered by a single priest if others could not be found (which suggests it was normally administered by two or more); the person should be at least 18 years old; a sick person could only be anointed once a year (even if ill many times); and it must be requested and not forced upon anyone. Furthermore, there was a prescribed method of anointing – the unction should be applied to many parts of the body or limbs, especially the head where the 'five senses chiefly reside'. If the person was confirmed, the temples should be anointed, and not the forehead. A priest was treated differently, and the backs of his hands should be anointed, and not the palms ('inside'), because 'they were anointed on the inside at his ordination'. Durandus finally tackles what should happen to an anointed person who recovered, or died. If the person recovered, 'the anointed places should be washed, and the water used thrown onto the fire'; but should the man die, 'his body ought not to be washed because of the recent unction' (Neale and Webb 1843: 179–80).

The biblical justification for the last rites came from the Epistle of James, Chapter 5, 14–15 which states that the Lord shall raise the sick. This was understood to mean that the administering of extreme unction conferred the forgiveness of sins. Anointing also absolved the sins of people unable to speak or make confession. The importance of the last rites was twofold: the first was to show that the person had perfect belief in Christ and the teachings of the Church; the second was to strengthen the soul to withstand the fiends that would soon assail it.

Around the dying person there were often many people, for example the priest, family, friends and doctors, who had their roles to play, but the dying person was also expected to take an active part. At set times the person was expected to reply in a standard or formulaic way to questions or actions. It was also expected for real emotion to be shown, especially reverence and humility, which in Henry VII's case was expressed as 'many knockings and beatings of his breast' (Duffy 1992: 324). The dying person was not a spectator, but a key player. To die well was so important that manuals (called *Ars Moriendi*) were written to describe the 'craft' of a 'good' death so that it would profit the soul. These manuals were very popular and followed many of the same themes, although there could be differences of content between them.

As death approached, the manuals advised that it was 'most necessary' to have a 'special friend' to pray for the soul and to counsel the sick. The friend could also remind the dying person of the Passion, or read some of the stories of the saints, and make sure a crucifix was at least in sight. To further deter the evil spirits who were waiting to attack the weakened soul, holy water could be sprinkled on the dying person. Both the dying person and friend could help more by saying prayers, which would also assuage the physical pain. That weeping and crying were considered acceptable at death is shown by the reaction of people to Margery Kempe, for 'though they loved not her weeping or her crying in their lifetime, they desired that she should both weep and cry when they should die, and so she did' (Meech and Allen 1961: 172). Others at the death-bed might include someone to write the will – for as we saw wills were often made only shortly before death – and family members. The death-bed scene was therefore full of action by a potentially large number of people and some manuals warned against the resulting distraction of the dying person (see below). William of Malmesbury recorded that when Fulbert, the Bishop of Chartres was dying, so many people visited the house that there was scarcely enough room to hold them all (Stevenson 1991: section 285). Caesarius related how in a monastery the brothers did not go to the bedside 'in procession' but rather stood 'round the bedside in no particular order, just as they ran up' (Scott and Bland 1929: 243). By the mid-twelfth century this seems to have changed with the monks arriving at the bedside in a more orderly procession.

The *Ars Moriendi* portrayed an idealised death, but in reality each death was different in detail and circumstance, although all technically followed the same basic pattern. A few death-bed scenes were recorded in detail, especially those of monarchs or high-ranking clergy. One such was that of Cardinal Wolsey whose death-bed scenes were described by his 'gentleman-usher' George Cavendish (Lockyer 1962: 219–34). After his dramatic fall from power, Wolsey was taken ill and was given an upstairs room in Leicester Abbey which was darkened by having the windows closed, but lit by 'wax lights burning upon the cupboard'. At first Wolsey was very angry at being asked to be confessed and absolved, but he eventually agreed and his confession lasted an hour. Outside events were still crowding in on him and a large part of the description gives Wolsey's conversations with Master Knighton about money which the king sought, and heretics. (These themes could fit into the general death-bed schema of setting one's worldly affairs in order and proclaiming the orthodoxy of one's faith.) It became obvious by the failing of his tongue, and when 'his eyes were set in his head', that death drew near, and 'Then we began to put him in remembrance of Christ's passion, and sent for the abbot . . . to aneal him [administer extreme unction] . . . and [the abbot] ministered unto him all the service belonging to the same' (Lockyer 1962: 227). Also in the room were Cavendish and 'the guard' who were witnesses to the death.

Cavendish stressed the role of Christ before Wolsey's death, and the Christocentric approach was a key part of the last rites. Christ's own death was prominently displayed before the dying person in the form of the crucifix, and Christ was constantly called upon to intercede for the soon-to-be-departed soul. Not only intercession, but also Christ's presence between the soul and the judgement of God the Father or devils was prayed for. The dying also took Christ's literal body in the form of the sacrament. In the later Middle Ages the Blessed Virgin Mary and saints could also be invoked, both during the last rites and in the preamble to wills, but it was Christ who was central. This emphasis upon Christ is remarkably similar to a death-bed scene recorded in the eleventh or early twelfth century by Anselm. In his work *Admonitio Morienti* Anselm gave a list of questions and responses to be said to and for a dying monk (Migne 1853: 636–7). After stating that the monk is glad that he will die in his habit, and that he has led a bad life and wants to correct his faults, the interrogator puts forward a case where God the Father acts as a stern judge. Christ is able to save the soul by interceding and placing himself between God and the soul: the soul says 'Lord God I place [literally "throw", *objicio*] between me and your judgement the death of our Lord Jesus Christ'. Christ's saving power is also invoked for other faults, such as the soul's sins, his 'bad merits', and the Lord's anger.

At the point of death there were two conflicting views. The first was that the behaviour at the time of death was crucial to the destination of the soul. This 'Final Moment' (often so with capitals), depended upon the dying person's mental attitude as to whether the soul would be saved or damned (Wunderli and Broce 1989: 262). In a striking image the Reformer Miles Coverdale likened it to the firing of a gun in which a single lapse in concentration results in all the preparations being in vain. One mental lapse at the point of death could result in despair, raging,

Conscious death

blaspheming and swearing: ammunition enough for the Devil to seize the soul (Wunderli and Broce 1989: 266). A 'good death' – emphasised by the popular *Ars Moriendi* – accepted bodily suffering patiently and without complaint, which in turn led to salvation. The importance of the Final Moment was that it gave the hope of salvation to every Christian, irrespective of the life led up to that point. The fate of even the most sinful soul could be *vs.* saved in the last moments, although the opposite meant that it was technically possible for a life full of Christian virtue to be lost at the last moment through mental lapse. The importance laid upon the 'Final Moment' was potentially contradictory with the second popular theme: that the soul itself was fortified by all its actions during its entire life, and the prayers and actions of *Angels* those left behind. These and the last rites could help it against the Devil, though it was left to angels to protect the soul, a feature which was often incorporated in medieval tomb design (Plate 3). The angels actively fought the devils who lay in wait for the small naked soul. The soul was therefore a passive participant in the centre of a combat between angels and devils. The angels were armed 'for that by help of them good men been often secured and defended in war and in battle of body and of soul' (Trevisa 1938: 479).

Although the immediate battle after the soul had left the body was artistically easy to illustrate, in reality the precise moment of death was not always easy to determine. There were several factors which complicated this. The first was the miracle stories attributed to saints who brought people back to life after they had died: these were ultimately derived from the biblical example of Lazarus (see Chapter 3). Many can be dismissed, especially in the saints' lives, as a miracle motif, although the account of the abbot who shouted in the ear of a dead monk 'I ordered you not to die until I came' whereupon the monk revived has a more truthful ring (Scott and Bland 1929: 245). However, some cases did exist where the dead came back to life of their own accord, sometimes whilst they were lying in their coffins. Normally in such accounts the dead revive to warn the bystanders, as in a case cited by Caesarius of Heisterbach: a rich cleric had died and was placed on a bier, when he suddenly sat up and in the hearing of all said 'The just judge had judged and condemned . . . and given over the condemned into the power of the wicked' whereupon he fell back and died (Scott and Bland 1929: 278). A well-attested case was that of Henry IV, who was thought to have died and was covered by a sheet, whereupon the future Henry V took the crown which was lying by the bedside. However, this was a bit premature and Henry IV revived and demanded to know why the crown had been taken whilst he was still alive. The encounter was memorably dramatised by Shakespeare in *King Henry IV, Part 2* (IV. v. 20–90). A more dubious claim was made by a noble lady who announced she had been raised from the dead. Unfortunately her only witnesses were found to be 'mendacious sluts' (Sumption 1975: 72). Whatever the truthfulness of such accounts, it was wise to make sure the person was truly dead before burial.

There were several methods to test whether a person had died. In some cases a feather or mirror may have been used in front of the mouth or nose to determine whether a person was still breathing (also depicted in Shakespeare's *King Henry IV, Part 2*). An alternative may have been a piece of straw. One preacher's story relates how when a priest's former mistress 'wanted to touch him to see whether he was still alive, he said: "Step back, woman, and take that straw away." ' (Wenzel 1989: 657). There were visible indications of death as well, and poems, categorised as the 'Signs of Death' were 'the most popular of all Middle English death lyrics'. The 'Signs' became a commonplace in both literature and sermons and were effective 'through their grim accumulation of disagreeable detail' (Woolf 1968: 78–83):

> When the head trembles,
> And the lips grow black
> The nose sharpens,
> And the sinews stiffen,
> The breast pants,
> And breath is wanting,
> The teeth clatter,
> And the throat rattles
> The soul has left
> And the body holds nothing but a clout—
> Then will the body be thrown in a hole
> And no-one will remember your soul
> (Wenzel 1989: 719)

A sub-category of 'Signs of Death' – which were copied into medical treatises – were those which detailed tests to determine whether a person would live or die. These tests included mixing urine with milk, or putting mugwort under the head of the dying person. Although the 'Signs' were initially medically inspired, they also were powerful moral verses to remind people of death (Robbins 1970). Once death had been confirmed, the body had to be buried. The first action was to lay it out. This could have the practical advantage that people could see that the person had died, which was especially useful for political enemies. In Wolsey's case the mayor of Leicester and the brethren viewed him 'to prevent false rumours that he was not dead but still living' (Lockyer 1962: 228). It was normal practice to wash the body, although in Wolsey's case this does not seem to have happened.

After death had occurred, the family, executors and friends could proceed to the burial, although the preparations were lessened if the deceased belonged to a religious guild. Guilds have been described as 'burial clubs', but although this was important it was just one function of many (pers. comm. D. Crouch). Each guild had different procedures, but the 1389 con-stitutions of St Michael on the Hill, Lincoln, show the care taken of guild members after they had died. At the member's death the Dean was required to go to the house with four wax lights, called 'soul-candles' and fulfil the usual ceremonies. A more prominent display of guild allegiance was also dictated:

> the banner of the guild shall be brought to the house
> of the dead, and there openly shown, that men may know
> that the dead was a brother or sister of the guild; and that
> this banner shall be carried, with a great torch burning,
> from the house of the dead, before the body, to the church.
>
> (Myers 1969: no. 624)

In 1529 Margaret Pepis of Cottenham left 8d. to every guild in the town 'So that they come with their banners to bring my body to burial' (Bainbridge 1994: 196).

The body was usually kept in the place where death had occurred – normally at home. In one of the earliest surviving wills in English, dated 1434, Margaret Ashcombe, a widow from London, asked for 'two tapers to stand at my head while my body resteth in my house of dwelling...' (Furnivall 1882: 96). If the body remained in the house overnight, a wake or 'night watch' could take place. In 1395 Robert de Crosse of York requested a 'night watch' and in 1535 R. Olyver, also of York, requested that there was to be no 'revel of young folks' during the night watch. At some point the body was appropriately dressed: in some cases this may simply have meant a shroud and such shrouding was usually performed by women. In 1514 Alice Bumpsted left 2d. to each of the 'two women that shall sew my winding sheet' (Dinn 1995: 154). In a small vignette by Simon Marmion the shrouding was also performed by women. The body lay on a bed with a lit candle at the head and the shroud was sewn along the centre and would eventually cover the whole body (Litten 1991: 59). In the Bedford Hours (c.1423), the shroud has been tightly wrapped around the body. In an English example of a stained-glass burial scene from Leicester the shroud was a large piece of cloth, put over the head and then tied at the feet. In the middle of the chest was a small cross (Clarke 1962). The shroud could be a source of dispute between the dying and the living. Several medieval stories survive about such disputes. In one a wife orders the maid to take an ell and a half of linen cloth to sew her husband's shroud. When questioned by her maid that this was too small, the wife replied 'Why should we sew that much for the rot'. Her husband then joined in, referring to the shroud as his 'shirt' (camisam) saying that it was too small. His wife answered: 'Shut up fool . . . I know you have a long hard way to go, and I have done this so you won't get your shirt dirty in the mud' (Wenzel 1989: 543). In his burial sermon, John Mirk also described the shroud: 'Then has he a white sheet on him, showing that he was clean shriven and cleansed of his sins by contrition of heart and by absolution' (Erbe 1905: 294).

It was very rare for a child to be portrayed in funeral art or on monumental brasses before the early fifteenth century (Page-Phillips 1970: 9–15), and the first child shown shrouded can be dated to 1467 (Litten 1991: 61). From the very late fifteenth century until 1552 (when the Second Prayer Book of Edward VI was introduced), babies who died under one month old might be shown wearing their 'chrisom'. The chrisom was a band of linen cloth tied across the forehead of an infant after baptism to stop the chrisom oil – which consisted of olive oil and balsam, applied after immersion in the font – running down the forehead and on to the swaddling clothes. Should a child die before it was one month old, the chrisom cloth was incorporated into the funeral swaddling clothes (Litten 1991: 61).

There were two alternatives to a simple shroud, both of which

43

were applicable only for the very rich. The first was for the person to be dressed in clothes of appropriate rank: Wolsey was dressed in, and probably buried with, 'all such vestures and ornaments . . . such as mitre, crozier, ring and pall, with all other things belonging to his profession' (Lockyer 1962: 228). The second was for the body to be embalmed: the body of Jane Seymour, was 'leaded, soldered and chested' (Byrne 1981: 180). Both of these methods were rare and only occurred for the highest ranks of society.

Once shrouded or dressed, the body may have been put in a coffin or laid on a hearse. It was at this point that the attendants to Jane Seymour 'put off their rich attire, doing on their mourning habit' (Byrne 1981: 180). Presumably it was when the body was put into the shroud or coffin that other sections of society also put on their mourning clothes. If the person was wealthy enough, the coffin could have been made specially and buried with the person. In an early Tudor example, a coffin was described as being 'waxed' for Richard Hunne, a rich London merchant (Cooper 1996: 243). For the poor a simple coffin was sufficient for the funeral service, but they would probably have been buried only in a simple shroud.

The body was usually moved from the house quickly 'lest the people there should die of its stench' (Wenzel 1989: 719) and moved to the church. In the thirteenth century there was still a debate about whether certain categories of person could be carried into the church. Durandus disagreed with some authorities that the body of a woman who died in childbirth must stay outside the church for her obsequies, because 'otherwise it would be as if she died in fault'. He did agree, however, that the body of anyone who died a violent death should not be borne into the church 'lest the pavement become polluted with blood' (Neale and Webb 1843: 106). Whether normally the body would simply be stored in the church until burial or be visible to people is unclear, although it could be politically useful to show the faces of the dead in church, as noted above. Polydore Virgil recounted that after the Battle of Barnet the Earl of Warwick and his brother were 'suffered to lie in coffins the space of two days' in St Paul's Church before burial so that all men might see they were dead and so no impostors could claim to be them (Ellis 1844: 147).

The movement of the body to the church might make a procession. At the front of such a procession a bell was rung; in the thirteenth century the parishioners of Worth and at Deal were called to account because the bell was either cracked or missing (Woodruff 1918: 82, 85). There were differences in procession according to the status of the deceased. If the deceased lived in an ecclesiastical house which followed the 'Uses of Sarum', a definite formula was prescribed. The procession passed through the middle of the choir and out of the south door of the church.

> The priest . . . [and] the attendant walk in albs, the choir however in black copes; and when the procession shall arrive at the appointed place, the priest shall sprinkle the body itself with blest water; then he shall incense it. Afterwards they shall return into the church, and if it be a canon whose body is borne, it shall be carried into the choir; but if not, it shall be left in the church outside the choir [i.e. the nave], the prayer having been said.
>
> (Jones 1883: 145)

If the deceased was a member of a religious guild, members might carry torches and the guild banner in the procession, as in the case of St Michael on the Hill in Lincoln. Testators sometimes specified in wills who was to be in their processions: in 1517 the York goldsmith William Wylson requested the four orders of friars, whereas John Wirrall the fishmonger specifically requested the Grey Friars in his will of the same year. The processions to church were an outward sign of power and prestige, as well as being a powerful reminder that prayers should be said for the soul. In 1524, Thomas Howard, Duke of Norfolk, was buried at Thetford. His body was escorted from Framlingham to Thetford by a procession of knights, gentlemen and friars in the company of four hundred men in hooded gowns (Marks 1984: 255). The carrying of the body did not always take place during the day. When Stephen Scrope, second Lord of Masham died, he gave instructions that his body was to be carried to York on the River Ouse on two consecutive nights (Hughes 1988: 59). If the transportation of the body was over a long distance, the body might rest overnight in a church; the body of Sir John Paston was placed in the church of St Peter Hungate, Norwich, on its journey from London to Bromholme (Richmond 1984: 196). The processions, especially the impressive ones, were a combined symbol of the unity of the household, which onlookers could participate in, and a 'triumphant voyage of the dead man's soul' (Hughes 1988: 59) which would be helped by the torches, bells and prayers. An impressive procession also helped the surviving family emphasise their continuing influence on earth.

By the sixteenth century, rigid rules of etiquette had been devised for the processions and the clothes connected with mourning. Sumptuary laws concerning clothes in general, and mourning clothes in particular, became common in the fifteenth century. Hoods could only be worn over the face by the nearest relations to the deceased, or those carrying out ceremonial duties, such as banner or canopy bearers (Taylor 1983: 77). Ordinances were issued for Henry VII's funeral, which were repeated throughout the sixteenth century. The outward signs of mourning were very important and if the proper attire was not available a person could be excluded from the ceremony. At the funeral of Queen Jane Seymour a girl could not take part because she had no formal burial gown (Byrne 1981: 180). A person's status was shown by the amount and style of mourning dress. Arthur Lisle, who served in the households of Elizabeth of York and Henry VII, attended both funerals. For Elizabeth of York's funeral he had the correct allowance of material – 5 yards – of mourning livery as befitted an esquire or gentleman. His two servants who followed him shared 6 yards of mourning material. When Henry VII died, Arthur had probably risen to be a Squire of the Body and he had the regulation 9 yards of material, and his three servants also had 9 yards between them, for the funeral procession (Byrne 1981: 148).

The act of carrying the body into the church was often a sign of prestige, especially when a saint or important person was involved. At St Hugh's funeral in Lincoln in 1200:

> The king of England and the rest of the magnates raised the illustrious load on to their shoulders. It was no small matter of congratulation for anyone to be granted the privilege of carrying the body of one whose merits could save from destruction the souls and bodies of those who rendered him this service and secure their admission into the kingdom of Heaven.
>
> (Owen 1971: 40)

In fifteenth- and sixteenth-century York, the pall-bearers are occasionally specified in wills, and of those specified almost all were aldermen of the city. The normal number was six, with the standard payment being 8d., although John Beisby of York was more generous with a total of 6s. in 1535. In Bury St Edmunds, the normal number was four, and priests always chose other priests to carry the bier. There are several instances of god-children being requested to carry the body of a god-parent, indicating that the god-children were reciprocating their joining of the Christian Church by helping their god-parents to join the community of the dead (Dinn 1995: 154–5). An alternative was to reverse this and have several paupers carrying the coffin, presumably as a sign of humility. John Lord Neville had twenty-four paupers carrying the hearse with his coffin on (Hughes 1988: 59). For the ordinary person it is assumed that the coffined or shrouded body would have been carried by family and friends, or on a cart.

After the body was carried into church the mourners would not have seen the shrouded body, except in extreme circumstances when it was politically expedient. Normally the body was placed in the hearse which was a metal stand or 'special funeral cart' (Dinn 1995: 154) with a coffin sometimes incorporated within it. The hearse was normally part of the equipment required by a parish; it could be free of charge, as was a re-usable parish coffin. Wealthy people often had their own more elaborate hearses instead of the simple parish one. For the duration of the service the hearse would probably have stood before the high altar in the chancel. Two medieval hearses have survived. The first – a semi-circular metal stand – encloses the body of Sir Richard Beauchamp, who is buried in the Beauchamp Chapel in Warwick. The second, complete with 'pricks' for candles, surrounds the Marmion tomb at West Tanfield in North Yorkshire. The hearse was given prominence by having a pall, or hearse cloth, draped over it, and lighted candles or tapers on it. Some palls were brightly coloured or had pictures on them, and in 1504 the priest William Place asked for a 'black cloth stained with the image of death . . . to be set upon my hearse in the day of my burying' (Dinn 1995: 154): this also indicates that the hearse cloth may not have been used before the day of burial itself. The usage of hearse and pall may have varied from place to place. The Beauchamp hearse could have been easily covered by a pall, but the size and the sharpness of the candle-holders at West Tanfield probably resulted in the pall being laid over the coffin (Plate 4).

A basic hearse cloth was a standard item of parish equipment, but if individuals wanted to be especially remembered by prayers at funerals they could donate a more luxurious one. Very few examples of hearse cloths or 'palls' now survive, although the London Livery companies have eight Medieval or Tudor examples. All are made of Italian velvet brocade and embroidered with English work of *c.*1500, with a central panel of a pomegranate and foliate design. A particular example was given by Mr Husee in 1539, which was described in the contemporary Vintners' Company Ordinance Book as 'an hearse cloth of gold with the arms of the Vinters [*sic*] and the arms of the said Mr Husee'. In return for this gift the chaplain was to pray for the souls of 'Mr Husee, his friends and all the brethren and sisters of the Vintners' four times a year, for which he got 4d. (Byrne 1981: 354).

Once the body lay before the altar the Office of the Dead could take place. A manuscript from Lincoln Cathedral shows a service in progress. A priest reads from a book whilst two clerks either read or sprinkle water. The coffin is draped in a hearse cloth and the candles are lit. The hooded mourners stand at one end of the coffin, (front cover). The Office consisted of two parts. The first was on the afternoon or evening before the day of burial. This evensong of the dead was known as the *Placebo* after the opening word of the service (Psalm 116: 9). During the night there might be a vigil over the body by the priests or clergy of the church, or in wealthier cases by paupers or other mourners. Early next morning Matins and Lauds, said as one office, were sung for the departed. This was called the *Dirige* (from which the English word 'dirge' derives) as it was the first word of the first anthem of the service (*Dirige Dominus meus in conspectu tuo viam meam*). Another service, such as the Mass of the Blessed Virgin Mary, or the Mass of the Trinity, was occasionally said. After breakfast a solemn Requiem Mass was celebrated. Increasingly through the fifteenth century the offices and Mass were sung ('by note'), although it was not yet universal (Burgess 1987a: 184).

Only then was the body interred: usually three days after death (Burgess 1987b: 841). There were other possibilities. In Bury St Edmunds the body seems to be buried the day after death ('While the body was still at home, the liturgical celebrations began on the evening before burial with *Placebo*', Dinn 1995: 154), and sometimes the period was longer. Nicholas Strelley requested candles to burn around his coffin and five paupers to watch over it for seven days (Hughes 1988: 60), and it took nineteen days for Jane Seymour to be buried (Byrne 1981: 180–1). The burial of the person does not seem to have been important in comparison to the last rites or the funeral service itself. There are few exemplar stories dealing with the burial: although there are stories of bodies being exhumed, these outnumber the stories about burial itself. Burial, however, was taken seriously by the church and irregular burials were reported. In the Hereford visitation returns of 1397 several cases were mentioned of irregular practice, including the stealing (*spoilavit*) of three corpses from another parish (Bannister 1929a: 287). A case of cursing was also reported, when the vicar said 'Lie there, excommunicate, in great opprobrium', etc. to the corpse of John Boley while it was being buried. A further two cases were reported of the corpses being buried without a mass or obsequies of the dead, and one where a chaplain refused to minister to the corpse 'without just cause' (Bannister 1929b: 447, 458). Sometimes the conscientiousness of priests over burial meant that other business was delayed. At some time between 1292 and 1294, Robert, the parish priest of Bridge, was suspended from his duties for not appearing before the bishop:

> Afterwards Robert . . . came running in great haste into the hall of the lord bishop of Hereford at Wymelyngeswelde, and asked to be restored, and since he offered a legitimate excuse, namely that he had a corpse to bury, the aforesaid sentence was relaxed . . .
>
> (Woodruff 1917: 175)

At the same time at Wodechurch, Roger the chaplain failed to appear also because he 'hath a corpse awaiting burial', with another one needing to be buried the next day (Woodruff 1917: 147).

The act of burial was surprisingly little represented in English art, even though it was one of the seven corporal Acts of Mercy. (Many more depictions are found in continental manuscripts – which may result from differing survival patterns (Fiero, 1984)). One fine English depiction is from a series of painted glass roundels from Leicester, which were probably made *c.*1500. The body, fully shrouded, with the shroud tied at the legs, is being lowered into a grave which has been newly dug, and has a scattering of bones beside it. The priest carries a sprig of hyssop with which he sprinkles the body with holy water as it enters the grave, and also touches it with a processional cross. The symbolism of the hyssop comes from Psalm 51: 7 'Purge me with hyssop, and I shall be clean: wash me, and I shall be whiter than snow', and Mirk in the fifteenth century described the sprinkling as depriving the fiends of power in the grave (Erbe 1905: 295). An acolyte stands beside the priest holding open a Breviary, from which the priest reads. Behind the priest stands the benefactor who holds a lit candle and a rosary, and is hatless. (The burial roundel is the only time he appears hatless out of the five surviving roundels.) The widow is also attending and watches the body being lowered into the grave (Clarke 1962: 25). It is unfortunate that the other remarkable set of the Works of Mercy, at All Saints North Street, York, does not include a burial scene.

Books of Hours and miniatures depicting scenes of burial show that the body could be physically lowered into the grave using different methods. In the Bedford Book of Hours the body is being placed in the grave head first by a person actually standing in the grave. In a drawing by Simon Marmion the body is being lowered in using a rope around the shoulders (Litten 1991: 58–9).

At some point during the proceedings a funeral sermon may have been given. Large numbers of sermons survive: from the single sermon for a local important person, for example, John de Colpepir of Pembury, knight of the shire of Kent (Devlin 1954: xix); to large collections for kings or important religious people. The sermons were occasionally repeated in a different language, especially if different groups of mourners were involved. The sermon at the burial of Sir Hugh de Courtenay in 1341 was first given in Latin and then in French, the latter presumably for the nobility (Owst 1926: 265). Sermons for national figures were often delivered throughout the country and formed part of a collective grief: many sermons remain for Edward I (D'Avray 1994: 71–9). Some sermons were given in the presence of the body; others were given elsewhere at different times and are classed as memorial sermons. These might be preached either at different geographical locations, or a month after death (the 'month's mind'), or on the anniversary of the death (Powell and Fletcher 1981, D'Avray 1994: 12). The content could be straightforward or made more challenging by use of biblical or classical illustrations.

The bare outline of the services was standard, but there was great potential to individualise the service through sermons or the instructions left in the testator's will. Services could be personalised by the number and type of mourners, lights, bells and Masses. Different people emphasised various elements: the Earl of Warwick wanted different Masses on different days of the week, for example 'Sunday of Trinity, the Monday of the Angels, the Tuesday of St Thomas of Canterbury' (Rosenthal 1972: 27–8). A similar request was made by John Beisby in York in 1535, who also asked for seven different Masses, which included Corpus Christi on Monday, All Saints on Tuesday and the Requiem Mass on Wednesday, to be said by the Franciscans. An alternative was to request seasonal changes: the Earl of Arundel requested changes of prayer between summer and winter (Rosenthal 1972: 27–8). Popular Masses often requested at burials were those of St Gregory, which was especially beneficial to the soul, and the Five Wounds. An alternative was for the Mass which was 'loved most in life' to be said as this would 'help him most when he is dead' (Erbe 1905: 296). If a Mass was to be said or sung thirty times, (usually one a day), it was called a 'trental'. In Bury St Edmunds the standard charge for the trental of St Gregory was 10s. Trentals could also be divided, and it was not uncommon for money to be given for half trentals (that is, fifteen Masses). John Mason, a glover of York, left five shillings to the four orders of friars for half a trental each, which resulted in sixty Masses for his soul.

The more money a person had, the more impressive the funeral was, although occasionally a testator deliberately reversed this. The trend of rejecting the pomp and splendour of funerals was especially popular around the early part of the fifteenth century. One obvious influence was the beliefs of the Lollards, a contemporary heretical group (Lambert 1992: 243–83) who rejected many of the teachings and worldliness of the Catholic Church. Except in extreme circumstances it is difficult to prove a connection between Lollard belief and funeral practice. In 1415 at Much Marcle in Herefordshire, Thomas Walwayn willed that his interment 'be held without pomp, which may not profit my soul' and in 1422 Lady Peryne Clanbowe requested to be poorly buried, without great cost (Furnivall 1882: 22, 49). In York a rector of St Helen-on-the-Walls went further than most by 'forbidding my executors to prepare for my body a wooden coffin or any other covering except a sheet in which to wrap my body' (Palliser 1980: 9). Except for these deliberate reversals, funerals were normally as impressive as a person could afford.

The most noticeable of the many important elements within a funeral were the number of mourners, the sights and sounds of the lights and bells, and the generosity of the testator. The number of mourners could be increased by additional priests and the charitable payment of the poor, who in turn were expected to attend the funeral, or to pray for the soul if too infirm or ill. At the funeral some of the poor could expect to receive gowns (sometimes bearing the insignia or heraldic device of the deceased), money or charitable gifts of food or drink. In Bristol, John Bannebury requested twenty-four priests and twenty-four paupers to attend the services on the day of his burial (Burgess 1987b: 843). The poor were an important part of the funeral, as it was thought their lowly and humble status meant that their prayers for the departed were especially beneficial. Torches stood around the hearse, and were often also borne in the procession with the body to the church. William Huby, a horner in York, specifically mentioned that four torches were to be carried in his procession in his will of 1531. As with the wearing of funeral livery, the poor were also involved in carrying torches, eight being bequeathed money to bear torches at the funeral of Bartram Dawson of York in 1515, who also specified that eight torches should burn about his body on the day of his burial. Twelve pence was given for three torches by John Chambelleyne, a butcher of York, in 1516 to 'burn around my body in time of my dirige and mass'. Another specific request, this time by Robert Lee the haberdasher, was that 10lbs of wax should be split into 5lbs to burn in the church and 5lbs around the body. Torches were also distributed more widely: to the parish in general, to the 'crafts' and to individual saints, for example the unusual bequest of torches to St Sitha made in 1531 by Thomas Glasyn, a capper of York.

Bell-ringing was also an important part of the service for two reasons. The first was to pronounce that the person was dead so that people would pray for the soul. The bell also indicated the exact status of the deceased: the numbers of strokes indicating the social status. For persons of note 'half an hour or more; for poor persons only a short time. Also less for children than men or women' (Bainbridge 1994: 197, quoting Rye 1887–8). The second reason was to frighten off devils. This is spelled out in a section of *The Golden Legend* concerning the processions of 'The Greater and Lesser Litanies':

> In this procession [of the Lesser Litany] we carry the cross and ring the bells to make the devils flee in terror . . . and so the demons who are in that murky air [are] sore afraid when they hear Christ's trumpets – the bells – and catch sight of his standards – the crosses. It is said that this is the reason for ringing church bells when storms are brewing, namely, that the demons who stir up the storms should hear the trumpets of the eternal King and flee aghast, letting the storms die down.
>
> (Ryan 1993a: 287)

The bells at funerals were to drive away the devils which might be attacking the departed soul. The importance of bells was such that, in some cases, the ringers were paid more than some of the clergy carrying out the service (Burgess 1987a: 188).

The bells were one method of proclaiming the death over a wide area, and another was to pay for a bedesman or bellman. (The word 'bede' derived from the Anglo-Saxon word for prayer.) The bedeman's task was to walk around the town or area either exhorting the people to pray for the departed, or to proclaim the obit, thus praying as he walked. This might have happened at the point of death (Dinn 1995: 154) or during the burial service. In Bristol it was usual to appoint a town official (such as common beadle or town crier) as a bedesman, for which he was paid 4d. The alternative name of bellman came from the fact that many rang hand bells as they walked (Burgess 1987b: 848). Rather than walking around the town an alternative was for prayers to be said only within church: in 1514 Alice Bumpsted left money for four 'bead women' to go to church on her burial day to pray (Dinn 1995: 156).

Prayers, torches and bell-ringing were important elements but there are other aspects which are much more obscure; notably the role of plants or flowers. In the late sixteenth century (after the Reformation), mourners carried small branches of bay, rosemary or other evergreens; coffins were 'covered in black with bunches of yew and rosemary tied to the sides' and garlands could be placed on the graves of virgins (Macquoid 1966:

149–52). It is tempting to project these practices back into the Middle Ages, though very little textual evidence has been found. Occasional archaeological excavations of coffins have discovered plant remains deliberately buried within them and exceptional references do exist, as when a lily was said to have grown from a monk's grave (Ryan 1993a: 201). The lily was a symbol of the Virgin, for whom the monk had a particular devotion, and it was used as a literary device to signify that the monk was in heaven.

Grief – feigned or real – was part of the normal expression of emotion after a death: it was normally shown by weeping. William of Malmesbury describes William the Conqueror 'weeping most profusely for many days, [which] showed how keenly he felt [his daughter's] loss' (Stevenson 1991: section 273). At St Hugh's funeral the King of Scotland wept bitterly (Owen 1971: 40). When a boy fell from a church tower the spectators shed many tears and the parents grieved by wailing, tears and much noise (Raine 1879: 329). Sometimes the emotion felt was part of a desperate desire on the part of the on-lookers to elicit some response and make the dying person see the sacrament or cross. In 1538 Alice Gysbye was probably in a coma and the priest and others present 'did cry and call many times unto the said Alice to look upon the sacrament then standing by her and knocked her upon the breast...' (Wunderli and Broce 1989: 269). This action of beating someone on the breast may have been commonplace, for Henry VII also had 'many knockings and beatings of his breast' (Duffy 1992: 324). There was also a contradictory attitude to grief, as often shown in the *Ars Moriendi*. The family was instructed not to be at the bed-side because their grief would distract the dying person from the spiritual tasks; grief also implied a lack of faith in the deceased's salvation (pers. comm. D. Tankard). Grieving was not always so passionate. Edward IV was only 'right sorry' for the death of the brother of the Earl of Warwick, which may not be surprising as he had fought against him. Occasionally grief was feigned: then the corpse normally had its revenge, especially if murder was involved. The Duke of Burgundy was present at the funeral of the Duke of Orleans dressed in black, 'showing very great mourning, as it seemed'. But the spectators said that the blood of the corpse flowed out of the body, which indicated foul play, and it transpired that the Duke of Burgundy had ordered the murder (Myers 1969: no. 95).

The colour most often connected with dying was black. Black

cloth was used in the house and in church. In 1451 a wealthy testator who died ordered that the church at Somerby by Brigg be put into mourning, 'the priests array the altars and over sepulchres with black altar-cloths and the "coverlid" of black and the cloths of gold ordained thereto' (Owen 1971: 103–4). In the Stonor Papers a memorandum gave details of the hangings required for a funeral – probably that of Thomas Stonor in 1474. It recorded 'black cloth for the house'; and in Pirton Church, Berkshire, the high altar was to have black ornaments on it, with silver candlesticks, censors and basins; the rector's choir clothes were to be black and white; and around the chancel and church were to be black hangings. Presumably in the centre of the chancel or church stood the hearse with the coffin. Over the hearse and coffin was a black cloth hanging to the ground, over which was a white cloth of gold with a cross of silver and gilt standing on it. Four tapers were around the hearse, with other lights on the high altar, on other altars and about the burial place, which was probably in the church (Kingsford 1919a: 143).

Black was also the normal colour for mourning clothes. In the fourteenth century, widows during mourning wore a 'black and simple dress' (Wenzel 1989: 601). At the burial or funeral black was also the norm (Hughes 1988: 60). In 1436, Thomas Bracebrig, a rich citizen and merchant of York, bequeathed to ten poor men a gown and hood each made up of $3\frac{1}{2}$ ells of black cloth, which had a white woollen lining. White linings to dark-coloured cloaks were common and may have had symbolic significance, although no reference has been found. The cost of making these gowns lay with the executors (Cook 1916: 8). Black gowns with white linings were still popular in York in the next century, for Sir John Gilliot, an Alderman of York, who made his will in 1509 gave the thirteen 'poor folk' who held the torches a lined gown and hood (Raine 1884). Although black was the norm, other colours could be used. At the anniversary of Blanche, Duchess of Lancaster, there is a strong possibility that the gowns were blue and white – the livery colours of Lancaster (Lewis 1937). In 1513 John Shaw, a merchant of York willed, 'to a poor woman a white gown in honour of our Blessed Lady' who was to wear it at his funeral. Other York people also specified white. Rauf Pullan, a York goldsmith, who made his will in 1540, requested white gowns for three men, and three white kirtles for women; and a former

York mayor, John Shawe, in 1538, requested twelve gowns, either black or white, for twelve poor men at his funeral.

The gowns may have been kept by the poor men after the burial, although when gowns were made for the anniversary of Blanche they were reclaimed after the services, possibly for use in other years or by Lancaster's retainers (Lewis 1937: 190). Sometimes the wording is ambiguous. Sir John Gilliot of York bequeathed gowns to the thirteen poor people holding the torches, but bequeathed sixty similar gowns (hoods are not specified) later in the will. These may have included a redistribution of the thirteen, or have been additional.

Other items could be distributed to the poor. Sir John Gilliot gave sixty shirts to the bed-ridden poor in 1509. In 1429 John Northeby, a citizen and merchant of York, requested the poor be given twenty pairs of shoes and twenty cauldrons of sea-coal (Cook 1915: 17). Bracebrig similarly leaves twenty shillings for forty pairs of shoes to the poor. Gifts to women could be specified separately, as ten shillings was left for twenty pairs of shoes to poor women. Bracebrig also left fifty shillings for ten cauldrons of 'sea borne coals' to be given to the poor, which were to be distributed so that each should have one 'mett' of coals. Bracebrig left 6s. 8d. for the carriage of the coal to the houses of the poor (Cook 1916: 11–12). The bequests of shoes and coal might reflect earlier beliefs – St Cuthbert wore shoes in readiness to meet Christ (see Chapter 4), and charcoal burials are known from earlier centuries (see Chapter 7) – although more practical considerations such as keeping warm and dry were probably more important. Bracebrig also bequeaths twenty shillings to buy up fallen branches (Cook 1916: 12) which would then be given to the poor, presumably as firewood. Similar requests were also made around the country: in Bristol John Richard left pairs of shoes for twenty-four paupers, as well as bread and thirteen gowns of Welsh russet (Burgess 1987b: 840).

The giving of gowns and other gifts was part of a unified system. The attenders and benefactors of the gifts were expected to pray for the person's soul, and so the more gifts given, the larger the number of prayers. On the social side of the equation, the impressiveness of the display revealed the social standing (real or sought) of the deceased or the relatives. The mixture of religion and social symbolism meant that funerals formed a focus for social interaction. The funeral was a formal occasion, and through the processions, services and procedures the order and hierarchy of the community was both defined and reinforced. After the burial there was usually food and one or more meals for the people involved, which could also be a social statement. There appears to be little religious symbolism in the content, although the bread and ale often given to the attenders and poor at the funeral might be a reflection of the bread and wine of the Mass. Details of one such meal have survived in the Stonor Papers (Kingsford 1919a: 143–4). On the day of burial, 'at the deriges' bread and cheese were given to the poor men, and the priests and gentlemen were given lamb, veal, roasted mutton and two chickens in a dish. For the following morning's breakfast the priests and other honest men were given a calf's head and boiled (*sode*) beef. Dinner was a much more elaborate affair. The meal was divided between two groups: the poor men and the priests in one group and gentlemen and more wealthy in the other. The poor men (whether 'men' is only men or includes women as well is not specified) received 'umbils' (that is, offal) of beef, roasted veal in a dish and roasted pork. The richer people and priests had two courses. The first course was a potage of capons, mutton, geese and 'custard'. The second course included a potage of broth (*jussell*), capons, lamb, pig, veal, roasted pigeons, baked rabbits, pheasants and *gelie* (chicken?). A list of necessary spices was also included, including saffron, pepper, cloves, mace, sugar, raisins, currants, dates, ginger and almonds.

The tableware, guests and servants had to be organised. Tableware included silver spoons and salt cellars for the most worshipful gentlemen, and cups, bowls and pots. To cook the food, cauldrons, pots and rakes were needed for the cooks, as well as a 'convenient place for the Kitchen'. Servants included the bottlers, a porter and 'a man to oversee the sad [*sadde*] purveyance of the church'. The list comes under the heading 'In Pirton Church' and it appears that the meal was held at the church. To cook the food a kitchen was set up in a 'convenient place'. Unfortunately there are no costs included, but the meals were obviously designed to impress and cannot have been cheap. The money spent on food, drink and tableware for John Trevelyan's funeral in 1492 was 935d., which was almost equal to all the other funeral expenses put together (1366d.). The most expensive single payment was for the priest's oil at £4 10s. (1080d.), followed by the wax, which cost 360d. The largest food or drink expenditure was of 480d. for a pipe of wine from Alson Tyeds (Collier 1857: 96–7). Of course the wealthier the deceased, the more money was spent. In 1542, £6 3s. 6d. (1482d.) was paid to John Skerynge, a waxchandler of London, for the provision of 'wax and other stuff' at the burial of Lord Lisle (Byrne 1981: 187).

There were numerous costs connected with a funeral, and unless the testator had decided on burial 'without pomp' (which may not have been followed by the executors of the will), generally the richer the person the more expensive the funeral. For the poor, guilds or the parish church may have had a common fund from which to pay the necessary expenses. In the 1389 guild regulations of Holy Trinity in St Botolph's, Aldersgate, any brother who died that 'hath nought of his own to be buried with . . . then that he be buried of the common box' (Westlake 1919: 69). For the wealthy there were expenses throughout: those determined by the will, the fees for the priests and church officials, such as the bell-ringer who was often a clerk, and any expenses for the meal afterwards. Although the priest could not demand payment for burial, some contribution was expected. Vicars in the bishopric of Exeter in the mid-fifteenth century could expect 'one penny from all oblations made at burials in the chancel, church or churchyard' and payment for the month's mind or anniversaries: 'all the pence from the reading of obits from the pulpit . . . and at trentals and anniversaries' (Dunstan 1967: 303). When disputes arose between chapels and mother churches, burial payments often had to be resolved to lessen the loss of revenue to the mother church. One such settlement occurred between the church of Churchstow and the outlying chapel at Kingsbridge in November 1425.

> Before every burial there one penny is to be paid to the rector [of Churchstow], together with the mass-penny after the gospel and offertory, when the oblations are offered; one third part of all gifts or bequests made by reason of any burial is to be paid to the rector, the other two thirds to the chapel; no lights belonging to the chapel, either of fraternities or the new one of All Souls or any other, are to be carried at funerals without the rector's licence and prior payments to him of an indemnity of two pence.
>
> (Dunstan 1963: 144)

Decisions also had to be made about the placing and cost of the grave. In the churchwardens' accounts of St Mary at Hill in London (Littlehales 1905) preparation of the grave usually varied from 24d., for an ordinary grave in either of the two churchyards (called the 'pardon' or 'great' churchyards), to 160d. for burial within one of the better parts of the church. These were generally standard amounts, although occasionally 8d. was paid, presumably for a very poor person, or 16s. 8d. was paid by a richer person. A document of 1498–9 lists the amounts received by the clerk, which gives a rare insight into how the standard burial fees were broken down after they had been paid. From a payment of 160d. or 80d. for a grave (*pyt*) in the church, 24d. would be paid to the clerk. Out of the normal 24d. fee for a grave in either of the two churchyards, the clerk would receive 8d. for a man's (that is, adult's) grave and 4d. for a child's. This differential presumably reflected the amount of work involved in digging the grave. It is unlikely to reflect the variable importance of an adult soul against a child's soul as 2s. was the standard burial fee of both adults and children in the churchyards (Littlehales 1905: 231).

The burial fees are given in more detail in the 1522–3 accounts, where although the overall burial amounts remain the same, the clerk's proportions have risen. The most expensive burials were in the two chapels of Saint Stephen or St Katherine (160d.): the clerk's fee had risen to 40d. The church was then further subdivided into areas which varied in cost. Burials outside the choir door of the chapels 'unto the west side of the aisle going north and south' paid 10s., and the clerk received 30d. The cheapest area for burial in the church was in the nave (sometimes called the 'church body' in the accounts) 'from the cross aisle to the west end of the church' which cost 6s. 8d. for which the clerk would get 20d. (Littlehales 1905).

From the churchwardens' accounts the receipts and costs can also be analysed. For example, in 1477–9 the three most expensive burials (each costing 160d.) were all for people buried in the church. These were for Sir Thomas Wilkynson, priest, Thomas Crulle, and the son of William Prune. Puzzlingly – and maybe significantly – the fourth most expensive burial (at 40d.) was 'for the burying of a strange man in the churchyard'. This is odd, for whilst strangers would have expected burial, their costs were usually very low. Quite why this 'strange man' was accorded an expensive burial is unknown, but it may be an example of burial as part of the Acts of Mercy (see Chapter 1). A further example probably occurred in the 1487–8 accounts when Margaret Bull paid 24d. for the burial of a 'strange child' and in 1512–13 a church memorandum was recorded for collecting alms for the burials of poor people and other deeds of charity (Littlehales 1905: 284).

Part of the fees for burial included the mortuary fee, which was also called the principal, corpse-present or foredrove. The mortuary fee was technically not a fee at all, but a voluntary gift of the testator for forgotten tithes. There are few details about when the mortuary was given and presumably there was some lee-way as to whether before, during or after the funeral. The fee was normally an object and generally was the man's best animal, such as horse or cow, and the lady's best piece of cloth. The 'gift' was often a prestigious one, especially from the wealthier in society. The mortuary fee, just as any other gift or right, could be abused or challenged. After Edmund, Duke of York, died in 1402 he was buried in the friary church at Langley. He was reputedly buried without any divine service being said for his soul (which would have been most unusual) and a further complaint was made by the local parson to the prior. The parson required from the prior 'the fourth part of the duke's armour and horse which will be offered for the principal and other oblations whatsoever to be made, as the common right of the Holy Church demands, and the prior denies him, saying he shall have nothing of this' (Myers 1969: no. 437). Mortuary payment was often deeply resented. A *cause célèbre* on the eve of the Reformation occurred in 1511 when Richard Hunne, a wealthy London merchant, refused to hand over to the cleric the christening gown of his five-week-old son, who had just been buried. The case went to court but Hunne was eventually murdered in 1514 (Cooper 1996, Brigden 1991: 98–103).

Occasionally the organisation can be discovered through the accounts. For the funeral of Henry VI the expense claims of two people have survived (Myers 1969: no. 191). Hugh Brice was paid £15 3s. $6^1/_2$d. ($3642^1/_2$d.) for funeral expenses (such as wax cloth, linen and spices) as well as the 'wages and rewards' of men carrying torches in the procession from the Tower to St Paul's, and then on to Chertsey. Richard Martyn was paid a total of £18 3s. 2d. (4358d.) which was divided into two halves. The first was for 'expenses incurred within the Tower at the last departure of Henry', for soldiers watching over the body and for the barges and crew to row to Chertsey. The second part, for £8 12s. 3s., was for obsequies, Masses and charitable works. This sort of logistical organisation is not often recorded. It is likely that these men were members of the royal household of Edward IV, as the burial was a politically sensitive one. It is possible that the people who administered the funds of permanent foundations also administered the anniversaries for which the foundations were funded. Many nobles and royalty gave churches permanent endowments of property to fund services and anniversaries, and the foundations had permanent officials to administer the often large sums (Lewis 1937: 182).

At the end of the fifteenth century, there was no evidence that specialisation had occurred (although the role of the College of Heralds was increasing, see Appendix 2) and the organisers were probably members of the appropriate households. Undertakers, who organised funerals, only emerged in the seventeenth century (Gittings 1984). However, the organisation of large funerals must have been a feat of logistics with many people playing a part.

The dead were not suddenly forgotten immediately after the funeral and there could be a period of intense activity where the focus of the living was on the recently dead. One reason for this was the belief in the timing of prayers. Theologically one Mass helped all souls equally, but popular belief required that a high level of Masses should be said soon after the death, which then tailed off. People could found chantries before they died, and Thomas Love of Norwich wanted the first ten Masses of a trental said whilst he was dying. Bishop Wakeryng requested a thousand Masses to be said on the day he died and John Shouldham of Norwich wanted twelve 'annuals' of Masses (presumably equivalent to twelve years of Masses) to be said in the single year after his death (Tanner 1984: 101–2, 106). Services were often carried out on the eighth day, after a month, or on the anniversary of burial, and prayers and services were sometimes said in the intervening periods. The eighth-day remembrance could take the form of a meal or a service, and in 1535 John Shawe of York requested in his will 'a dinner on the eighth day after burial to which the Mayor and Brethren are invited'.

More common was the 'month's mind', possibly because in traditional belief the soul was still regarded as lingering in the vicinity of the body during the first thirty days after burial, a situation needing extreme caution (Gittings 1984: 162–3). Some testators requested daily bell-ringing for a month, others requested Masses or a daily *Placebo* and *Dirige* (Loades 1994: 209). Conservative testators provided for this 'trigintal' period by ordering a black cover for their coffin or grave (Cressy 1989: 104). At the end of the month it was usual to have a secondary service, dole, and funeral feast for the soul. It was not uncommon in wealthy households for the month's mind to be as grand as the original burial. The month's mind of John Trevelyan was a third more expensive than the expenses connected with burial. The original expenses, totalling 2301d., consisted only of food and direct burial expenses (priest's oil, buckram for the hearse and wax). The month's mind consisted of a wider range of items and cost in total 3166d. Food and drink were again important and included fish, wheat, chickens, pigs and bread. Brewers cost 5s. and two people were hired to help in the kitchen. There was, however, a wider range of expenses for the month's mind than the original burial (assuming that a full set of both accounts exist), and the additional expenses included the 'making of the hearse' and wax (347d.); the making of the black mourning gowns (96d.); and the expensive purchases of the black livery cloth itself (1912d.). Just to make sure John Trevelyan was recognised, a dozen 'papers with arms' (that is, coats of arms) were bought for 48d. The month's mind seems to have been visually a much more spectacular affair than the burial. Torches were also carried, and the poor people attending the ceremony were paid 204d (Collier 1857: 96–7).

A year after the death or burial an anniversary service – which could be called an anniversary, obit, yearday, earthday or earthtide – could be held (Dinn 1995: 161). In some cases 'the rich frequently benefited from more than one anniversary annually' (Burgess 1987b: 846). There could be potential problems if the death occurred on a particularly holy day (such as Easter) when it would be inappropriate, and some people asked for specific days. In 1506 John Cropley asked for his obit to be celebrated on 16 April every year (Dinn 1995: 163). The service was to be an exact repetition of the funeral with the obsequies and the Mass (though without the body or burial) (Burgess 1987a: 191). Following the funeral liturgy the *Placebo* was said on the evening before, followed by the *Dirige* and the Requiem Mass. By the early sixteenth century, it appears to have been standard to celebrate the services with music, chanting or singing (Burgess 1987b: 846–7). Many elements of the original burial service were also in evidence, such as the hearse draped in the hearse cloth, bell-ringing, bedesmen to walk round the town and lit candles around the hearse; the candles being the responsibility of the vicar to provide. Alms-giving was also important and could cost as much as half of the total expense in the wealthier cases (Burgess 1987b: 847). The scale of the anniversary could vary enormously, ranging in Bristol from a meagre 2s. to £3 (Burgess 1987a: 192) and in Bury St Edmunds from 1s. to £2 (Dinn 1995: 161).

In the more important households hundreds of pounds could be spent on each anniversary. Fortunately, a detailed set of accounts survives for the expenses of one anniversary service for Blanche, the Duchess of Lancaster in 1374 (Lewis 1937). This set of accounts is the only survivor from a service which took place annually between 1370 and 1399, when the Duke himself died. The only other expenditure given in the other years are the costs of the services, which keep steady at about £40 per year until the late 1370s and then tail off to around £10 in the 1390s. The services were all held in St Paul's Cathedral, with at least fifty-one priests and other people, as well as bell-ringers and other servants of the church. St Paul's was draped with black cloth, brought from the Duke's home in the Savoy. Twenty-four poor men dressed in the gowns of Lancastrian livery stood round the tomb holding torches. Whether the service was open to the public is unclear, though the bell-ringing would certainly have encouraged people to pray for the Duchess's soul. The payments in 1374 total £45, in four parts: the supper at the Savoy (847$\frac{1}{4}$d.); refreshments at St Paul's (423d.); the preparation of the church (4803d.); and alms and payments for the clergy and the poor (2382d.). The largest costs in the preparation of the church were for the wax and torches, and the gowns of the poor men. The cloth for these gowns was bought and made up, and then worn by the poor during the service. However, they were then reclaimed and taken back to the Savoy, as revealed by the costs of carting them back. This adds to the theory that the gowns were in the livery colours of blue and white, for after the service they could be reused, whereas black gowns would have been more difficult to reuse.

As well as individual anniversaries, the guilds and voluntary fraternities organised group anniversaries for their members, often near or on the feast day of the Saint subject to their devotion. The fraternity of Corpus Christi in St-Mary-in-the-Fields, Norwich, 'celebrated daily masses for its members, and observed an annual procession in the octaves of Corpus Christi with a collegiate mass and a dinner' (Rubin 1992: 242). The Masses for particular groups and anniversaries for individuals were part of a larger system to help the soul through Purgatory: from the death-bed, to the funeral services and then periodic remembrance. The physical death of a person was but a stage on the soul's journey, but although life on earth was transitory it made a crucial difference to the soul's ultimate destination. All the actions around the death-bed and at the funeral were attempts to help the soul reach its desired goal: Heaven.

3

THEMES OF DEATH

Unsurprisingly, many of the themes and practices of medieval funerals and burial were reflected within contemporary literature. In Malory's *Le Morte D'Arthur* there are descriptions of the funerals and burials of Queen Guinevere and Lancelot. Guinevere was 'wrapped in cered [waxed] cloth of Rennes, from the top to the toe, in thirtyfold; and after she was put in a web of lead, and then in a coffin of marble' (Malory 1995: 42). There is more description of Lancelot's death-bed scene and the funeral service. When Lancelot's companions discovered him dead:

> Then was there weeping and wringing of hands, and the greatest dole [sadness] they made that ever made men. [The next morning the bishop gave a Requiem Mass and then took the body to 'Joyous Gard' on a horse bier with one hundred torches burning about him.] . . . And there they laid his corpse in the body of the choir, and sang and read many psalters and prayers over him and about him. And ever his visage was laid open and naked, that all folks might behold him.
>
> (Malory 1995: 46–7)

In all, Lancelot's body remained unburied for thirty days: fifteen for the journey and fifteen in the church (Malory 1995: 46, 48). These literal descriptions would have been familiar to a medieval audience through personal experience.

There were, however, some predominantly textual and artistic forms which featured death and burial outside normal human experience. The earliest, and arguably the most influential, was a re-enactment of the biblical account of the Resurrection. The emphasis was upon the discovery of the empty tomb at Easter by the three Maries, which formed the introduction, or Introit, to the Easter Mass. In the tenth century St Ethelwold gave detailed instructions about its re-enactment as an 'Office' (*officium*), rather than a play or game (*ludus*). At the moment when the Maries came to the tomb:

> When therefore he who sits there [in imitation of the angel, and holding a palm] beholds the three approach him like folk lost and seeking something, let him begin in a dulcet voice of medium pitch to sing *Quem quaeritis . . . ?* [Whom do you seek . . .?] And when he has sung it to the end, let the three reply in unison, *Ieshu Nazarenum.* So he [says] *Non est hic, surrexit sicut praedixerat. Ite, nuntiate quia surrexit a mortuis* [He is not here, he is risen as he predicted. Go, tell that he has risen from death]. At the word of his bidding let those three turn to the choir and say *Alleluia! resurrexit Dominus!* [Alleluia, the Lord has risen]. This said, let the one, still sitting there and as if recalling them, say the anthem *Venite et videte locum* [Come and see the place].
>
> (Wickham 1987: 38)

The instructions continue until the tomb has been visited and the cloth in which Christ was wrapped has been shown to the congregation.

The Easter depiction at the tomb was the most popular theme for plays and over 400 versions of the Visitation of the Sepulchre still exist (Marshall 1972: 35). By the fifteenth century the re-enactment had become a standard way of celebrating Easter. Wooden Easter Sepulchres (and more rarely stone) were the main focus for the Easter story within almost every parish church (see Chapter 1). The most fundamental Christian message, that Christ had risen and so defeated death, was emphasised not only through the liturgy, but also in such physical re-enactment. Through religious drama, the invisible truths of medieval religion had been illuminated for the greater benefit of all Christian souls (Potter 1975: 8). Gradually other religious events also began to be performed from the eleventh century onwards. The Christmas story in the eleventh and twelfth centuries centred on the coming of the Magi, rather than the Nativity itself (Marshall 1972: 35), and it was Saint Francis of Assissi's innovation to introduce the crib, ox and ass. By the fifteenth and sixteenth centuries, full cycles of plays were performed by trade guilds (*mysteries*), which depicted the Creation to the Last Judgement. The 'Mystery Plays' depicted God's plan for all Creation, and every soul within. At the other end of the scale were the morality plays which concentrated on the redemption of the individual. These plays illustrated the traps the Devil set for the unwary and how, with Divine Grace, the soul might avoid them and obtain salvation.

In morality plays, Death was ever present. It was accepted that Death was the penalty paid for the original sin of Adam and Eve in the Garden of Eden. Through their sin they were cast out into a mortal, and physically and spiritually corrupting, world. Whether Death was sent by God, or the Devil, was unclear, with no universal agreement. In the fifteenth-century play *Everyman*, Death says

> Almighty God, I am here at your will,
> Your commandment to fulfil
> (Cawley 1990: 209)

whereas in the poem 'Death and Liffe' Death is called 'Dame Daughter of the Devil' (Tristram 1976: 176). The difference may be determined by the final resting place of the soul; whether Heaven or Hell. Death could arrive in different ways. One of *The Canterbury Tales*, the Pardoner's Tale, describes how three young men in Flanders unknowingly meet Death at a stile in the form of an old man, who tells them that they can find Death under a tree. They find instead a large amount of money and in their eagerness to acquire it murder each other – thereby finding death. In *Everyman*, Death is the agent by which Everyman is forced to examine his soul, and so, through the central part of the play he moves from a state of sin to a state of grace (lines 463–654). The first step to a state of grace was to feel remorse, which Everyman felt after Fellowship, Kindred and Cousin, and Goods leave him alone. Even his Good Deeds, which should have been able to help his soul, were bound by his sins. Rather than actively helping him, Good Deeds can only refer him to Knowledge, who takes Everyman to Confession. Confession accepted his contrition and said that Everyman should scourge himself as a penance in remembrance of Christ's sacrifice, which he does after praying to Christ and the Virgin Mary. In this way Everyman has made the transition into a state of grace. When Everyman eventually died, his last words matched those of Christ's:

In manus tuas, of mights most
For ever, *commendo spiritum meum*
(Cawley 1990: 233)

before his soul is taken by an angel to Jesus (Potter 1984: 135–6).

The start of the play *Everyman,* and a popular theme throughout religious literature, was the arrival of Death when least expected.

Everyman: O Death, thou comest when I had thee least in mind!
In thy power it lieth me to save;
Yet of my good will I give thee, if thou will be kind –
Yea, a thousand pound shalt thou have –
And defer this matter till another day.
Death: Everyman, it may not be, by no way
[. . .]
I give thee no respite. Come hence and not tarry
(Cawley 1990: 210)

In all the morality plays, and wherever Death featured strongly, a central theme was the need for repentance. As Death could strike at any time, repentance was not something that could be left until later.

Sermons also urged the sinner to repent. Preachers used many powerful images to contrast this life and the next. Bromyard, the Dominican preacher, related how a fat man had become fat, not – as he thought – as a sign of pomp and good favour, but to feed the worms more royally and to fan the flames of Hell. The loneliness of death was also stressed. Companionship was worthless and all that remained were good deeds and weaknesses. Bromyard compared death and the journey of the soul with a visitor leaving court: the visitor/deceased left the court/life with friends around him or her, but was then left alone on the journey (Owst 1933: 527–8). The grave itself was also used to emphasise the loneliness and lack of companionship of the body. The 'grave-as-house' occurred frequently in sermons and poems. The theme was used to stress that the body was alone – and that no one would visit to admire the body's new home. The image was taken further: the smallness and poverty of the grave contrasted with the splendid residence of the body when it was alive. The grave had low walls, no doors and a roof which lay immediately above the chest and chin (Woolf 1968: 82–5). It was in this house that the worms would eat the flesh and the body decompose. The friars were also responsible for another powerful depiction of death: the Dance of Death. The Dance was led by a skeletal figure who guided the deceased on a merry dance. The emphasis was that no one – whether popes, kings, emperors, the old, the young, the rich or the poor – could escape. Some, like labourers or the old, welcomed death, whilst others feared it. The Dance was first developed in Germany and France, where it was always more popular than in England. Franciscan and Dominican friars seem to have been especially attracted to the theme, and it has been documented in friaries in Germany, Switzerland and Italy. The Dance probably grew out of the preaching tradition: during sermons on death the Dance may have been mimed or spoken. The most famous instance of a performed Dance was that in 1453 at Besançon, France, under the auspices of the Franciscan friars (Potter 1975: 21); the most famous painted example was at the church of the Holy Innocents in Paris (a regular place for preaching by friars), which in turn inspired the picture on the cloister walls of St Paul's Cathedral. Other depictions were also known in England, as at Salisbury Cathedral, and thirteen English texts have survived of the Dance (Warren and White 1931). It was, however, always more popular on the Continent where it continued to develop. One French version dealt exclusively with the dance of women (Wemple and Kaiser 1986).

The universality and unexpectedness of death was also evident in the legend of the Three Living and the Three Dead, again originating on the Continent. It became popular in the fourteenth and fifteenth centuries in England and over fifty depictions survive in parish churches. The legend involved three living men who came across three animate skeletons or semi-decomposed corpses. The corpses addressed the living with the words: 'What you are, so once were we; what we are, so you shall be'. This sentiment was a powerful reminder of mortality and was used widely as a *memento mori*.

The *memento mori* was extended to the physical decomposition of the body in the grave. A particular type of tomb, called the cadaver tomb (see Chapter 7), depicted the body in a state of decay and sometimes with the accompanying worms, toads or snakes. This image also extended into literature. In a fifteenth-century poem, 'Disputacione betwyx the Body and Wormes' (partially quoted by Tristram 1976: 160), the worms with an 'insatiable and greedy appetite' devour the corpse of a once beautiful woman, who laments her former Pride of Life. In the end she accepts the worms with the realisation that her glorified body would be resurrected at the Last Judgement:

> At the Day of Doom before the High Justice.
> With the body glorified to be.

There was also an extensive and long-lived literature of dialogues between the decomposing body and soul. In England these dialogues are known from the Anglo-Saxon period, throughout the Middle Ages and beyond into the post-Reformation literature of the seventeenth century (Osmund 1990). The basic theme was a debate between the body and the soul, both accusing each other for the sins committed during life. The debate revealed two opposite views of the body: the soul accused the body of actively sinning in the pleasures of life, whilst the body replied that it was merely passive matter, and that even if it had sinned, the soul should have exercised greater control (Osmund 1990: 55, Woolf 1968: 89–100). The final outcome was that devils dragged the soul to Hell, and the body was left to rot. A variation was for the body in the grave, either personally or via an epitaph on the tomb, to inform a living reader of the body's present state:

> [My figure] Now turned to worm's meat and corruption
> Both foul earth and stinking slyme and clay
> (Horrox 1994: 347)

A sense of humility and the transience of life was thus powerfully instilled within the reader.

A further group of texts which mentioned death were poems, songs or carols. These references could be direct, as in Lydgate's 'Death's Warning' where Death speaks directly to the poet (MacCraken 1933: 655–6), or where the poet thinks of the disturbing or frightening nature of death: Lydgate wrote one of the many existing medieval poems based around the sentiment *Timor mortis conturbat me* (the fear of death frightens me) (MacCraken 1933: 828–32) – a sentiment which was even incorporated into some carols (Chambers 1971: 102). As well as these direct references to Death, there were more oblique references of which the most famous is the beautiful medieval English poem 'The Pearl'. The poem is an allegorical dream-vision on the death of a young child. The dreamer encounters the dead child in a beautiful land and, through his questions and her answers, when he awakens he is able to cope better with his own grief. The 'Pearl' poet is thought also to have written 'Sir Gawayne and the Green Knight' where death and survival – in the form of beheading (see below) – form a central crux to the poem.

The cause of death itself could indicate whether the soul was destined for Heaven or Hell, as the type of death symbolically represented the previous life. Fore-knowledge, and the associated preparations for death, were very important symbols of holiness, and fore-knowledge was frequently granted to saints. St Cuthbert knew when he was going to die and

> He passed a quiet day in expectation of his future bliss . . . And after receiving the sacraments . . . He fortified himself for his death, which he knew had now come . . . And raising his eyes to heaven and stretching out his hands aloft he sent forth his spirit in the very act of praising God . . .
>
> (Colgrave 1985a: 285)

Sudden death was feared because the lack of preparation was possibly injurious to the soul in the afterlife (see Chapter 1 and Chapter 2).

Once the themes had been established – that fore-knowledge of death was good, and sudden death was bad – there was only a very short logical step to assuming that good people would have fore-knowledge, and that bad people, or pagans, heathens or non-Christians, would die suddenly. Spiritual truth – which was if anything more important than factual truth – meant that people died in certain ways. Several themes were so consistent that they can be studied in detail, especially drowning; thunder, lightning and earthquake; falling; and beheading.

Drowning was always portrayed as a cause of death for non-Christians: Christians could not drown. Biblical precedent was very strong. The Egyptians drowned in the Red Sea after the Israelites had crossed; Jonah was saved by the whale, which in turn pre-figured Christ rising from the dead; and Noah rode out the Flood whilst those who did not believe were drowned. In the New Testament, Christ walked on the water. Peter joined him, until he doubted, and then began to sink. Christ took his hand and said 'O thou of little faith, wherefore didst thou doubt?'

(Matthew 14: 29). An interesting conflict arose when literal truth (that a Christian drowned) clashed with the spiritual truth.

Anglo-Saxon Christian writers followed the biblical traditions; the poem 'Exodus' vividly depicted the Egyptians drowning in the Red Sea after the Israelites had crossed (Bradley 1982). The contrast between drowning and a good Christian death can be seen by a comparison between the 'Exodus' account and the death of Saint Cuthbert. The drowning of the Egyptians covers over fifty lines of verse (lines 447–516, some may be missing) and starts 'people were afraid' (*folc waes afaered*) (line 447) of the horror of death and their spirits were miserable (*geomre*). Furthermore, the sound of the uproar/clamour (*hream*) and the 'reek of carnage' – literally the 'mist of death' – (*waelmist*) all add to the general chaos and horror of the situation. This is in direct contrast to Cuthbert who had time to prepare for his death in a peaceful way. As the waters close over the Egyptians, they are described as cowards (*herebleade*) who wanted to return home (*hamas findan*) in the face of death. They therefore have no respect for God or their souls, but are only interested in saving their physical bodies from the flood. Again Cuthbert is different: though death is described as the 'Queen of the Terrors' (Colgrave 1985b: 137), Cuthbert waits anxiously for it and 'sent forth his spirit in the very act of praising God . . .' (Colgrave 1985a: 285). Cuthbert does not try to escape, and he decides to stay alone, although sorely tormented by devils. After the death of a saint, sometimes a light is seen stretching from earth to heaven as the soul ascends to heaven, and choirs of angels sweetly sing. In contrast, the sounds in 'Exodus' are of despair and chaotic confusion with the turbulence (*storm*, line 460) rising high into the skies and, far from the blissful sound of angels, 'a most mighty cry of despair [arose] from the army' and the air darkened above them. Furthermore, nowhere in the poem is there the idea that the Egyptians were 'saved' because they drowned. Death by drowning was not considered a symbolic baptism. Those who drowned died in a terrified state and 'lost' their souls. The bodies were also lost in the deep. The danger of the body not being recovered was a tragedy for relatives of those drowned in shipwrecks.

In 1120, William, Henry I's son and heir, perished in the White Ship disaster. Henry was grief-stricken not only by his loss, but also by the knowledge that his son would be eaten by sea-

monsters. William of Malmesbury wrote: 'The calamity was aug-
mented by the difficulty of finding the bodies, which could not
be discovered by the various persons who sought them along
the shore; but delicate as they were, they became food for the
monsters of the deep' (Stevenson 1991: section 153).

In devotional writings, however, Christians did not die by shipwreck or drowning, which has the biblical precedent set by Saint
Paul who survived a shipwreck (Acts 27). Jacobus, the author of
The Golden Legend, written *c.*1260, included many examples from
the lives of the saints (Ryan 1993a, 1993b), examples which were
often closely followed by John Mirk in his English sermons in
the fifteenth century (Erbe, 1905). In the life of Saint Mary
Magdalene a ship was sinking and one woman called upon
Mary to save her. 'At once a woman of venerable visage and
bearing appeared to her, held her up by the chin, and, while the
rest drowned, brought her unharmed to land' (Ryan 1993a: 382).
Even attempted drownings were doomed to failure. Saint Christina (Ryan 1993a: 386) had a large stone tied around her neck
and was thrown into the sea: 'but immediately angels bore her
up' and Christ came down and baptised her. Alternately the water
could simply disappear. When Saint Blaise was about to be thrown
into a lake to drown, 'he made the sign of the cross over the
water and instantly it became like dry, firm land under him'.
When the pagans were asked to walk on water, 'sixty-five men
walked in and promptly drowned' (Ryan 1993a: 153). The theme
of pagans drowning frequently occurred: the pagan Maxentius
tried to trap the Emperor Constantine, but was defeated by his
own ruse and 'drowned in the depths of the stream' (Ryan 1993a:
280). Similarly, Christian relics floated or returned to shore,
whilst pagan or magical objects sank: the books of Simon the
Magician were thrown into the sea and sank (Ryan 1993a: 342).

Occasionally the theme was reversed for dramatic effect and
Christians appeared to have drowned. In the 'Life of St Andrew'
(Ryan 1993a: 15–16) some potential converts were travelling by
sea to be converted by Andrew. Before they managed to arrive,
they were all 'drowned' by a storm raised by the Devil. Fortunately
their Christian intent probably saved them for they were washed
up on to the shore, and the apostle Andrew quickly brought
them back to life. A more powerful example occurred in the
'Life of Saint Peter Martyr' (Ryan 1993a: 262)

At Sens in . . . France, a girl fell into a swift-flowing stream and was in the water for a long time, finally being pulled out dead. Her death was proven by four facts: the length of time in the water and the rigidity, coldness, and blackness of the corpse.

Up to this point the text would have been deeply puzzling to a medieval audience, for Christians could not die by drowning, but here in the life of a saint was someone who had drowned. Jacobus proved her death by the four cited reasons. 'Still, some people carried her to the church of the friars, and when they commended her to Saint Peter, she was restored to life and health.' In the last five words, the previous illogical paragraph was turned the right way up.

The role of water was also important in the disposal of the body. The bodies of Christians were saved from rivers or polluted water after they had died. One of Saint Petronilla's (unnamed) companions (Ryan 1993a: 315) was thrown into a sewer; and Saint Nicodemus was beaten to death with leaden rods and his body thrown into the River Tiber. Both bodies were retrieved and were buried honourably by other Christians. Saint Barnabas was killed by putting a rope around his neck, dragging him out of the city and burning him alive. Even so, his Jewish persecutors were not satisfied. 'They stowed his bones in a leaden urn, intending to cast it into the sea', but his followers acquired the relics.

Sometimes people were so evil that the demons of the water rejected the body. The body of Pontius Pilate, who was depicted as being extremely evil in medieval texts, was weighted down by a huge stone and then thrown into the River Tiber. The foul spirits of the river, however, would not allow it to rest, and 'made sport with it . . . plunging it into the water and snatching it up into the air.' (This can be contrasted with Saint Christina who was raised up and then baptised.) The vivid impression given of Pontius's body thrown and tossed about was in direct contrast to a normal burial where the body lies still and resting under the earth. The hurling of the body also caused 'awesome floods in the water and lightning, tempests and hailstones in the air, and widespread panic broke out among the people'. The body was not only in perpetual motion, it turned the natural order of the world upside down: from calmness to floods and tempests. The Romans therefore pulled the body from the Tiber. It was carried in contempt to Vienne, which was translated as 'the road to Hell', and was dumped into the River Rhône. There again the 'wicked spirits' caused the same disturbances, so the population carried the body for burial in the territory of Lausanne, and sank it in a pit surrounded by mountains where, some say, 'diabolical machinations still make themselves felt'. Jacobus was aware that the story was not true – his last sentence was: 'thus far we have quoted the aforementioned apocryphal history: let the reader judge whether the story is worth telling'. However, he told it because it *ought* to be true. Pilate, and other evil people, could not have a peaceful and normal burial: their evil had to be displayed after death as well as in life (Ryan 1993a: 213).

The almost complete universality of drowning being connected with non-Christians caused some problems when it was known that a Christian had literally drowned. Literal fact clashed with spiritual truth. One of the most remarkable examples was the Venerable Bede's account of Peter the priest who was drowned in the Bay of Amfleat. Bede followed the general theme of only non-Christians drowning with consistency, but Peter's death caused a problem. The only way to resolve it was by a miracle. Bede related how Peter's body was found on the shore – finding the body after drowning is itself unusual – but the inhabitants gave it an unworthy burial because they did not know who he was. It took a heavenly light to indicate that Peter should be honourably buried. The miracle was also important as it was one of the very few that Bede located on the Continent (Colgrave and Mynors 1981: 115–17).

Thunder, lightning and earthquake as a cause of death were always depicted as an instant and severe punishment for evil people. In the 'Life of Saint Andrew' (Ryan 1993a: 15), a mother falsely accused her son of incest with her. Andrew, who supported the son, prayed to God, whereupon a huge thunder-burst terrified all the accusers, an earthquake threw them to the ground, and the mother 'struck by lightning, shrivelled up and crumbled to ashes'. After Emerentiana, the foster sister of St Agnes, was stoned to death by a group of pagans, 'at once God sent an earthquake with lightning and thunder, and a large number of pagans perished' (Ryan 1993a: 103). The wrath of God was portrayed as immediate, frightening, widely proclaimed (through the thunder) and highly directional (by the lightning). In the 'Life of Saint George' (Ryan 1993a: 241), the combination of fire and earthquake destroyed temples, idols and priests. In the 'Life of Saint Ambrose' a rich man boasted that nothing untoward had ever happened to him, whereupon an earthquake swallowed him and left not a trace behind. In the 'Life of Saint Matthias' a literal explanation was given as to why earthquakes were connected with pagan deaths. When some people obstinately resisted his preaching, he said to them: ' "I give you notice that you will go to hell alive!" And the earth opened and swallowed them' (Ryan 1993a: 171).

Literally descending to Hell was also part of a larger theme connected with non-Christians, that of falling. Falling does not have such good biblical parallells, although they can be found: Jezebel was thrown from a window and died (2 Kings 11: 33). In Anglo-Saxon works, the saints were tormented by devils trying to throw them. Devils tried to fling Cuthbert from a high rock, and Guthlac was thrown by devils into the muddy waters of the black marsh. If Christians did fall, they could be saved by a miracle: a mason who was building the church at Hexham 'slipped from a pinnacle of enormous height . . . was dashed upon a stone pavement' whereupon the other masons thought he was dead. He was carried to the church and prayed for by Saint Wilfrid and so revived. The cross, in the poem 'The Dream of the Rood', stated: 'I did not dare to collapse to the ground and fall to the surfaces of the earth, but I had to stand fast' (lines 42–3, Bradley 1982: 161). As the rood supported Christ, a direct link was made between not falling and being Christian.

Both drowning and falling were consistent in meaning: a more complicated theme was that of fire and burning. An explanation was given by Cynewulf at the end of his poem 'Elene' (Bradley 1982). Cynewulf described how God will destroy the world by fire, and that the souls will divide up into three groups. The first group will be the righteous and steadfast (soðfaeste, line 1289), who will be in the upper, pleasantly warm part of the flame. The sinful (synfulle, line 1295) will be punished by being placed in the middle of the flame. The final group will be the damned (lease leodhatan, line 1300), who will be bound up in the flame's grip forever. These categories also apply to methods of death. Fire cannot burn holy objects or people. In the poem 'Daniel' (Bradley 1982) the three Hebrews were thrown into an 'absurdly huge' fire, but to them it was like 'the weather in summertime when a sprinkling of raindrops is sent during the day . . .', a motif which is also used in the poem 'Juliana' (Bradley 1982). Whereas flames cannot harm the holy, they can kill the sinful; in both 'Daniel' and 'Juliana' the flames turned upon the heathens outside the furnace and burned them up. Even the threat of dying by fire is enough to force the deceitful Jews to hand over Judas to Elene: 'Then they were under the prospect of death, of fire and their life's end, and there and then they pointed out the one ready versed in the traditional accounts . . .' (Bradley 1982: 179). The amount of burning could be in direct ratio to the amount of sin committed in life. In 'Christ and Satan' Eve says that she and Adam are 'cruelly scorched' (*þeale onaeled*, Bradley 1982: 96). Bede gave a clear example from Fursa's vision, when an angel explained after Fursa got burnt: 'You were burned by the fire you had kindled. For if you had not received the property of this man who died in his sins, you would not have burned in the fire of his punishment' (Colgrave and Mynors 1981: 274–5). The last category were the damned who were forever tormented by fire. Bede described Dryhthelm's vision, in which Dryhthelm saw globes of fire shoot up and 'The tips of the flames as they ascended were full of human souls which, like sparks flying upwards with the smoke, were now tossed high and now, as the vaporous flames fell back, were sucked down into the depths (Colgrave and Mynors 1981: 490–1).

To heighten the effects of the miracles, themes were sometimes combined. In a famous account, Bede described how the men of a drought-stricken starving population 'Would go together to some precipice or to the sea shore where in their misery they would join hands and leap into the sea, perishing wretchedly either by the fall or by drowning' (Colgrave and Mynors 1981: 374–6). Drowning and falling were powerfully combined, but immediately after Saint Wilfrid arrived and converted the starving to Christianity a gentle rain fell and food once again became plentiful. A similar combination of falling and drowning occurred in *Beowulf* where 'They shoved that reptile, the dragon, over the ramparts of the cliff and let the waves carry him away and the water close over [him] . . .' (lines 3131–3, Bradley 1982: 493). In the Anglo-Saxon poem 'Andreas', Andreas defeated his heathen adversaries by using a flood, but fourteen of the most sinful were sucked into the abyss.

Fire from Heaven might be an added element. In Nennius's story about Vortigern, one version of Vortigern's fate was that

'The earth opened and swallowed him up on the night when his fortress was burnt about him, for no trace was ever found of those who were burned with him in the fortress . . .' (Morris 1980: 33). A similar fate was reserved for Thunor – itself a suspiciously close corruption of the name of the pagan god Thor – in an account by Simeon of Durham. Thunor had two princes killed and for his deeds he was 'struck by a bolt from the almighty . . .' and fell to the ground. 'Immediately the very wretched Thunor was swallowed up, with his horse and arms, in a frightful chasm of the earth.' This has several of the same elements as the Vortigern story: the fire from Heaven, and the disappearance of the body. The result would have no doubt been the same, for Thunor's soul was thought to have gone to Hell and was passing from the 'pangs of snows to devouring flames' and was 'suffering the penalty of torments'.

Both the lightning and earthquake consumed the body in an instant: there was no fore-knowledge, with the associated preparation, repentance and last rites; and no formal burial. These aspects of speed and unpreparedness for death are important indicators to determine whether a cause of death is associated with Christians or non-Christians. By these criteria many other methods of death can be seen to be associated with Christians or non-Christians. Strangulation was an occasional form of non-Christian death. The wicked Carpasius, who sought Saint Urban, was himself seized and strangled by a demon (Ryan 1993a: 315). Another evil spirit waited until a knight forgot to say his *Ave Maria* so that the knight could be strangled, but a holy man thwarted the attempt (Ryan 1993a: 202). In a general passage about martyrdom (Ryan 1993a: 98), Jacobus specifically equates strangulation with the Devil: 'the devil thinks he conquers, . . . [but] while he strangles he is killed'.

Christian methods of death were not so various and tended to be based on biblical examples, or the deaths of saints or martyrs. The archetypal Christian death was by crucifixion, of which Christ was the prime example. Other disciples were also crucified, such as, in Anglo-Saxon tradition, Simon (Garmonsway 1982: 9). Beheading was a common method of Christian death. Although the biblical parallels are less numerous, there are some obvious examples. The head of John the Baptist (Mark 6: 27; Matthew 14: 10) was brought to Herod on a plate or 'charger'. This powerful image was certainly depicted in stained glass and as wall-paintings, and in some parts of England alabaster 'St John's Heads' were a common reminder of the beheading (see Chapter 1; St John Hope 1890). A further biblical reference occurs in Revelation (20: 4), 'and I saw the souls of them that were beheaded for the witness of Jesus, and for the word of God'.

In the 'Physician's Tale', in *The Canterbury Tales*, a spotless maid was beheaded by her grieving father to preserve her chastity from an evil judge. This tale is effectively a 'pagan saint's life' (pers. comm. D. Daniell) and followed the convention that a suitable way for martyrs to be killed was by beheading. The 'Second Nun's Tale' involved the martyrdom of Saint Cecilia, who continued to preach despite her neck being almost hacked through. In *The Golden Legend* a large number of martyrs were beheaded after suffering terrible tortures. Faith, a daughter of Saint Sophia, was beaten by thirty-six soldiers, had her breasts torn off, was thrown on to a red-hot grid-iron, and then put into a frying pan full of oil and wax. None of these tortures killed her, but finally she 'was beheaded'. Her sister, Hope, was tortured by being put into a cauldron full of pitch, wax and resin, drops of which fell on some unbelievers and cremated them. She survived and the only way that she could be killed was 'with a sword' (Ryan 1993a: 185). Saint Matthias was being stoned (a good Christian role model had been given by the first Christian martyr, Saint Stephen (Acts 7)), when 'he was beheaded with an axe' (Ryan 1993a: 170). The list of those beheaded also included these saints and martyrs: Juliana, George, Boniface, Gordianus, Pancratius and Julitta (Ryan 1993a: 161, 242, 290, 308, 311, 324 respectively) and, in England, Alban.

There was a good reason, however, for the number of Roman Christians beheaded. In the account of St Peter the apostle, Jacobus wrote: 'Then Peter, being an alien, was condemned to be crucified, while Paul, because he was a Roman citizen, was sentenced to beheading' (Ryan 1993a: 345). The number of saints beheaded therefore owed more to their Roman citizenship than holiness. Perhaps inadvertently, an iconographic link was made – many saints were beheaded, therefore it was a Christian way of death.

Beheading as a cause of death was not only a sign of martyrdom, but had other connotations in other societies. In England, the Celts had revered the head, and in Anglo-Saxon and medieval periods it was seen as a legal punishment and as a method of destroying evil. As the former, the Anglo-Saxon Chronicle entry for 1053 recorded that: 'It was decided that Rhys, the Welsh king's brother, should be killed, because he was causing injuries; and his head was brought to Gloucester on the eve of the Epiphany.' As the latter, in the Anglo-Saxon poem 'Judith', Judith cut off the head of Holofernes and his soul went straight to Hell; and after Beowulf had cut off Grendel's head he carried it from the mere and placed it in front of Hrothgar as a 'token of victory' (*tires to tacne*). One of the most remarkable medieval poems, 'Sir Gawayne and the Green Knight', has beheading as a central theme. The Green Knight rides into the court of King Arthur and challenges the knights to a beheading pact: a challenge taken up by Sir Gawayne who cuts off the Green Knight's head. Sir Gawayne then rides to his castle to fulfil his vow, before returning and confronting the living Green Knight after a year. The Green Knight's survival of the beheading is a fundamental mystery at the heart of the poem (pers. comm. D. Daniell).

The history of beheading can be developed further through the Middle Ages. The basic posture for being beheaded from at least the twelfth century until the late fifteenth century was kneeling or standing (either erect or with head bowed). The martyrdom of Thomas Becket in Canterbury Cathedral was artistically shown by him kneeling or standing to receive the blow. Those who were beheaded as a legal punishment usually knelt with no support. Some were also blindfolded and had their hands tied behind the back. The swordsman swung at the neck. A depiction was given in *The Luttrell Psalter* of the execution of Thomas of Lancaster, which showed him kneeling at prayer and not blindfolded. The executioner rested one hand on Thomas's head and swung the sword (Backhouse 1989: 13).

The use of the slab or the block was a great dishonour. The earliest example found concerned four detested knights connected with Richard II. They were killed, dragged through the streets and had their heads cut off on a fishmonger's slab. Their heads were then put upon pikes and their bodies were hung on gibbets (Brereton 1968: 457). The earliest example of the use of a block occurred when the Duke of Suffolk was beheaded in 1450. The events were described in a letter from William Lomnor to John Paston (Myers 1969: no. 144). The Duke of Suffolk, who learnt of his death sentence, attempted to escape by ship. The ship was stopped in the English Channel:

And in the sight of all he was drawn out of the great ship into the boat, and there was an axe and a block; and the one most ignorant of the ship bade him lay down his head, and he should be fairly treated, and die by the sword; and the man took a rusty sword, and smote off his head with half a dozen strokes, and took away his gown of russet, and his doublet of velvet sewn with metal rings, and laid his body on the sands of Dover. And some say that his head was set on a pole by it, and his men were disembarked with great ceremony and deference. And the Sheriff of Kent watches the body and has sent his under sheriff to the judges to know what to do . . .

In 1478 John Paston had compared the Duke of Suffolk to the evil Herod (Cawley 1990: 109). Suffolk's beheading was therefore deliberately degrading and contemptible to one of such high rank: one of the most ignorant performed the task, the sword was rusty (therefore a block was used), and it took several strokes to complete the task. In the Tudor period the block became more common. The change in method of death seems to have been politically inspired. It is a salutary reminder that politics (and especially Tudor politics) could play a significant role in changes to actions and culture about death.

There were other literary and religious themes and motifs connected with death and dying; two of which were the dead coming back to life, and a living death on earth. The ability to bring back people from the dead was known in medieval literature, for Christ had brought Lazarus back from the dead, and Christ himself lay dead for forty hours before the Resurrection. This ability was a commonly reported miracle in connection with saints and Jacobus stated in *The Golden Legend*: '[The Holy Spirit] is sent to give life to the dead . . . Because it is the spirit that gives life; Ezek. 37: 4 "O dry bones, hear the word of the lord. Behold I will cause breath to enter you and you shall live" ' (Ryan 1993a: 307). Holy objects also had the power to bring the dead back to life. Helena, Mary (mother of Christ) and Judas (the disciple) discovered three crosses under a temple. They were uncertain as to which was the cross that Christ had died on, so they held each of the three over the body of a young man who had recently died and was being carried to burial. He 'immediately came back to life' (Ryan 1993a: 282) when the correct cross was placed over him. A later example occurred in 1252 when a woman, after her fourth miscarriage, invoked the help of the recently martyred Dominican Saint Peter, and her dead son came back to life. The time-scale of a person's waking-up from the death could vary considerably, from a few days, to many years. Jacobus related the story of Saint Paul promising that Saint Peter would bring the Governor of Antioch's son back to life after he had been dead for fourteen years (Ryan 1993a: 163). On being told what he had to do, Peter said 'that's a hard promise to keep, ... but God's power will make it easy', and after prayer the son 'came back to life immediately'. The longest suspension of death was that of the pagan who was brought back to life by St Erkenwald. The uncorrupted body in the tomb had lain there since 354 BC, or 1,740 years, awaiting baptism. After the ceremony

> And all the beauty of his body blackened like mould
> As foetid as fungus that flies up in powder
>
> (Stone 1977: 42)

The souls of those people brought back to life probably resided either in Hell or Purgatory. (It would make little sense for souls in the bliss of Heaven to return to a corrupting world.) Christ raised Lazarus from Hell and in an account Jacobus stated that Lazarus's soul 'took off like an eagle, springing up with unbounded agility and getting away' (Ryan 1993a: 223). Jacobus did not mention Purgatory in this context, but presumably most Christian souls who were brought back to life would have gone there. In the fifteenth century, Reginald Pecock also discussed the issue of people being brought back to life. The soul had two possibilities; either to be joined to a mortal, corruptible body, or an incorruptible heavenly body. Pecock wrote that it was possible for a soul to return to its earthly body one hundred times, but in the end it would migrate to its heavenly body (Hitchcock 1921: 128).

Death could be postponed by someone being brought back to life, but it could also be accelerated by the body undergoing death whilst still living. The most common group who suffered this fate were the evil or diseased, but in one instance the flesh was depicted as rotting from the body of the hermit Romuald. In the eleventh-century *Life*, Peter Damian described Romuald going into a corrupting swamp: when he left he was swollen and his hair had fallen out; his flesh had gone green – a green of rotting flesh. He was literally in a process of advanced decay (Phipps 1985: 72-3). This image was specifically aimed at Romuald's adversaries – the monks – who have not gone through the same degree of temptation or mortification.

The physical rotting of the flesh in a holy man is unusual, for normally the outward appearance of the body is taken to be a sign of the inward health of the soul. Thus Saint Anthony fought demons in the desert for twenty years, but when he was seen, 'the old comeliness of his members persisted as if no time had passed' (quoted by Phipps 1985: 72). In *The Golden Legend*, evil people suffered an implicit internal death by the 'unclean spirit within' (Ryan 1993a: 232). The body of the Emperor Hadrian 'rotted and he wasted away to death' as a punishment for putting the daughters of Saint Sophia to death (Ryan 1993a: 186). Herod of Ascalon, who had the Holy Innocents murdered, fell ill with a deadly disease at the age of 70. 'Being tormented by high fever, an itch all over his body, incessant pain, inflammation of the feet, worms in the testicles, a horrible smell, and shortness and irregularity of breath' (Ryan 1993a: 58). In the York mystery plays, Herod states that his 'guttes will out-thring' or burst out. This was the fate of Judas who hanged himself and then he 'burst asunder in the middle and all his bowels gushed out' (Acts 1: 18.) This is paralleled in the Old Testament by Jehoram who wrought evil in the eyes of the Lord (2 Chronicles 21), for which the Lord smote him with an incurable disease in his bowels and after two years 'his bowels fell out ... [and] he died of sore diseases'. Evil people might also be eaten from the inside by worms. In reality intestinal worms were probably quite common to the medieval population, but in Christian literature they symbolise evil. Herod was struck down by worms in his testicles, and various miracles relieved people suffering from worms. Saint Peter Martyr's cloak caused a nobleman, who suffered violent convulsions, to vomit up a worm 'that had two heads and was covered with thick hairs' (Ryan 1993a: 257). The Emperor Vespasian suffered from worms up his nose and could only be cured by invoking Christ, whereupon 'the worms fell out of his nose and he received his health then and there' (Ryan 1993a: 274). One remedy for worms (which symbolised evil) was myrrh (Ryan 1993a: 149), given to Christ at his birth.

Whilst most types of death, and accompanying symbolism, can be categorised in some way, there is a large group of exceptional examples. Some are probably literal fact: Charles, the king of the Franks, was gored by a boar – the only recorded example in the Anglo-Saxon Chronicle. Other causes verge on the borderline of fact and fiction. William of Malmesbury related how Henry I's sister-in-law died because the midwife ordered her breasts to be bound too tightly 'on account of her copious flow of milk', which, if true, might in reality be suffocation (Stevenson 1991: section 389). William of Malmesbury also recorded one of the most bizarre causes of death: mice. In one story a group of mice attacked a boat with the intent of urinating on a wounded man bitten by a leopard. In this way the man would die. The mice rowed 'in the rinds of pomegranates, the insides of which they had eaten' (which gives a charming mental image), but were drowned. The preceding account by William related how a group of mice swam out to a boat, gnawed the planks and forced the occupants to shore, 'whereupon [the mice] entirely gnawed [a man] in pieces' (Stevenson 1991: sections 290, 291).

Such unusual causes of death highlight the problems of textual transmission and where the themes originated. The most powerful influence was biblical example, a clear instance of which was the theme of drowning. The Bible was the most important source, but other texts helped to spread the themes. A large, and certainly the most influential, group of saints' lives in the Middle Ages were those written by Jacobus de Voragine in his popular work *The Golden Legend*. Written about 1260 it was possibly 'the only book more widely read than the Bible'. There are around 1,000 surviving manuscripts; with printing, the numbers increased still further (Ryan 1993a: xiii). Its popularity was such that it was referred to by William Langland in *Piers Plowman*; and about 1485, Cecily, Duchess of York, was said to read it and other holy works daily. Jacobus consistently followed the conventions regarding the deaths of Christians and non-Christians, and the book is a rich repository for further research. Dissemination also took place through exemplar used in sermons: John Mirk borrowed heavily from *The Golden Legend* (Erbe 1905), and William of Malmesbury's twelfth-century tale of a witch's burial also appeared in a fourteenth-century preacher's manual (Wenzel 1989: 583). Two other exceptionally influential works in fifteenth-century England were Chaucer's *The Canterbury Tales* and Langland's *Piers Plowman*, both of which contained powerful portrayals of death: The Pardoner's Tale about finding death (see above), and the account in *Piers Plowman* of Christ's harrowing of Hell and defeating Death. Cultural influences also played a part in the development of themes. Within England the new influx of continental contacts around the Norman Conquest may also have brought new themes. Thunder, lightning or earthquake as causes of death were rare in Anglo-Saxon literature (especially early Anglo-Saxon texts), although occasionally occurring in Celtic texts. The increasing continental contacts after the Norman Conquest may have introduced it as a literary theme. William of Malmesbury, writing after the Conquest, used the lightning motif retrospectively, describing how Godwin's mother 'paid the penalty for her cruelty (of purchasing slaves from England for Denmark), [by] being killed by a stroke of lightning' (Stevenson 1991: section 200). A further theme may also have been introduced through continental influence, that of being trampled to death by horses. Another retrospective example might be that by Florence of Worcester, a twelfth-century chronicler, who described how a raiding party in 1052 killed men, women and children by trampling on them with their horses.

Throughout the Middle Ages the consistency and persistence of many themes is noticeable. Those with the biblical precedents were the strongest and longest-lived, being used in almost any Christian religious context throughout the Middle Ages and into the Reformation. In 1547 Cranmer published a set of sermons, or homilies, which were to be read throughout the kingdom. The sermons have been compared to the Book of Common Prayer and the Thirty-Nine Articles as one of the earliest statements of the Reformation. The same themes were used. In *An Homilie of Whoredom and Unclennesse,* Cranmer described how only Noah and seven others were saved, but all the rest of the world 'perished' because it was 'overflowed with waters', an 'example worthy to be remembered, that you may learn to fear God' (Bond 1987: 182). Similarly the 'filthy sin of uncleanness [of] Sodom and Gomorra' was destroyed by the 'fire and brimstone from heaven', the equivalent of a lightning strike. The Reformation and the English Renaissance, however, do seem to have caused a break in the literary tradition that certain types of people died in certain ways. The Duke of Clarence (in *Richard III*) and Orphelia (in *Hamlet*), were rare examples of death by drowning in Renaissance literature, and it was unlikely that the audience thought of either as non-Christian or evil simply because they drowned. Sometimes the themes continue; in Marlowe's play *The Jew of Malta*, the wicked protagonist falls to his death. The overwhelming desire, however, of Renaissance authors to equate different deaths to categories of people no longer existed.

4

THE GEOGRAPHY OF BURIAL

The place of burial was dominated by two factors: which church (or, exceptionally, other place); and then where in the holy ground. Within these two basic decisions lay a host of other considerations: the wishes of the dead person; the views of surviving relatives; social expectations; the desires of friends or enemies, and the decrees of the authorities, whether secular or religious. For most people the only option was to be buried in the parish cemetery or church, but there were still many choices as to exactly where to be buried. The choices, and conflicts, were most readily apparent in the more wealthy and privileged burials, not only because better documentation survives, but also because the churches had the most to gain or lose by these burials, whether in terms of patronage, prestige or money.

Some of the factors involved were highlighted after the Norman Conquest when a choice could be made between burial in Normandy or England. In 1230 Gilbert de Clare died in Brittany and, following his wishes, his body and entire household made the long journey from Brittany to Tewkesbury Abbey for his burial (Golding 1985: 68). Alternatively, decisions by family members could override the wishes of the dead, as in 1189 when the last male de Mandeville was buried at the family abbey of Mortemar in Normandy rather than his preferred choice of Walden in England. The stated excuse was the difficulty of the journey, although family politics probably intervened (Golding 1985: 67). One of the most famous cases of non-compliance by an heir was by Edward II's treatment of his father's body. Edward I requested for his heart was to be sent to Palestine, and a later, possibly apocryphal, account recorded that he asked for his body to be boiled in a large cauldron: his flesh was then to be buried, and his bones carried into battle against the Scots (Prestwich 1988: 557). In reality, Edward II built an unremarkable tomb in Westminster Abbey and the body was buried there. These two examples are confirmation that a person's last wishes could be changed if friends or relatives desired otherwise.

Death during the Crusades, fighting in the East, or pilgrimage to the Holy Land meant that decisions had to be taken about the long-distance transportation of the body. There was no standard pattern. There were examples of people being buried where they died, such as Sir William Neville and Sir John Clanvowe who died in Constantinople in 1391. An alternative was to carry the body back to England. Lord John Roos died in Cyprus in 1393 and was buried in Rievaulx Abbey in Yorkshire, as was his uncle William who was buried there in 1352, having died in Syria. A further alternative was to bring back just part of the body: the heart and bones of Hugh, Earl of Stafford, were returned to England. Disinterment at a later date was also an option: John Mowbray, killed by the Turks in 1368, was originally buried with the Dominicans in Galata. In 1397, his son Thomas recovered his father's 'bones or relics' and had them transported to England for reburial (Luttrell 1991: 180–1).

Before any of these decisions could be resolved, the desired burial place had to have authorisation of burial. The right to bury people came about in two ways; either through established tradition, the origin of which was lost in the mists of time; or it was granted. A major source of conflict arose between the parish church and one or more of its outlying dependent chapels. At a county level, the chapels could outnumber the parish churches. Before the Reformation, Lancashire had 100 detached chapels in fifty-nine parishes; and in Cornwall it has been estimated that there were 700 chapels, in 209 parishes. Even in more densely populated areas chapels could be numerous: in Kent there were 500 parishes and 300 chapels before the Black Death (Rosser 1991: 175). The chapels were often distant from the parish church, were supported by the laity or powerful lord, and had acquired rights over time, rights which often did not extend to burial.

Chapels, dependent on the parish church, could apply for burial rights, but these were often fiercely contested because burial was profitable. The most common reason for the application was the length and difficulty of the journey carrying the body from the chapel to the parish church. In 1427 the people of Highweek, in the diocese of Exeter, complained of the 'dangerous' journey to the parish church for burial, even though 'their dead were taken first into the chapel [of Highweek] for the requiem mass, and the customary oblations'. The only thing missing from the list of funeral rites was the burial itself (Dunstan 1971: 281). Other reasons could also be cited. In 1429 the chapel of St Ives, Cornwall, applied for burial rights and to be upgraded to a parish church. The reasons were more varied than in normal applications: that mothers in childbirth had hastened to the parish church at Lelant to receive sacraments but had died on the way; that on funeral journeys, the men – who were seafarers, merchants or craftsmen – had to forsake their occupations, and when they had a funeral in Lelant their homes were easy prey to pirates (Dunstan 1971: 260). Economic reasons were not uncommon and at St Sidwell, Laneast, in Devon, distance, flooding, the hills and the wet and muddy road were given, but also that it was 'vexatious' to the traders, husbandmen or 'articifiers in the mechanical arts' to be called away for a burial (Dunstan 1967: 235). Economic reasons were also explicitly mentioned at Revelstoke when funerals were sometimes delayed because 'the general economy could not sustain long absences' from the work of fishermen and labourers (Dunstan 1971: 314).

Once burial rights were granted, the cemetery could then be consecrated. A series of Italian woodcuts, dated to 1520, show the process (Riley 1908). The rubric stated that there should be a cross at each corner of the cemetery, and one in the middle. Before each of the crosses, which appear to be over head-height, were three lit candles. The bishop made his way round the churchyard, and sprinkled holy water on to the cross and then censed it. He then, using a ladder in the illustration, placed three lit candles on top of each cross.

A formal ceremony also had to be performed if the cemetery was polluted by bloodshed or some other offence. A polluted churchyard was serious, as it disrupted the life of the community and meant that the church lost burial and funeral fees. Normally it was required that a public penance should be performed by the perpetrator – which could not be bought off with a monetary payment. The attacker may also have been expected to pay the reconciliation fees: in 1320 William of Colburn asked absolution for pollution of churchyard by violent assault on John Cresse. As he had nothing to pay the reconciliation fees of the church-yard, he swore on the gospels that when he came to fatter fortune he would pay three shillings by instalments (Leach 1898: 381). Pollution of a cemetery meant that no one could be buried there until the pollution had been spiritually removed by reconciliation. On 2 November 1306 (All Souls' Day) the Minster Yard at Bever-ley was reconciled after being polluted by the bloodshed of Peter of Cranswick. For the two years the cemetery remained polluted, no one could be buried there. Unusually, some of the details of the reconciliation have survived. The archbishop blessed the water for sprinkling (the churchyard or crosses?) in a tent, which was fixed on to the ash-trees at the churchyard gate, towards the archbishop's manor. The fees were also included. The archbishop was paid 40 shillings, the marshal 5 shillings and the clerk 2 shillings (Leach 1898: 166). After bloodshed or pollution it was possible for cemeteries to be unreconciled for one or two years (Durandus 1671: 69), and presumably the length of time reflected the seriousness of the case. A deputy could stand in for the archbishop, but only with papal permission. In 1426 a papal bull from Martin V allowed the Bishop of Exeter to reconcile churches and cemeteries by deputy, that is 'by a priest using water episcopally blessed' (Dunstan 1963: 159).

Burial rights could be extended to sailors, travellers and strangers as well as parishioners. Parochial rights, including burial, were given to the priory at Lynn for all sailors on ships mooring at Lynn, and on 6 April 1206 further rights were granted by Pope Innocent III of burial to all men drowned between North Lynn and Stapleware. At Plymouth an agreement was reached in 1438 between the vicar of Plymouth and the Carmelite priory about the burial of strangers (Dunstan 1966: 123), who were presumably sailors. The written agreement itself may have been contentious for it was stolen by being cut out from an old missal in St Katherine's Chapel at Plymouth.

Disagreements were not uncommon, even at the most local level. In the diocese of Exeter a dispute arose when different treatment was given to two sets of servants in the same priory: servants resident in the inner court or house of the cell were buried in the priory, whereas those living in the outer court were buried in the parish church (Dunstan 1967: 296). Some-times disputes flared into open hostility when two rival factions battled (sometimes literally) for the body. In 1152 the hermit

Wulfric died at the village church in Haslebury, Somerset, but the monks from the nearby Cluniac priory of Montacute tried to seize his body. They were repulsed by the prompt action of Osbert the priest and a quickly mobilised gang from Crewkerne (Mayr-Harting 1975: 348). The monks failed to get the prestige and financial advantages they had sought.

To stop this sort of open hostility, agreements were reached between parish churches and other institutions with burial rights. In Ely, the Hospital of St John had its relations with the parish laid down by episcopal ordinance which limited its burial rights to brethren and inmates. This restriction was just part of wider concerns over money and the hospital was also prohibited from receiving money from parishioners' bequests or offerings (Rubin 1987: 132–3). Other hospitals were also forbidden to ring bells, as they might attract parishioners from their own churches (Rubin 1987: 104). Where hospitals had burial rights a compromise was usually reached with the local parish church. In many cases the hospital could only bury parishioners who had requested hospital burial in writing. When hospital burials took place there was a danger that the parish church would lose financially, but this was rectified by a payment to the parish church to which the dead person belonged (Rubin 1987: 105–6). Some regulations have survived concerning compensation for the parish church when burial took place outside the parish. In the Statutes for the London Archdeaconry (dated between *c.*1229 and 1241) the payments were laid down. If a chaplain was without a cemetery to bury a body, he could bury it in the cemetery of another parish church for half the burial offering. If a cemetery was available, but another cemetery was chosen, the first church received all the offerings. Similarly, if the original church did not have a cemetery, and so a conventual church was chosen, the original church should receive all the offerings (Powicke and Cheney 1964).

Disputes over burial, and other religious matters, were common when a new group, whether monks or friars, became established in an area. If a monastery was founded or wanted prestige then there might well be a dispute with the local parish church (as with Wulfric, see above). A more extreme example of conflict occurred in 1392 when the monks of Abingdon hijacked a funeral cortège making its way to an illicit burial ground beside the town's parish church, and then proceeded to disinter sixty-seven people from the parish burial ground and rebury them at the monastery (Rosser 1991: 180–1). The monasteries, however, complained bitterly if the new orders of canons or friars buried important people. The monasteries saw themselves as the natural choice for important burials and were affronted when people chose to be buried elsewhere. The Walden chronicler spoke of the 'vain new things' of the Gilbertines in obvious disgust. However, a much greater threat came from the new orders of friars after they arrived in the thirteenth century. In 1298 William IV de Beauchamp, on the advice of the friar John de Olney, changed his will and so chose to be buried in the Franciscan church in Worcester, rather than in Worcester Cathedral – the traditional burial place of his ancestors. The shocked chronicler wrote of the body being carried through the city as if it were 'the spoils of war' and the body was buried 'in a place which had not been used and where in wintertime he could be said to be rather drowned than buried' (Golding 1985: 64). The horror of this last statement becomes more apparent when the beliefs connected with drowning are considered (see Chapter 3).

A study of the favoured burial places of the Beauchamps, the earls of Essex, and the Berkeleys in the thirteenth century shows that the most important reasons behind the choice of burial place was to show family stability and permanence (Golding 1985). The monasteries were the preferred choice, not because the person might have been a generous benefactor, but because it was the family's traditional resting place. This is well shown by Isobel, Countess of Gloucester, who was very generous to Tewkesbury Abbey, but was buried in Beaulieu to continue the family tradition. When conflicts of burial place arose, one solution was to divide up the body and distribute the parts to different churches. Isobel's heart was buried in Tewkesbury and her entrails were buried at Missenden, which was favoured by her husband's brother, Henry III. The body of Richard of Cornwall, brother of Henry III, was buried in his foundation, Hailes Abbey, but his heart was interred in the choir of the Franciscan church in Oxford.

A permanent shift in burial place was most likely to occur when there was a change in dynasty, rather than depending on an individual's personal religious affinity. A dynastic change threw up another choice: the new family could adopt the old family's burial place (as giving authority to their own cause) or continue in their usual place of burial. In the fifteenth century the newly entitled first Duke of Norfolk chose to give authority to his Mowbray possessions by being buried at Thetford Priory in Norfolk (Robinson 1982). A similar switch occurred in the thirteenth century with the house of Clare. Originally based in East Anglia, the Clare family switched their burial place to Tewkesbury Abbey after they inherited the Gloucester possessions, thereby validating the new inheritance (Golding 1985: 68–71). Burials away from the dynastic churches were likely to be for negative reasons, such as personal disagreements, rather than positive support for the different church. The change of burial place by an individual could be viewed with outrage by the monks and other family members because it threatened the monks' income and prestige, and the family's image of stability and permanence.

In the thirteenth and fourteenth centuries another new group moved on to the religious scene: the friars. Rather than the rural isolation of many monasteries, the friaries were deliberately placed in towns and were in an excellent position to receive burials of the richer members of society. In Toulouse the friars were very successful, receiving between a third and a quarter of burial requests, but in Norwich the figure seems to have stabilised at around 10 per cent of burial requests (Tanner 1984: 95), the same percentage as friary burial requests in the diocese of York (Hughes 1988: 61). This was a large enough number to cause complaints against the friars from the parish clergy. This trend may have seemed more serious because many members of the East Anglian county families were buried in the friaries of Norwich (Tanner 1984: 95). Other groups also were buried together. Occasionally churches could be designated as the burial place for foreigners or non-parishioners. One surprising group was 'Slavonian' traders, named after the 'School of Slavonia' in Venice, who brought cargoes to Southampton and the south coast. Slavonians who died in England were buried at North Stoneham Church in Hampshire (Kitchin 1894).

Once buried, there was no guarantee that the body would remain in the same church or churchyard for ever. The saintly or politically important were especially likely to be moved. The prime example, although Anglo-Saxon, is that of Cuthbert, whose body was carried around the north of England, the outer limits of which were Lindisfarne, Yorkshire, the North Sea coast and the coast of the Irish Sea. Eventually the body settled in Durham, but even there the body was moved to different locations within the church. The removal of bodies had been going on for centuries, and there is a theory that the pagan Anglo-Saxons brought the cremated remains of their ancestors over to England with them when they migrated. Although there are no examples to match St Cuthbert's journeys in the later Middle Ages, the translation or removal of both secular and religious bodies was not uncommon. In 1197 Beatrix de Say was buried in the Gilbertine priory of Chicksands, to the annoyance of the Cistercian house of Walden, but then her husband moved her body to his own Gilbertine foundation at Shouldham (Golding 1985: 64). In 1392 the Earl of Pembroke was removed from the Dominican church in Hereford to the Franciscan church in London, with the official sanction of the Bishop of Hereford (Capes 1916: 16). Bodies could also be removed if the person was thought to be inappropriate. A mistress of Henry II, Rosamund, had been buried before the high altar at the nunnery at Godstow, but Hugh of Lincoln ordered the body to be moved into the Chapter House of the nunnery (Anderson 1964: 150).

The removal and reburial of nobility was obviously for prestige and political reasons, but translation or exhumation could happen to lesser mortals. In 1334 a faculty was given to the Abbot of Shap

> to exhume the body of Isabel, wife of William Lenglays of Appelby, from the present tomb and re-inter it in a more suitable place in a church or churchyard, because of her honourable life and conduct; the bishop wishes her remains to be venerated.
>
> (Ross 1993: 30)

Practicalities might also dictate re-burial; two possible causes were the disputed consecration of a cemetery, or if a defiled burial had occurred and the remains needed to be dug up and reburied. In the diocese of Winchester the Carmelites were forbidden to bury people in their church – the one known burial was ordered to be exhumed (Douie 1969: 129–30). In 1440 there was an examination of the burials which had taken place without authority at the chapel of Templeton. They should have taken place in the parish church at Witheridge. Two or three graves had been dug at the chapel, although only one woman had been buried there. The burial had been ordered by a certain John Whitefield, senior, and the chapel had been illegally consecrated by a friar. The collector of the parish tithes had noticed two graves (one inside the chapel, one outside) but had not done anything 'because of the fury of John Whitefield and others'. The rector of Witheridge had the body exhumed and the woman was properly buried in consecrated ground at the parish church (Dunstan 1966: 211-12). This is a very odd account for two reasons: first, why were several graves dug while there was only one burial (unless they were to disguise the real burial); and second, why was it so important to John Whitefield to have the woman buried in the chapel? Both questions remain unresolved.

A medieval church can be described as a series of concentric rings. The most holy area was the high altar at the east end; the holiness lessening towards the west end and into the churchyard. All the holy areas were enclosed within the boundary of the cemetery. The concentric rings were not uniform, and even within the cemetery some areas were more holy that others (and therefore desirable). Within the church, the east end of the church – nearest to the high altar – was the most desirable, followed by the rest of the chancel, and then the nave. In the nave there were further divisions: altars, the font, rood screen and votive candles, which also acted as local foci of holiness. In some of the larger churches a favoured location was to be buried near a saint's shrine.

The power of this spiritual geography was shown by the way that people jostled or displaced people in burial. William Courtney, Archbishop of Canterbury, requested in his will:

> My body which will be corrupted and decay I wish to have buried as quickly as possible in a worthy manner in the nave of the cathedral church of Exeter at the place where there now lie three deans in a row before the great cross. . . . I wish that those three deans who will be removed because of my burial be interred at some other honourable place in the same church and wholly at my expense.
>
> (Dahmus 1966: 266)

For Courtney, burial before the great cross was the most honourable in the whole church. Even previous burials were no hindrance as they could be moved and buried elsewhere. Though the deans were to be buried 'at some other honourable place in the same church', it is obvious that Courtney had chosen *the* desirable burial location. It was rare in a will that the removal of bodies was described in such blatant terms, but the request highlighted the desire of important people to be buried in honourable places. Ironically, Courtney was eventually buried in an even more honourable spot: near Becket's shrine in Canterbury Cathedral.

The burial of the religious was fairly easy to determine. The priest was often buried in the chancel near to the high altar where he celebrated Mass every day. Abbots were often buried in the chapter house, which was the meeting place of the monks: at St Albans eleven abbots were buried in the chapter house, with two priors, a cellarer and Robert of the Chamber – the father of the only English pope, Nicholas Breakspear (Biddle 1979: 14–16). The chapter house could also be the burial place of laity who were accorded special devotion, but were not saints. This trend was evident in the twelfth and thirteenth centuries. The chapter house tomb of Rosamund, Henry II's mistress, became the centre of a cult of young people in love and women desiring children. The young boy William of Norwich was translated from the monk's cemetery at the south-east of the church into the chapter house, and was later interred in a shrine within the church (Anderson 1964: 149, 193). This reference to a young boy being buried in the chapter house is particularly interesting for at the Dominican priory in Oxford, children aged less than 15 'are almost entirely confined to the chapter-house' (Harman 1985: 188). Monks and canons usually had their own cemetery, often at the east end of the church. (One excavated example is that of the Gilbertine priory in York (Stroud and Kemp 1993)). Although the burial of the religious was usually well defined, there were exceptions and variations. The Cistercians, for example, had the right to bury two lay 'friends' in the exterior cemetery (Astill and Wright 1993: 132), which could cause demographic problems in assessing the monastic population.

The position of lay burials was potentially much more problematic. Once again honour, prestige and money were of concern. In the Statutes of Chichester 1292, there was an injunction that there should be no indiscriminate burials in the church or chancel except for those of the lords of the village, patrons of the church, and their wives, and the rectors and vicars. This was so that the church could accrue honour and nobility (Powicke and Cheney 1964: 117). A similar mandate was issued to the Dean of

Carlisle in 1342 by the Bishop, which prohibited burial of 'any body within the walls of a church, save those of patrons and rectors, without the bishop's licence' under penalty of excommunication (Ross 1993: 125). As well as honour and prestige, there might also be financial reasons behind this mandate as a licence would probably have to be bought.

To determine the important factors concerning the geography of holiness and lay burial in church, an analysis of place of burial for 4,700 wills between 1389 and 1475 was undertaken by the author. The wills are from the diocesan Exchequer Court of York and cover Yorkshire (except Howdenshire on the Humber) and Nottinghamshire. Will-making was not compulsory between these dates and they therefore form a random sample: the reasons for making a will, its registration at York, and survival rates are all unknown. Furthermore, there is a heavy bias towards York (1,612 wills) and the other urban centres of Hull (173), Scarborough (158), Nottingham (67) and Doncaster (54), which may mask different urban/rural patterns. Another bias is the high ratio of male adults to females. Further, it was only the more prosperous who made wills. Two other elements also affect the figures: there is no certainty that the wishes of the dead were carried out, and the outcome of requests to be buried 'Where God wills' or at the discretion of the executors remains unknown. The random and biased nature of the sample means that the figures cannot withstand detailed statistical analysis, but they do show broad trends of where it was desirable to be buried.

The most popular place for burial – with 388 requests – was in the choir (*choro*) of the church. Unfortunately the definition is confused, for as well as the high choir in the east end, the nave itself seems to have been called the 'choir' in some churches and there may have been choirs in the chantry and guild chapels. A much more precisely defined area was the chancel, in which only certain people could be buried. Out of a total of 126 requests (specifically either the chancel or near the high altar), 105 had accompanying occupations, which allows an analysis of the figures.

Rector	51
Vicar	23
Chaplain	9
Gentleman, Knight, Esquire	9

Widow, Lady, Daughter	5
Burgess, Citizen	4
Cleric	2
Canon	2
Grocer	1

These figures clearly show the heavy predominance of clergy burials within the chancel. Only the richest and most important lay people, and their wives or female relatives, were granted burial in the chancel. The grocer Thomas Catlynson of York, who was buried in 1498, may be indicative that the rigid system was breaking down, but his burial was probably more an indication of wealth rather than a slackening of the rules.

Whereas the chancel was an area to aspire to, the altars in the rest of the church, such as the nave, aisle and chantries, were within reach of more people. In all there were 187 requests for burial near altars, 81 of which gave an occupation. The trades represented show a much greater variety, including for example a baker, a girdeler and a draper. The shift away from the clergy and nobility to the trades can be shown by a comparison of the number of requests:

Citizen, Merchant, Tradesman	26
Gentleman, Knight, Esquire, Lord	20
Chaplain	19
Widow, Wife, Daughter	10
Rector, Parson	6

The low figure for the number of rectors who wished to be buried outside the chancel shows how far away the area outside the chancel was considered to be from the spiritual centre of the church.

The analysis of burial requests near altars spread around the church can be broken down further by altar dedication. Out of 163 known requests, the most popular was the Blessed Virgin Mary (44 requests). Surprisingly, no women requested to be buried near an altar dedicated to the Virgin, nor near altars dedicated to St Anne (4 requests in total). This may reflect the small number of women in the sample, as it is surprising that women rarely asked to be buried near altars dedicated to female saints: out of 12 requests to St Katherine, only 2 were by women. The second most popular saint was St Nicholas (14) near to whose altar four women requested burial. Altars to St James were requested 10 times (2 women), the Holy Trinity 9 times (no women) and John the Baptist 8 times (no women). Presumably such a list shows the power of each dedication – Mary occurring first as the Queen of Heaven, followed by Saints Nicholas and Katherine. Perhaps surprisingly, St Michael the Archangel, who weighed souls to determine whether they would go to Heaven or Hell, only received three requests.

After altars, images around the church were the next popular, with 66 requests. Once again the Blessed Virgin Mary is the most popular with 32 requests, which included one wife and one widow. The next most popular were St Katherine (4 requests) and the image of the Cross (4 requests). All Saints, John the Baptist and the Holy Trinity received 3 requests each. St Nicholas only had 1 request, as did an image of Thomas Becket.

The differences and similarities between altars and images is interesting. The Virgin Mary was by far the most popular in both cases, but then different patterns emerge, for example St Nicholas had 14 requests for burial by an altar, and only 1 by an image. The reasons are not easy to give. Being buried by an altar may have been seen as more influential in helping the soul get to heaven, and 163 people requested burial by an altar, as opposed to 66 by an image. A further reason may be that one altar in one church was very popular, with numerous bequests, thereby giving a false impression of popularity. The skewing of the figures can be shown not to be true. Of the 14 requests to Saint Nicholas, 12 different churches were involved. In the 12 requests to St Katherine, 11 different churches were involved, and in the case of St James (10 requests), 7 different churches were involved. Although the numbers are quite small out of a total sample of 4,700, there does seem to be a difference in trends between being buried near an altar or buried near an image.

It is possible that cemeteries also were divided into more and less desirable areas: the south side being more favoured than the north, and the churchyard cross being a magnet for burials. Whilst these examples are often cited, especially from folk tradition, there is remarkably little medieval evidence to back up these beliefs. A slightly stronger case can be made for the role of the cross than the south/north divide. Out of a total of 1,065 requests for burial in the churchyard, only 13 people (12 churches) wanted to be buried near the cross – just over one per cent. Only one person wanted to be buried directly 'before' the cross. The other requests used it as a locational marker: to the west of the cross (2 cases), to the left or east, (1 case each), or simply near the cross (7 cases). Although the cross was an obvious landmark, it does not seem particularly relevant to the position of burials in the diocese of York, although in an unpublished report of burial requests in Worcester, the churchyard cross does seem to have been more popular (pers. comm. C. Kightly).

An alternative request was to be buried in a liminal situation, for example across a boundary or near an edge, which may equate with the soul crossing the boundary from earth to the afterlife. In pagan Anglo-Saxon England, territorial boundaries were sometimes used as burial places, although it is usually not clear whether the burial or boundary came first. Physical boundaries were also important, and Beowulf's barrow was deliberately constructed on a cliff overlooking the sea. Sea-shore burial of Christians was very rare, especially in the later Middle Ages, but there is one apocryphal, but very interesting, example in *The Golden Legend* (Ryan 1993a: 378). In the account, various motifs clash: a wife on her way to Rome could not be drowned because she was a Christian (see Chapter 3), but she appeared dead and so was laid on the sea-shore. Many years later she was awoken, and discovered she had given birth to a son. Two resurrections have been accomplished: herself being brought back to life, and her son's birth. The sea-shore was a temporary place of burial, neither at sea nor in a graveyard. So long as the body was on the shore there was hope of recovery.

In Christian terms the churchyard defined the area of burial, but even so, liminal burials were possible. The two key areas were the thresholds between the outside and inside of the church (which, if there was a porch, was a larger area than simply the doorway); and the rood-screen, and especially its door, between the more secular nave and the holier chancel. Burials crossing these thresholds are not uncommon. At Chester, a 'prestigious' burial 'cut the line on which a screen might be expected ... and perhaps indicates the position of a doorway' (Ward 1990: 28). One of many documented examples was that of the Abbot of Gloucester, John de Wygmor, who requested to be buried at the entrance of the choir on the south side near the pulpit (Myers 1969: no. 463). A less obvious boundary was that between the aisle(s) and the nave. This was particularly marked at the Dominican friary in Chester where there was a strong bias to burials in the aisle, whereas burials in the nave were very sporadic (Ward 1990: 121). The same trend was discovered at Oxford Black Friars where nave burials were 'well spread out' but a 'very much higher concentration' of burials were found in the south aisle (Lambrick 1985: 143).

There were also vertical boundaries between Heaven and Earth. In medieval Christian terms this is symbolically represented by burial as close as possible to the high altar or a shrine. These places had the power to draw down holy influence from Heaven, which was sometimes represented in art by a ray of light. A burial under the feet of the priest by the high altar was on a direct vertical line to Heaven. At the most holy point of the Mass, the transubstantiation, which turned the bread and wine literally into the body and blood of Christ, it was hoped that the religious power of the miracle would emanate to the deceased's soul and so help it through Purgatory. A more tangible vertical belief related to being buried under the eaves drip of churches; the rainwater being sanctified by the church roof. One possible example was discovered at Norwich when a grave was found outside the church but close against the junction of the nave and chancel walls (Ayres 1985: 58).

The geographical areas of holiness were important, but of near equal weight was being close to one's family. It is occasionally written that burial beside a relation or even in the same tomb was mainly a post-Reformation Tudor phenomenon. 'After the Reformation, areas of the church became identified as the resting place of particular families, suggesting a new orientation, more secular and familial, in the face of death' (Gittings 1984: 87). Whilst it is true that after the Reformation altars and lights were no longer important in the placing of burials, family ties feature strongly in medieval requests for burial. This has been shown by the lure of the noble family mausoleum in monasteries (see above), but the same powerful incentive to be near one's relations can be shown for non-nobility as well.

The most popular request was for a wife to be buried near, or actually with, her husband. From the 4,200 wills studied there were 150 such requests, which compares favourably with the 187 requests to be buried by an altar. Next came requests of a husband to be buried with his wife (117 requests), or wives (2 requests), or a wife and children (4 requests). Burial near parents was the next most popular: near or with the father (54 requests), mother (24) and 36 with both parents. In one case a woman wanted to be buried with her parents and husband. Parents also wanted to be buried near their children (40 requests) and 13 people wanted to be buried beside their brother or sister. In terms of burial the family was a close-knit one. The only mention of an extended family came with four requests to be buried near an uncle. There were no requests for burial with an aunt, grandparents, godparents or close friends. The nearest example to a request for an extended family was a request for burial with 'ancestors'. Sometimes requests were made for burial near predecessors (such as the 2 requests for burial near Treasurers of York Minister), or former teachers (11 requests). A similar pattern of a close-knit family group specified at death was discovered from an analysis of prayers within wills of the nobility (Rosenthal 1972: 21–3) and from a study of burial requests from 500 London wills between 1380 and 1520. A high number of requests to be buried near family members (18–60 per cent of yearly totals) was found in London and a particular desirability was to be buried with a spouse, though not necessarily the last one (Harding 1992: 127).

In terms of a map of burial the holy sites inside the church came first in preference (and also cost), followed by burial with other family members. However, the mental map was more diverse than a straightforward choice, because different elements could be included in one request. In 1472 Robert Coke asked to be buried near the image of St Saviour, at the altar of the Blessed Virgin Mary in the south porch. This single request combined an image, altar and 'liminal burial' in the porch. A more complex example over several generations was the Ecop family from York, who had connections with St Helen-on-the-Walls. Robert Ecop asked to be buried next to the altar of St Nicholas and the grave of his children in 1460. Eight years later, his wife Margaret asked to be buried beside him, but does not mention the altar or children's tomb. In 1472, William Ecop, who was the rector of Heslerton, made a donation to St Helen's because his parents were buried there. (What relation William was to Robert – whether brother or son – is not clear). Even though there may be multiple elements which need untangling, what is given greatest relevance in the wills is illuminating: Robert wanted to be buried near the altar first, then his children, while

Margaret only cited her husband as the reason for her choice of burial location.

Whilst there was some variation about where a body could be buried, it was expected that a Christian would be buried in consecrated ground. Any exceptions were most unusual: the most remarkable were those who had to be buried during the Pope's Interdict against King John. The Interdict affected the whole of England and meant that consecrated cemeteries could not be used. This forced local churches and monasteries, such as Meaux Abbey and St Albans, to designate unconsecrated ground for burial. No one was excluded and even the bishops of Durham, Rochester and Bangor, and the chancellor of Lincoln, were all reputedly buried in unconsecrated ground (Cheney 1966: 163–4). This was an extreme measure in exceptional circumstances. In most cases Christians could only be buried in consecrated ground, and burials in unconsecrated ground could be removed. The burial at Templeton (see above) was removed because the chapel was not consecrated. A potentially confusing situation could arise if the church was consecrated, but not the cemetery, or the other way round. At Fairfield it was reported that

> the church was never dedicated, and the altars in the chancel are of wood badly put together, also the walls of the chancel are in bad condition [*debiles*] because they are full of holes in the lower parts; moreover the churchyard is dedicated, but not the church, because it is of wood and daub.
>
> (Woodruff 1917: 162)

One further reason for a cemetery being theologically unfit for burial was that it had become polluted by, for example, the shedding of blood. The only way that burials could continue was for the churchyard to be reconsecrated.

The perimeter of the churchyard was a boundary between the Christian and the non-Christian in death. Various writers had different ideas of who should be excluded from the graveyard. John of Burgo listed pagans, heretics and excommunicated people. Others defined the group to be buried outside the cemetery more widely. In the fifteenth century the priest John Mirk excluded from burial women who died in childbirth (see Chapter 5), thieves who had not made 'satisfaction' or were slain whilst thieving, lechers, and the 'cursed', who, if buried, were to be 'cast out' of the churchyard (Erbe 1905: 298). Those who died suddenly were also excluded, unless they were good people, were drowned by mishap, or accidentally slayed themselves 'by mischief against [their] will' (Erbe 1905: 298–9).

Lists of groups who were to be refused burial in cemeteries were also incorporated into statutes. The first Statutes of Salisbury (dated between 1217 and 1219) gave those who should not receive burial, the Eucharist, confession or other sacraments. The list included manifest usurers (*manifestos usurarios*), named excommunicates or the indicted (*interdictos*) and also, surprisingly, strangers to the parish (*alienos parochianos*). Some of these categories can be expanded and added to. In the Church's attempts to make the clergy celibate, the concubines of clergy were included in the lists. The Statutes of Winchester (1224) stated that concubines should leave the parish and vicinity. If they remained, they would be excluded from the sacraments and the communion of the faithful. If they still continued they would be whipped and, at the last, denied a church burial. This ruling was evident throughout the thirteenth century. In connection with celibacy the church attempted to regulate marriages by banns, but only the first and second Statutes of London (both dated 1245–59) specifically denied burial to those who married without banns. Perhaps this issue was particularly important in a city with a large, mobile and ever-changing population. The lack of similar statutes elsewhere shows it was probably a peculiarly London problem. Perhaps the statute was unworkable for it was not repeated later in the century (Powicke and Cheney 1964: 66, 132, 631, 643).

A group not mentioned in the statutes were those who died as a result of tournament or duel. The church's official stance was stern: anyone killed in a tournament or duel could not be buried in a church or churchyard, but could be given the last sacrament and extreme unction. The policy of non-burial was very rarely enforced and most were honourably buried in a church or cemetery. The only widely publicised case of refusal (which was later rescinded) occurred in Germany in 1175. In England there was little dispute and such men as Geoffrey de Mandeville (killed 1216), Gilbert Marshall (1241), Hugh Mortimer (1227) and John Mortimer (1318) were all buried with due reverence. The most important example was that of Geoffrey of Brittany, the son of Henry II, who was killed in a tournament in 1186 and was buried in the cathedral at Paris, even though it was only seven years after the last prohibition (Barber and Barker 1989: 142). A second group were also omitted from the statutes: suicides. Not only were suicides not mentioned in terms of burial, they were not mentioned in any legislation (Powicke and Cheney 1964: index). Initially this seems surprising. However, there was more leniency towards suicides in the Middle Ages than later in the Tudor era. Suicide was an act of violence against God and was therefore condemned, but there were various gradations of act and intention. There seem to be three types of suicide: the active suicide; the loss of the will to live; and suicide through madness.

The first type was condemned, though not as vehemently as in the Tudor period. In *The Golden Legend* there are two versions of Herod's death. The first is that after 'a violent coughing spell [he] turned his knife against his breast, looking round to see that no one could prevent him from killing himself' but his nephew prevented him from stabbing himself. The second version, cited from Remy's commentary on Matthew, was that Herod did indeed stab himself (Ryan 1993a: 59). Although the act was committed by a very sinful person, there was not the deep horror in the accounts that was evident later. The second type of suicide was the loss of the will to live. This does not seem to have been condemned as such – presumably because it happened over a long time and was therefore seen as God's will. In the case of St Agatha, after she had endured unbearable torture: 'having finished her prayer, she called out in a loud voice and gave up her spirit' (Ryan 1993a: 156). This seems to be in the same category as 'migrating' to the Lord, or 'falling asleep' with the Lord and was deemed to be part of God's will.

The third type was death through madness or despair. In England the church was curiously silent about suicides. In *c*.1000 there was a canon which prohibited normal burials and funerals for suicides, except madmen: but the next official canon concerning suicides was in 1662. Despair, however, was seen as the main reason for suicide and was allegorised in literature: in *Piers Plowman*, Avarice fell into despair, was about to hang himself and was only saved by the arrival of Repentance. If deliberate suicide was proved, there was also a severe financial implication as the crown acquired the property and lands of the deceased. The combination of the dishonour and financial implications meant that it was rare for a jury to convict a person of suicide; especially as, if suicide was suspected, a verdict of madness or misadventure was likely to be given. This makes suicide rates difficult to calculate accurately (MacDonald and Murphy 1990: 19–23). A good example of leniency was that of Maud, the widow of John Hoper. In 1420 an accusation was made that her burial, as a suicide, had polluted the churchyard. It was decided, however, that she was insane before and at the time of her suicide and so burial in the cemetery was allowed (Dunstan 1963: 13). An extraordinary case occurred in 1351 when it was reported to the Bishop of Exeter that a parish priest, Richard Boyle, who had committed suicide, was being revered as a saint by his parishioners. Local people were making pilgrimages to his tomb and twelve miraculous cures had been reported (Sumption 1975: 269). The reverence paid to the suicide was exceptional, but even though the church frowned on this type of death, it was unusual for a person who committed suicide to be buried outside the cemetery. The harsh and strict punishments of suicides after death, which resulted in the stake through the heart, and burial at a cross-roads, were only rigorously enforced from the late fifteenth century onwards. The reasoning was twofold; the stake would stop the body walking, and even if it did, it would get confused as to which way to go. This type of burial was not uncommon in the sixteenth century: in 1573 Thomas Maule was buried at midnight at the 'nighest' cross-roads with a stake in him because he hanged himself from a tree after a drunken fit (Cox 1910: 114).

For the worst cases of heresy and witchcraft, burning was an option. The theological reason for the use of fire was that it cleansed the soul on its journey. One other possibility was that it was a remembrance of past traditions of cremation. Stevenson noted that around the time of the Norman Conquest, a popular notion about ghosts or the undead was that the devil reanimated the corpse and then used it to play a variety of tricks on the living. The only remedy was to dig up the corpse and consume the body with fire (Stevenson 1991: section 124). A more suggestive example comes from France, when a fire was reported to have started in a grave and so turned the corpse to dust. This was interpreted as signalling the hopeless fate of the sinner buried there (Menache 1990: 96–7). The Lollards and sixteenth-century Reformers were often burnt: even after death. The body of Wyclif was posthumously exhumed and burnt. Burning could also be used as a punishment for witchcraft. To the medieval mind this was a terrible death for the fire consumed everything. (As noted in Chapter 3: being struck by lightning was only reserved for evil people.) A famous case which resulted in the burning of a witch occurred in 1451 when Dame Eleanor Cobham confessed that she had used the sorcery and witchcraft of 'a woman called the witch of Eye'. The result made the Duke of Gloucester love Eleanor and then wed her. 'Wherefore, and also because of the relapse, the same witch was burnt in Smithfield' on the 27 October (Myers 1969: no. 514). It is difficult to know how burnt the body actually was. Death by burning can range from total cremation, to death by smoke inhalation and only slight singeing of the body. Total cremation requires a great deal of wood because of the body's water content and it is therefore likely that some or all of the body would be left.

In very exceptional cases, mass burning of the dead was an option after battle. William of Malmesbury reported that the Crusaders heaped up the bodies of Turks and 'evaporated by means of fire' for the pragmatic reason that 'putrifying in the open air, they should pour contagion on the flagging atmosphere' (Stevenson 1991: section 369). Battle, siege and plague could also result in the non-burial of the dead. During the Agincourt campaign it was reported that bodies lay unattended in the streets during the siege of Harfleur (Hibbert 1964: 65). To the medieval mind, the impact of the image was compounded by the neglect of the bodies, as death and burial were normally communal events. Only rarely were the unburied bodies connected with disease and pestilence. During the siege of Jericho, William of Malmesbury reported on: 'the stench of the unburied dead bodies, the fumes of which exhaled in such a manner as to infect the sky itself. In consequence, a contagious pestilence spreading in the atmosphere, swept off many of the new comers' (Stevenson 1991: section 374). The physical lack of a body also meant that the normal funeral services could not take place. One of the most common causes was drowning at sea. Henry I's grief at the loss of his son in the White Ship disaster was probably heightened because not all the bodies could be found even by those who searched along the shoreline. 'Delicate as they were, they became food for the monsters of the deep' (Stevenson 1991: section 419). Bodies found on the sea-shore, however, could be buried in church (Erbe 1905: 299).

Burial carried out in secret was also treated with revulsion. In chronicle accounts, secret burials were often revealed by Divine intervention. William of Malmesbury recorded how Egbert, King of Kent, had some near relations murdered and buried in a rubbish tip. It was only when the 'eye of God . . . brought the innocents to light' that the neighbours dug the rubbish tip and formed the heaps of turf into 'a trench after the manner of the sepulchre, [and then] they erected a small church over it'. William also wrote of the murder, secret burial, and rediscovery of St Kenelm and the young boy Wistan (Stevenson 1991: sections 209, 211, 212). Occasionally factual accounts occur: between 1422 and 1442 Richer Lound of Norfolk was killed by two people, and his body was buried in the garden next to a hall. The grave was dug 6 feet deep and the ground was replanted carefully to prevent discovery. However, the fact that the case was recorded suggests that a search had been carried out and that the body had been found. Two people were condemned (Maddern 1992: 121–2). A spectacular case of secret murder and burial, which was later used as Tudor propaganda, was that of the young Edward V. The Tudor author Rastell wrote in his *The Pastime of People* (1529) that the bodies of Edward V and Richard, Duke of York, had been put into a heavy chest, and then dumped into the sea on the way to Flanders. This death has the double connotation of not only being secret, but also of drowning and being eaten by sea-monsters. An alternative was that the children had been persuaded to hide in a chest and were buried alive in it in a great pit under the stairs. Later they were disinterred and thrown into the sea (Hanham 1975: 104). This version has the additional element of being buried alive, a terrible fate at any time in history.

A final category of burial might be classed 'the odd and unusual', which may hark back to earlier rituals (see also Chapter 7). A striking example was the burial of Owen Glendower's cousin who was reputedly placed in a hollow oak tree (Rees 1985: 20), although this may have been used to explain a haunted oak (pers. comm. C. Kightly). Other references exist to tree trunks, and in a striking comparison the supposed body of King Arthur was also 'encoffined in a hollow oak' (Rahtz 1993: 43), as witnessed by Geoffrey of Monmouth. That the monks had probably buried Arthur a little time before seems to show the use of hollow oaks was still common. At both Barton upon Humber and York bodies were buried in hollowed-out tree trunks (Panter 1994: 31). Other inexplicable burials have also been recorded, such as the 'boy [who] was found dead in an earthen pot in a pit' in 1218 (Stenton 1937: 344), a possible reference to a prehistoric urn burial.

The horror of a non-cemetery or non-church burial was such that in practice few people were exempted. The cemetery in the Middle Ages was, after the church, the holiest place in most towns and villages. It was also a social place, and the conflict between the holy and the social gave rise to many disputes between the church hierarchy and the local population, who used it for games, markets, pasturing animals and refuge. These secular uses were unacceptable to the church hierarchy and gradually throughout the Middle Ages the solely religious use of the churchyard gained ground.

There were two commonly used Latin words for the graveyard: *coemeterium* and *atrium*. *Coemeterium* reflects the nature of resting and sleep as it derives from the Greek word for bedroom. The second is derived from the Classical Latin and originally meant 'a reception room in a house partially open to the sky', but it came to mean an enclosed space, or cemetery. This word was especially popular in both Picardy and Normandy. The idea of an enclosure also highlights the role of the cemetery as a pro-tected (if sometimes only spiritually) place of refuge or sanctuary (Barrow 1995: 79). The cemetery as a refuge was especially important in times of war, and during the anarchy of the twelfth century William of Malmesbury recorded that the men of Flanders and Brittany were rapacious and violent, and 'made no scruple to violate churchyards or rob a church' (Stevenson 1991: section 14). In peacetime too a churchyard could be used as a storage place. In 1218–19 the constable of Tickhill and his uncle took the corn of William de Buoles which was stored in the churchyard at Laughton en le Morthen (Stenton 1937: 209).

Despite the cemetery's holiness, there was a very strong tra-dition of secular use. These traditions, which can sometimes be traced back to at least Anglo-Saxon times, proved stubbornly resistant to reforming bishops and ecclesiastical statutes. The statutes and decrees form the largest coherent body of evidence for lay activities in the churchyard, although contemporary refer-ences give supporting evidence. An individual statute, however, cannot be plundered for evidence without consideration of how it came to be formed. The vast majority of statutes borrowed heavily from earlier ones and it was not uncommon for a bishop, when he moved diocese, to republish his previous statutes in his new diocese. A comparison of statutes shows this process in action. The synodal Statutes of Salisbury (1217–19) have been described as 'some of the most important diocesan legislation of Medieval England' (Powicke and Cheney 1964: 57). The writer, Bishop Richard Poore, was translated to the bishopric of Durham in 1228 and the statutes were reissued in his new diocese. These statutes had therefore been published in dioceses of both the provinces of Canterbury and York and were widely copied by contemporaries.

As well as republishing from a single source, statutes could include elements from many different sources. The wholesale borrowing of ideas, phrases and items allows the influences upon individual statutes to be analysed. The second synodal statutes of Bishop Peter Quinel of Exeter (16 April 1287) are an excellent example. (Roman numerals indicate first, second, etc.) Powicke and Cheney identified within Exeter II elements of the statutes of: Salisbury I (dated to between 1217 and 1219); synods of an unknown diocese (1222–5); Exeter I (1225?–37); Salisbury II (1238–44); Worcester II (1240); Wells (1258?); Worcester III; Lincoln (1239?) and Winchester III (1262–5). Quinel also brought his statutes up to date and was familiar with the great councils of Oxford 1222, London 1237, London 1268, Reading 1279, Lambeth 1281 and also had knowledge of papal councils and decretals (Powicke and Cheney 1964: 984). This range of influence is unusual, but most statutes were based at least in some part on precursors. It is therefore difficult to determine whether the statutes are an accurate reflection of the position within the parishes, or whether they were a list of possibilities which may, or may not, have happened at the local level. The repetition of an item – between many statutes and a wide geographical spread – may simply indicate that it was contained in an original statute, rather than that the practice continued. Even though the statutes may not reflect the reality at a local level, they do throw light on the concerns of the bishops.

A frequent requirement within statutes was that cemeteries should have defined boundaries. The Statute of Winchester III (1262–5) ordered that the cemetery was to be enclosed by a ditch or bank (*fossato*), a wall, or a hedge (*sepe*) (Powicke and Cheney

1964: 708). Many statutes were anxious to prevent 'brute animals' or swine entering a cemetery. When they entered they not only ate the grass, but trampled on dead bodies and even dug or snuffled them up (Powicke and Cheney 1964: 379, 1005). The sight of animals digging up decomposing bones (possibly of one's relatives) cannot have been pleasant. The official complaint described the problem in terms of reverence: that the bodies of the holy (*sanctorum*) were resting until the 'salvation' and people should show reverence to them. The responsibility to enclose the cemetery was that of the incumbent, who was to be forced to comply by censure if necessary. The visitation returns recorded the problem in reality. The returns of the diocese of Canterbury (1292–4) discovered badly fenced churches at Womanswould, Aldington and Smeeth, and Loose. At New Romney it was reported that the churchyard fence 'is out of repair and in the same condition as it was last year' (Woodruff 1917: 149, 169, 178; 1918: 85).

Sometimes the attitudes of the local inhabitants or incumbents were also a problem. At Aldington and Smeeth the 'vicar pastureth his horses in the churchyard'. As a penalty he was bidden to keep the church gate shut. Another incumbent, at Westwell, pastured his tithe lambs in the churchyard in spring. (This conjures up a morbidly amusing image of spring lambs leaping amongst the graves.) Other farming practices could also take place, and at Deal the rector was found to winnow his corn in the churchyard (Woodruff 1918: 85). These violations do not seem to have been heavily punished, but a more serious case concerned Robert Byng at Deal who was accused of making the churchyard a common pasture and grazing his animals on it. He confessed that this had once happened, and swore it would not happen again. Despite this promise he was flogged three times (Woodruff 1917: 178; 1918: 86, 89). The cemetery was therefore used a resource and even a source of income. It was not uncommon for the incumbent to be granted the trees in the churchyard. In 1436 a new chapel and churchyard were built at Callington and the rector alone was granted the right to dispose of trees growing in the churchyard (Dunstan 1966: 90). A dispute about the ownership of the trees occurred at Worth (1292–4) when it was reported that the trees in the churchyard had been felled and sold by the parishioners. This was contested by the rector, who claimed he had the sole right (Woodruff 1918: 82). A dis-

111

pute, and the lengthy agreement, was also recorded between the vicar and parishioners of Broadhempston. The first statement followed canon law and stated that all the trees and grass were church property, especially in this case as the trees acted as a wind-break. This was then modified by saying that the parishioners could cut down trees, after a licence had been granted, for the repair of the nave: the clergy could cut down trees for the repair of the chancel. The hedges or hedge-row trees could be cut back without a licence, so long as the wind-breaks were not damaged (Dunstan 1967: 310).

Buildings within the cemetery were only permissible in wartime and at all other times houses or cottages (*casis*) must be pulled down. In 1240 the Statutes of Worcester III stated that only in time of war should buildings be allowed in the cemeteries, and then immediately torn down; and even in time of war the builders must have a licence from the rector to build (Powicke and Cheney 1964: 193). In bishoprics with borders on the Welsh and Scottish frontiers the threat of war was greater, although the various civil wars in England might have given rise to some building in cemeteries for protection. In the Statutes of Norwich (1240–3) (Powicke and Cheney 1964: 353) the reasons for building included an incursion by the enemy (*hostiles incursus*) or 'sudden destruction by fire' (*incendia repentina*). In peacetime, buildings in churchyards were generally frowned upon. In the Statutes of Norwich, buildings were banned on two counts: first, the worldly living which took place in the cemetery (*inmunditam fornicationis vitandam*); and second, on the occupation of the cemetery, which indicates the worry of the church about the encroachment of lay buildings.

As well as the property in the churchyard, the cemetery land itself could be disputed. In densely populated urban areas building land was often in short supply, and the high land prices were an encouragement to sell cemetery land. Alternatively a cemetery fell within different jurisdictions, and – as the land and burial rights were profitable – disputes ensued. A disagreement arose between the Abbot of Pershore and the Abbot of Westminster over the possession of a tenement in Pershore built in the cemetery. A further complication was that the Abbot of Westminster complained about the last burial which had been presided over by the Dean (Baildon 1890: 48). In this one case, the two abbots and the dean seem to have different jurisdictions within the same cemetery.

An alternative was lay encroachment upon the cemetery. A blatant attempt was reported by William of Malmesbury in 1139 when Bishop Roger of Salisbury began to build a castle which was partially on the land of the cemetery and scarcely a stone's throw from the main church (Stevenson 1991: section 19). A similar castle-building scheme over a part of a cemetery was discovered during archaeological excavations at Norwich (Stirland 1985). A much more common form of encroachment, and more insidious, was the small piecemeal eating-away at cemetery land by the laity. The problem was described, and the penalties, in the Acts of Exeter Cathedral in 1390, whereby 'the laity who fixed pales and posts in the graveyard and closed certain portions of it with the walls of their houses ... [should remove poles and palings under] pain of excommunication' (Myers 1969: no. 453).

Markets and trading held in churches or cemeteries were also condemned in the statutes. The biblical example of Christ ejecting the buyers and sellers from the temple was often cited, for example in the Statutes of Wells (1258?) (Powicke and Cheney 1964: 601), and another common reason was that the church should not be made into a 'cave of robbers'. The churchyard and church of St Paul's Cathedral was a traditional place for business and in 1385 Bishop Braybrooke acted against people who traded in the Cathedral itself, and, implicitly, against traders in the churchyard (Stone 1977: 32). In rural Lincolnshire, bishops acted against trading in churchyards in 1239 and in 1392 (Owen 1971: 105).

Games were also condemned. In the twelfth century

> on the day after Christmas there were gatherings in the cemetery, wrestling bouts and matches between the Abbot's servants and the burgesses of the town; and from words they came to blows, and from buffets to wounds and bloodshed.
>
> (Butler 1949: 92–3)

As a punishment the people involved were stripped naked, scourged and the Abbot 'publicly forbade gatherings and shows in the cemetery'. Bishop Grosseteste of Lincoln prohibited martial games, specifically the jousting at a quintain on wheels (Owen 1971: 105). In the Statutes of Exeter II (1287) (Powicke and

113

Cheney 1964: 1009) it was stressed that the bodies of the dead should be honoured, and that the priest should denounce dishonest games. Under this heading was also included theatre (*teatrales*) and spectacles (*ludibriorum spectacula*) which took place on the vigils and feast days of the saints. These should be detested as they polluted the honest churches. That they happened can be shown by a miracle story from Beverley when a young boy fell from the minster roof whilst watching an Easter play being held in the northern part of the cemetery (*polyandri*) (Raine 1879: 328–9).

In the Statutes of London II, dated between 1245 and 1259, games or plays (*ludi*), singing songs, wrestling (*lucte fiant*), ring-dancing and wanton behaviour were all forbidden because reverence should be shown to the bodies of the dead (Powicke and Cheney 1964: 649). These types of restrictions were stated many times and across a wide geographical area. This was probably a reflection of the seriousness of the situation, for instances from other sources are known, for example, the monk who climbed up a gate to behold the pipe-players (*fistulatores*) and the ring-dancers (*ducentes choreas*) in the churchyard of the parish church (Thompson 1915: 24). A decree in 1384, by William of Wykeham, Bishop of Winchester, condemned the pollution of cemeteries by dissolute dances and 'stone-castings' (Chambers 1971: 72). 'Stone-casting' is an enigmatic phrase, but the range of explanations spans the merely athletic to ancient pagan rituals. Also forbidden was the playing of tennis, which occasioned the 'brawling, contention and shouts' in the churchyard of the collegiate church of Ottery St Mary in 1451 and so disrupted those trying to pray for departed souls (Dunstan 1967: 119). The game was to cease under threat of excommunication.

Religious or 'honest' gatherings were acceptable in the cemetery and at Beverley a night procession in the cemetery was the occasion for a miracle (Raine 1879: 323). At Waddesworth church in 1498 an indulgence was given on forty days to those who – when they heard the great bell rung – knelt in the church or the churchyard and said the Lord's Prayer and Angelic Salutation (Barker 1976: 243). The cemetery could also be used for official business, such as preaching and proclamations. This was normally intentional, although when Master Robert of Derby locked out a visitation commissary, the visitation had to take place in the churchyard (Woodruff 1917: 171–2). The most prestigious churchyard in England was at St Paul's Cathedral, London, and it has been described as a 'mirror of Medieval life and thought' (Owst 1926: 208) where important announcements were regularly made, a tradition which continued into the seventeenth century (Maclure 1958). The Ordinances of 1311 were first proclaimed there, and then a tablet was erected so that the memory of them was not lost (King 1979: 95), and preaching, processions and punishments in the churchyard were commonplace (Owst 1926: 209). Occasionally, preaching could be detrimental to the church if the preacher happened to be a Lollard or Reformer. In the churchyard of St Frideswide in Oxford, in 1382, the Lollard Nicholas Hereford preached many 'wicked and detestable things in the grave-yard . . . exciting the people to rebellion' (Myers 1969: no. 501). The church was aware of the dangers of unauthorised preaching, and in 1409 the Constitutions of Archbishop Arundel stated that 'If anyone should preach in any church, graveyard, or other place in the province of Canterbury without licence [then that place shall] lie under an interdict' (Myers 1969: no. 506).

The Church was keen to distance the heretical and secular elements from the holy ground of the churchyard. The cemetery was portrayed as a place where the dead could rest in peace, without interference from the outside secular influences of snuffling animals or lascivious living. Religious processions and preaching were acceptable as they respected the dead. The choices connected with burial also show tensions between the purely religious and secular: groupings of burials around altars or lights, and the social influence of family graves. The decision where to be buried was not straightforward: many factors made a potential impact. It was only after the Reformation that the dilemma was partially resolved by the removal of many of the religious foci and an increased emphasis on the family grave.

5

THE BODILY EVIDENCE

The importance of carefully excavating and analysing the evidence of human remains has increased markedly over the last few decades and is now a flourishing area of study. In the 1960s, however, skeletons were often given little attention. This was highlighted in the excavation report of St Mary Le Port, Bristol, excavated in 1962 and 1963. Not only was there limited time and money, but

> in the early 1960s the importance of investigation of Medieval Christian cemeteries had hardly been realised. The general impression, including the 'official' view of central government and local museum sponsorship, was that we knew all we needed to know about Christian burial, that in any case they had no finds, and that there was an element of impropriety in disturbing or even looking scientifically at interments of a community whose religious beliefs and mortuary practice were at least nominally those of our own day . . . vaults [were] emptied by unskilled workers, [and] any coffins [were] smashed in the process. In one case a lead coffin was attacked by vandals . . .
>
> (Watts and Rahtz 1985: 128)

Although the official attitude may have changed, a lack of respect for the dead can still exist and the archaeological press in 1994 reported the treatment of lead coffins, which echoes that from the 1960s: 'Sub-contractors break open a 19th century child's coffin at Sevenoaks, before reburying the body in a plastic sack in a mass grave' (Morris 1994: 9) The accompanying picture to the article shows two heavily protected people prising open the (lead?) coffin with a spade.

Even where archaeologists have been informed, cases may still occur where investigation can not be carried out. In 1973 the graveyard of the redundant St Giles's Church, Colchester (Crummy *et al.* 1993: 221), was dug by machine, which destroyed a mass of intercutting burials. Thankfully this sort of complete unrecorded destruction is rare, although a suspicion remains that this case was truthfully reported, whereas other instances may remain hidden.

The variable conditions of cemetery excavation and dating are exemplified by two other groups of burials from Colchester (Crummy *et al.* 1993). The lay cemetery of the Crouched Friars was known from historical evidence and previous discoveries. During excavation sixteen burials were identified, but stratigraphic relationships could only be established when one grave intercut another. Grave-cuts were difficult to distinguish and there was no evidence of any grave-goods or coffins to indicate date of burial or status. The archaeology revealed 'an intensively-used and long-lived cemetery' which indicated that burials occurred before the burial licence was granted in 1402. The cemetery could not be dated within precise time limits: giving a general dating of 'late medieval to early sixteenth century'.

The dating of cemeteries from historical sources (and archaeology in general) is problematic; for example, the historical sources usually indicate only when a cemetery or church was already in existence. Even a burial licence does not necessarily indicate when the first burials took place: the licence might confirm a previous practice. Occasionally the archaeological dates of a cemetery are so wide as to be meaningless, as is shown by the cemetery at St Benedict, Norwich. During excavations, 37 skeletons were discovered which had a sex ratio of 11 males, 9 females, 2 unsexable, and 15 skeletons less than 13 years old. The potentially interesting data were rendered useless for the burials ranged in date from pre-Conquest to twentieth century – on average only three per century. An interesting case of rickets was probably a result of twentieth-century slum life (Wells 1982: 25).

Occasionally graves can be closely dated and the skeletons survive in excellent condition. Fifteen skeletons were recovered from St John's Church in Colchester. They could be closely dated to between 1133 and pre-1171, as the new church of St Giles, and its associated burial ground, was in existence from at least

117

1171. The skeletons remained undisturbed, as later burials and the associated intercutting of graves took place in the new cemetery.

Once human remains have been discovered their burial positions can be determined. The significance of burial position is problematic as there does not seem to be a universal trend across cemeteries. The most common positions are with the hands over the pelvis, arms crossed on the chest, or arms by the sides of the body. These positions were found at the Dominican friary at Chester, with fourteen, nine and six examples respectively (Ward 1990: 124). At St Nicholas Shambles, out of 234 skeletons the 'position of the hands ... does not seem to vary significantly' (White 1988: 18) as they all had their arms by their sides. Burial trends sometimes occur within cemeteries. At Chester, juveniles were buried with their hands by their sides. At Hull a small number of burials in the chancel area, who were probably the priors of the Augustinian friary, were buried with their hands on their chests, perhaps in a praying position (pers. comm. D. Evans). Towards the end of the Middle Ages, the burial position was increasingly represented on monumental brasses and sculpture, with the body sometimes depicted in its shroud. The most frequent position was with the hands in an attitude of prayer, followed by a crossing of the arms over the chest, and finally the hands over the groin (Litten 1991: 60). Standard burial positions do seem to vary over time but the reasons and chronology for the changes have yet to be fully explored.

Occasionally a completely unexpected burial position is encountered, for example a prone burial (which can also be called a 'face-down' or 'live' burial). These are more common in the pagan periods, and a remarkable sequence of peculiar burials has been discovered at the pagan Anglo-Saxon cemetery of Sutton Hoo (Carver 1995). A prone burial was discovered at the Anglo-Saxon cemetery at Sewerby, and whilst there has been some debate about the burial, there is no intrinsic reason why the woman was not buried alive (Hirst 1993: 41). In the later medieval period such burials were extremely unusual within a churchyard setting. One exception was discovered at Guestwick in Norfolk where a 'gruesome' burial was partly buried face down and was horribly contorted: the person was probably killed violently (McKinley 1987: 74). It is unfortunate that the only dating possible for this burial was 'late- or post-medieval' as literary examples from the sixteenth and seventeenth centuries are known of 'gruesome' burials of suspected vampires (Barber 1988). A medieval example would have been particularly interesting.

The burial position can often be determined even in skeletons with minimum preservation, but for cemetery studies in general the survival rate of skeletons is critical. The survival rate can be influenced by two factors: the conditions of burial and decomposition, and the later disturbance of the grave.

The amount and type of soil a body is buried in has an important effect upon the rates of decomposition. It has been calculated that an average burial will displace two cubic metres of soil (Rodwell and Rodwell 1977: 42). In very acidic soils the body might be dissolved away, leaving only a body stain or silhouette. The most dramatic examples in England are those from the pagan Anglo-Saxon cemetery at Sutton Hoo (Carver 1995). Good preservation may result in even the smallest bones of the human body – in the ear – surviving. At Chichester a total of 136 ear bones survived from 89 individuals (Bruintjes 1990: 627). The best soils for preservation are alkaline soils, such as chalk, where gall or bladder stones, or even hardened arteries may be preserved (Rodwell 1981: 148), although rapid drainage of ground water may lead to very poor bone preservation even on chalk.

The general processes of bodily decomposition are known; but there are numerous factors which influence the rate of decomposition. A body left in the open air will decompose much more quickly than in a coffin; a body with open wounds or septicaemia will decompose more quickly than one without. The agents which determine speed of decomposition are not fully understood, and in one modern case two people, who were killed together and buried in adjacent graves, had different rates of decomposition (Garland 1989). The way the body is buried is also important. A coffined burial – which is shielded from the soil – will decompose at a different rate to a body buried in the soil. If the coffin is completely sealed then decomposition may stop altogether. A sealed sheet of lead was found at St Bees in Cumbria; the processes of decay had stopped and a medieval middle-aged man was perfectly preserved. Preservation of Anglo-Saxon saints – the most famous being St Cuthbert – may also have been caused by sealing the coffin, though in both the St Bees and St Cuthbert examples the nearly complete lack of food in the stomachs probably helped in the preservation. This halting of decomposition was uncommon, as the majority of medieval coffins had drainage holes in them, and the food in the stomach would have added bacteria so that decay would have started internally.

In medieval England it was very rare for a person not to be buried. Exceptions might be criminals hung up and left to rot, bodies left to rot on a battle field, or the heads of victims being stuck on poles. After the battle of Wakefield during the Wars of the Roses, the most important people had 'their heads, put upon stakes, [and were] carried to York for a spectacle of the people' before being put upon one of the city gateways (Ellis 1844: 109). Even so, criminals were normally buried after death. At Norwich those who were hung as a punishment were buried in the churchyard of St Margarets in Combusto (Ayres 1990: 56–9). For the vast majority of the population it was normal for the body to be buried.

Once death has occurred the body quickly begins to decompose as a result of the heart stopping. This leads to the lack of cell renewal, and lytic enzymes are released. This process is called 'autolysis' and has been defined as the 'postmortem fermentative processes which operate without the participation of bacteria' (Garland 1989: 22), in other words, a natural bodily decay without any external bacteria.

The next stage, putrefaction, is the progressive breakdown of body tissue. The body cavities swell and eventually the tissue liquefies and leaves the skeleton, which is held together by ligaments, which slowly decompose (Garland 1989: 22). A coffin has a marked impact on the decomposition of the body. If the coffin is sealed, the body will be lying in body liquids. Eventually a chemical equilibrium will be formed within the coffin, at which time decomposition will probably stop. In an unsealed coffin, or when a coffin itself begins to rot, the rotting coffin, and the chemicals, water and organisms from the soil all influence decomposition. Physical damage to the skeleton may also occur if the coffin lid collapses into the coffin. Such cases have been found at Colchester (Crummy et al. 1993: 215–17).

Normally the body naturally decomposes, although several techniques can be used to stop or slow down the processes. The first is mummification, in which embalming fluids were used to help preserve the body. The most famous are the Egyptian examples, although embalming and preservation techniques were known in medieval England. In an apocryphal account, the medieval chronicler William of Malmesbury described how the body of the classical hero Pallas was discovered at Rome, having escaped corruption because the body was embalmed. After its discovery the body was leant against a wall and was dripped upon by rain water, resulting in 'corruption common to mortals; the skin and nerves dissolving' (Stevenson 1991: section 206). It was not uncommon for medieval royalty to use preservation techniques such as the removal of the internal organs. Other methods are by desiccation, where the body survives because it is dried by heat or cold; or in waterlogged conditions. Well-preserved bodies have been discovered in Greenland buried in the permafrost, and in England where the body was deposited in a peat bog, for example 'Lindow Man' where preservation was exceptional (Denison 1994b: 3). Even in relatively normal conditions some parts of the body can unexpectedly survive. At the Augustinian friary at Hull fifteen medieval brains survived. They were shrunken and 'spongey' but still recognisable (Denison 1995a: 4). Although a rare survival, it is not unique, and brains were also discovered during the excavation at Sandwell Priory (Hodder 1991: 115).

After the body liquids have been absorbed by the soil, the bones remain in the grave. Bones have a much better survival rate than soft tissue, but they too are subject to decomposition. The key factor determining the survival of the bone is the relationship between its protein and mineral constituents. The assessment of bone decay, called 'diagenesis', has many techniques, such as electron microsopy. In a study of eighty-eight adult Romano-British skeletons the variable survival rate of different bones was analysed. The smaller and more vulnerable bones – such as those of the hands, feet and base of spine – were poorly represented. One surprising result was that the bones on the front of the body (such as the patella (knee-cap) and sternum (breast-bone)) were also under-represented (Garland 1989: 26).

The processes of decomposition, and bone changes whilst living, were known in general terms by medieval people, although the explanation was often described in religious terms. William of Malmesbury makes a direct link between prayers and affliction of the knees. One of William the Conqueror's daughters died and a 'hard substance, which proved the frequency of her prayers, was found upon her knees after her decease' (Stevenson

1991: section 276). The study of anatomy slowly became more sophisticated during the Middle Ages with many operations being carried out, such as healing skull fractures and cauterising wounds (Jones 1984: fig. 43, plate 9).

Occasionally, particular organs were given special treatment, the most common being the heart. Burial of the heart was a popular practice at the time of the Crusades, possibly because the heart was easy to carry back from the East, and because of its ancient symbolism and biblical references (Gill 1936: 11). Hugh, Earl of Stafford, died at Rhodes on his way back from Jerusalem. His heart and bones were brought back to England by his squire John Hinckly for burial at Stone Priory (Luttrell 1991: 181). There were various means of storing the hearts for burial. King John's heart was kept in a silver vessel (Welander 1991: 142), and an ivory heart case, purported to be of thirteenth-century Sicilian work, is at York Minster. Archbishop Walter Gifford's heart was deposited in two leaden dishes soldered together (patens?) and preserved with spices. Angels often decorated the heart shrines, for example that of Eleanor of Castile (Gill 1936). Hearts are not uncommonly depicted on monumental brasses, normally in someone's hands, though this may equally be religious symbolism, as much as an actual heart burial.

Other parts of the body could also be treated separately, though this practice was not so common. The body might be boiled and the bones sent back to England for burial, or alternatively embalmed or, after the vital organs had been removed, stuffed. The body of Eleanor of Castile was stuffed with barley (Gill 1936: 14) and Bishop Geoffrey Rufus of Durham (died 1140) was disembowelled and preserved from decomposition by salt (Carver 1980: 13). The Bishop of Hereford, Thomas Cantilupe, died in Italy in 1282 and his heart and his head were carried back to England. His heart was buried in Hereford Cathedral, and his head was buried in Ashridge, Hertfordshire. When Robert de Ros – who was one of the signatories of the Magna Carta – died, his heart was buried at Croxton Abbey, and his bowels before the high altar of Kirkham Abbey (Gill 1936: 8). The practice of dismemberment was condemned by Boniface VIII (1294–1303) who described it as cruel and profane, shocking to the faithful, abominable in the sight of God and impious to the deceased (Brown 1981). It might be for this reason that in 1312 the head of Piers Gaveston had to be sewn back on to the body before burial (Denholm-Young 1957: 28). The practicalities of burial, however, meant that Boniface's successor, Benedict XI, modified this stance: Pope John XXII (1313–24) was more practical still and made money by issuing licences for the division of the body.

There is only fragmentary archaeological evidence for the medieval practice of dismemberment or heart burials. The body of Robert the Bruce was reportedly found at Dunfermline Abbey 'with his breast bone carelessly sawn through' (Gill 1936: 4). At Hulton Abbey one skeleton had cut marks on many bones, his body split down the middle and his head cut off. It is possible that the reason is superstition against the dead, but more probably it was the result of the massacre by the Welsh of an English force. The body has tentatively been identified as that of William Audley, who died whilst attacking Anglesey in the thirteenth century (Klemperer 1992: 86–7). An alternative explanation is that the body was dismembered after death. Earlier evidence is even rarer, though a sixth-century example, exceptional for the time, has been suggested from Maiden Castle (Brothwell 1971).

Even after burial there was a strong possibility that the body would be disturbed. Statutes were passed to maintain boundary walls and ditches to keep out animals, but complaints were still made: in the cemetery of St John Baptist, York, dogs and birds were attracted by a great heap of offal put there by the butchers. Bones, probably both human and animal, were reportedly scattered across the churchyard (Raine 1955: 82). A more human threat was the cutting through of bodies when digging new graves (Plate 5). This can be a severe problem in modern archaeological excavations. At St Nicholas Shambles, London, only thirty-six skeletons were complete out of a total of 234, and half the skeletons were 'deficient in the head region' (White 1988: 29). A very high degree of skeletal completeness came from St Andrew's, York, where over half were 80 per cent complete and less than 10 per cent had less than one quarter of the body represented (Stroud and Kemp 1993: 160). For St Helen-on-the-Walls, York, no precise figures were given, but in addition to the relatively complete burials (Plate 6) a 'great number of disarticulated scattered bones or part bones were found both with skeletons to which they did not belong or in other contexts in the general graveyard area' including charnel pits (Plate 7) (Dawes and Magilton 1980: 25–7).

Even if the degree of completeness is very high, analysis of the cemetery as a whole is complicated by other factors. For example, an assumption cannot normally be made that the skeletons form a cross-section of the local population, as the majority of cemeteries are not completely dug, and the excavated graves cannot be precisely dated (Stirland 1989: 62). Various estimates have been attempted to determine the possible number of bodies buried, or the size of the population settlement. One estimate is that from a population of 200 people over 1,000 years there would be 6,000 burials (Rahtz, quoted in Shoesmith 1980: 53). If the population was relatively stable, dying, for example, three times a century, a settlement size could be worked out over time. This of course is fraught with complications (migration, plague, population fluctuations), but such estimates might be a useful starting point. If several cemeteries are completely excavated in a small area, a regional picture may be built up of population size.

The smaller the area of cemetery excavation, the more difficult it is to make general conclusions about demography and life expectancy. During excavations of the north-east bailey of Norwich Castle, a cemetery was discovered, but no boundaries were found, which limited the accuracy of population estimates (Stirland 1985: 49). Even in large-scale excavations, such as St Helen-on-the-Walls, York, where a minimum of 1,041 bodies were discovered, it was estimated that only two-thirds of the site had been dug (Dawes and Magilton 1980: 9). At St Andrew's, York, more burials were thought to exist to the south and west of the site (Stroud and Kemp 1993: 130), and the same is probably true of St Nicholas Shambles (White 1988: 7). The same lack of completeness can be replicated on many other sites. It is generally assumed that the higher the number of burials found, the more representative the sample is of the parish or local population as a whole. This may be a correct assumption, but a potential flaw occurs if the bodies were buried in distinct groupings within the cemetery, the cemetery had defined 'zones' for certain burials, or burials took place from other settlements outside the parish.

Zoning of burials is relatively common, especially in the case of child burials. Burial of children should be very common as the infant mortality rate was very high, and in some cemeteries this is evident in the archaeological record. At Winchester out of 260 bodies there were 116 adults, 125 children and 19 indeterminate (Kjølbye-Biddle 1975: 105); and at Barton Bendish,

Norfolk, the largest single category, with seventeen examples, was children aged 0–5. However, a frequent feature of excavated medieval cemeteries is that children or infants are under-represented. At St Helen-on-the-Walls, the excavator expressed surprise that so few baby skeletons were found, and those that were found were buried with adults (Dawes and Magilton 1980: 27). At St Nicholas Shambles, London, only 17.5 per cent of articulated burials were juveniles (0–12 years old) when the proportion has been estimated at 30–50 per cent for pre-industrial society (White 1988: 30). This pattern has been discovered elsewhere, for example at the Augustinian priory site at Taunton (Rogers 1984).

The reasons for the low numbers of child or infant burials have been extensively discussed. Reasons that have been put forward include the burying of children elsewhere or in a different way, the shallowness of child graves which makes them susceptible to disturbance, and the fact that children's undercalcified bones are less resistant to degradation and the soil's chemicals than adult bones (White 1988: 52). The explanation could be a mixture of all three; but the lack of children's graves, with and without bones, might indicate that children were buried elsewhere or in a different manner (pers. comm. T. O'Connor).

In pagan societies, such as Roman or Anglo-Saxon societies, children were occasionally buried outside the predefined cemetery, for example under floors in Roman times. These are generally described as 'secretive' burials, and the rare medieval discovery of a baby under the floor of a house in the medieval village of Upton, Gloucestershire, probably supports this view (Spence and Moore 1969: 123–4). However, the baby was also buried with a shell, found only in the Mediterranean and, possibly, a spindle whorl. The shell is reminiscent of the scallop shells brought back from pilgrimage to Mediterranean lands (Rahtz 1969) and may have been included as a religious symbol. For non-Christian societies, however, the supposed secrecy has been strongly challenged (Scott 1992). It is difficult to determine the number of child burials at Anglo-Saxon cremation cemeteries, such as Spong Hill, simply because the bones are more susceptible to fire (McKinley 1989: 241). In Roman and Anglo-Saxon societies there is also evidence – documentary and archaeological – for infanticide (Mays 1995: 8).

In medieval cemeteries it is not unusual to find a foetus with a female skeleton, either still in the womb or beside/on top of the body (Plate 8). Examples include cases from St Helen-on-the-Walls, York (Dawes and Magilton 1980: plate IVb), and at the Augustinian friary in Hull, where a woman was buried in a coffin, and a child was buried in a tiny coffin by her leg (pers. comm. D. Evans). At St Nicholas it has been suggested that a woman had been in labour for several hours, or even days, and died of maternal exhaustion (Wells 1988: 71–3). Although scientific archaeology does not deal in emotions, this case vividly highlights the human pain and suffering that must have been experienced.

It has long been recognised that monastic burials are predominantly male. Sometimes the difference is extremely marked, for example at the Cistercian monastery of Stratford Langthorne only one burial was that of a female out of a total of ninety-five (Stuart-Macadam 1986: 68). It is not surprising that a monastery, full of males, should produce figures of higher male burials. Yet this poses another problem: if it is assumed that the population was roughly equal between male and females, it would be expected that – to make up for the large number of monasteries, all with a higher proportion of male burials – the local parish population would have a correspondingly higher female presence. In fact the numbers of male/female burials from six parish cemeteries are remarkably similar (544 males, 546 females, 421 sub-adults; see 'Primary Sources' (pp. 209–10) for the parishes). Occasionally there is a higher number of female burials, as at Rivenhall, (31 male burials, 40 female), but they do not make up the shortfall. Nunneries are not the answer either, because there were fewer than monasteries – although not many have been excavated.

There are several problems with this sort of analysis, one of which is the assumption of a 10 per cent bias towards sexing a skeleton as male, but even so this does not close the gap. One answer is that there was widespread infanticide, especially of girls, which occurred in medieval England (and continued until the twentieth century). This could be done easily, for example through hypothermia. Supporting evidence is that the medieval church repeatedly banned infanticide, even down to the parish level (Mays 1995: 9). Abortion is also an unknown factor, although as the sex of the child would not have been known prior to birth, this would have presumably affected both sexes equally. Documented cases are rare, although c.1340 an accusation was made against Thomas Lengleys that he attacked his wife when she was pregnant and 'he so injured her that he killed the child in her womb'. Whether the death was deliberate was not stated (Ross 1993: 113).

A further possible complication is whether the child was baptised. Baptism was an important sacrament. In 1440 John Palfryman remembered his father saying that 'sometimes the Templeton people ran with their babies for baptism to a church nearer than Witheridge when their lives were in danger . . .' (Dunstan 1966: 211). Baptism was a defining moment when the child, and the soul, was brought into the society of the church and the community. There was a difference in treatment between a baptised and an unbaptised child in terms of infanticide and burial practice. In the fifteenth century John Mirk wrote: 'A woman that died in childing shall not be buried in church, but in churchyard, so that the child first be taken out of her and buried outwith churchyard' (Erbe 1905: 298). The removal of the child from the womb to be buried elsewhere may have been considered harsh, for archaeological examples are found of women with children in their wombs (White 1988). That infants – especially unbaptised infants – were buried elsewhere is a stronger possibility. A child buried under the floor at Upton may not have been baptised. At St Helen-on-the-Walls, the theory of a zone for unbaptised children in the (unpopular) north side of the cemetery was tested, but no such group was discovered. The conclusion was reached that unbaptised children were 'excluded . . . [from] the confines of the church cemetery' (Grauer 1991: 71).

This result is supported by remarkable archaeological evidence from Hereford. In 1398 a royal licence was given to enclose the Cathedral cemetery. Part of the stated reason was to stop 'the secret burials of unbaptised infants'. This implies that unbaptised children were excluded from cemeteries and so had to be buried 'secretly'. They were indeed excluded from the normal burying places. This is especially interesting because the last group of burials at Castle Green, Hereford, were a group of twenty-four children:

> some were buried with care, but most of the others were in small, shallow graves dug with little or no attempt at regularity and with a wide variety of orientation . . . It is therefore suggested that the twenty four infant interments are an

indication of this late use of consecrated ground for the burial of small, unbaptised children.

(Shoesmith 1980: 51)

There are several aspects of this which are important. Technically there should have been very few children who were not baptised, for it was allowed for even the midwife at birth to baptise a child if the child was in danger. This sample of children may show that unbaptised children were not that uncommon. Second, it shows that children between the ages of 0 and 2 remained unbaptised (Shoesmith 1980: 29) even in a cathedral city. The third aspect is that special areas were designated (with, or without, sanction) for unbaptised child burials. This in turn may explain the absence of the expected numbers of child burials in parish cemeteries. This example is the nearest medieval equivalent to the postulated 'infant cemeteries' both in the Roman period at Hambledon (Scott 1992: 78–9) and in the Anglo-Saxon period at Whithorn (Crawford 1993: 89).

The designation of special areas for child burials is sometimes found in official burying places. In Anglo-Saxon Christian cemeteries children might be buried under the eaves of churches, possibly so that the water running off the 'holy' roof would 'double-bless' them. Clusters of child burials have been found at Raunds, Whithorn, Jarrow, Winchester, Hartlepool (Crawford 1993: 88) and possibly at Norwich (Stirland 1985). This custom seems to have died out post-Conquest – it would be interesting to know why – but the west or east ends of the church were still often favoured. At Taunton 85 per cent (17 out of 20) of infant burials were found at the western end of the excavation, whilst only three were found in the eastern half (Rogers 1984: 195). The west end of the church was also favoured at St Margaret's in Combusto, Norwich, where the few child or infant burials were found close to the west end of the church (Ayres 1990: 59). At Kellington a group of juvenile burials was discovered at the east end of the chancel (Mytum 1994: 22). At St Andrew's, York, or St Nicholas Shambles there were no obvious areas for child burials, although at St Nicholas some infants and adults (possibly parents) were found at the south-western limits of the site. The example of child burials is just one way that zoning of burials in a cemetery can have a dramatic impact on the perceived nature of the cemetery.

Once a cemetery or part of it has been excavated, the analysis of the remains can be used to analyse demography and life expectancy of the population. In this analysis there are four main considerations: completeness of the skeletons and area of cemetery excavated (discussed above); the age of the population; sexual ratio; and disease, injury, pathology, stature and general health of the skeletons. Of course the larger the sample of skeletons, the more general the conclusions that can be made: in some cases a 'sufficiently large' sample can be as low as forty-four individuals (Stirland 1985: 49).

The age of death is important in determining individual life-expectancy, and general demographic trends. However, determining the age at death is an inexact science. The primary determinants are the teeth and the fusion of bones. There are two indicators connected with the teeth: eruption and attrition. Ageing by eruption of teeth is helped by humans developing two sets of teeth: the milk teeth and then the permanent teeth. There are several stages of eruption. The first starts from birth and continues until 4 years when the child has a full set of milk teeth. These are then lost and by 12 years old a full set of permanent teeth has erupted. The final eruptions, from 21 onwards, are the wisdom teeth which may, or may not erupt (Brothwell 1972: 64). Age can be determined with considerable accuracy using teeth eruption especially for infants, children and sub-adults.

Once adulthood has been achieved, tooth eruption loses its significance and reliance has to be given to attrition (how worn the teeth are): the assumption being that the greater the wear, the older the person. This makes several assumptions in turn – especially where burials occurred over a long period. One assumption is that the diet of the population remained constant, for example that the bread had a constant amount of grit in it. Eruption and attrition ageing relies on the good preservation of the head and teeth. If this is not the case, as at St Nicholas Shambles where over half the skeletons were 'deficient in the head region' (White 1988: 31), teeth analysis and then correlating known results with the whole population becomes very difficult.

Other techniques have been developed to age skeletons, especially the amount of fusion there is between bones, especially the sutures on the skull. (A suture is a non-movable joint between two bones). In early life there is a thin edge between them, where the bone has not joined (Brothwell 1972: 43). This edge may remain unossified until adulthood, and, in rare cases, indefinitely. Although a certain degree of ageing can be determined, for example whether the person reached adulthood, there is little uniformity in suture closure to allow more specific ageing to be assessed. The technique was abandoned, but recent studies have shown that suture closure does give an indication of age within a fairly broad band-width (Key *et al.* 1994: 206).

An alternative analysis is that of the fusion of the epiphysial cartilege to bones. This is a thin layer of cartilege which slowly turns to bone and becomes completely ossified by about 25 years of age. This process is called the 'fusion of the epiphyses'. A general guide has been worked out for certain bones, for example between 12 and 22 years old for foot bones, or between 16 and 23 for the bones at the knee. Even though this technique is useful in general terms, there are significant differences between individuals and between population groups (Brothwell 1972: 67–70).

One specific bone which has been much used for ageing skeletons is that of the pubic symphysis in the groin. This changes in shape over time and is potentially of use because it changes shape in the later decades of a person's life. Its shape is possibly affected by childbirth, so an agreed ageing structure has so far only been worked out for males (Brothwell 1972: 68–70). Other useful bone changes include the end of the ribs at the breast-bone (sternum) and the widest part of the hipbone (technically called the 'auricular surface of the ilium'). However, results from one cemetery or skeleton should not be taken as universal, as many variations occur. At St Andrew's, York, the changes to the male ribs complied with previously described phases of change; those for females did not. Also at York the auricular changes of the ilium were also as good as the better known one of the pubic symphyseal ageing technique, with the advantage that they had a better preservation rate and change continued beyond the fifth decade (Stroud and Kemp 1993: 168–9).

Whilst each technique to determine age has its advantages and disadvantages, they should never be looked at in isolation, but rather in combination. Skeletons discovered at Taunton were aged by using the eruption of teeth, dental attrition and fusion of the epiphyses (Rogers 1984: 195). On only 29 of the 266 adult skeletons assigned an age at St Andrew's, York, could all five techniques be used (change at the pubic symphysis, changes to the auricular surface, changes to sternal ends of the ribs, dental attrition and suture closure), the other skeletons being assigned an age by a combination of techniques (Stroud and Kemp 1993: 162). The bones at St Nicholas Shambles were aged using dental development and sutures, and the condition of the pubic symphysis (White 1988: 28).

As with all bone studies there is a danger that modern data are used which are not true to the populations of the past. Fortunately this has been largely overcome by the examination of a recorded population from the eighteenth century removed from Spitalfields church crypt in London (Molleson et al. 1993). The skeletons were all coffined and the records were such that many could be individually identified. This group provides a remarkable sample on which to test the accuracy of present archaeological methods, the results of which can be tested by documentary evidence. The work is on-going, but has so far ranged from the examining the growth rate of teeth in children aged 0–5.4 (Liversidge 1994: 31–7), to testing methods of ageing by cranial suture closure (Key et al. 1994: 171–92).

As well as determining the age and number of burials, the sex of each individual has to be determined. As with ageing skeletons, the science of sexing skeletons can be imprecise, though the difficulties are reversed: it is more difficult to sex a younger skeleton than an older one. For children and sub-adults a category of 'unsexable' is often assigned. Five categories of sex can be applied to a skeleton: positive male, positive female, doubtful male, doubtful female, and unknown.

A very high success rate – estimated at between 96.8 and 100 per cent – of skeletons can be sexed if the skeletons are complete, although the guarantee that the correct identification was made is lower. Thereafter the greater the number of diagnostic bones that survive, the greater the accuracy. At some time or other every bone has been studied, but the two most important are those which have a role in reproduction or are genetically influenced: the pelvis and the skull. Combined, the pelvis and the skull can have an accuracy of 97–8 per cent, and the pelvis on its own has an accuracy rate of 90–6 per cent (Henderson 1989: 79). Ideally both pelvis and skull should be used, but occasionally one contradicts the other (at St Andrew's, York, 12 skulls indicated a sex contrary to the pelvis) or the skull is ambiguous in its sexing (c.105 skeletons out of 315 at York) (Stroud and Kemp

1993: 165), in which case the pelvis was used as the determining factor.

Of all the bones the pelvis is the most important and reliable. The key difference is that the female pelvis is adapted for childbirth and from this fact there are significant sexual differences. A particularly important one is the 'sciatic notch' which is wider and shallower in the female pelvis, which in turn helps in childbirth. The other excellent indicator is a groove on the pelvis called the pre-auricular sulcus. Two types of groove are possible, one of which is purely female and possibly occurs during pregnancy or childbirth (Brothwell 1972: 62). These two are the most important, but there are numerous other potential pelvic indicators of sex, for example the ratios of angles within the pelvic structure: the results for an Inuit population showed an impressive difference between male and female pelvic characteristics (Brothwell 1972: 62–3).

After the pelvis the skull is the next best guide to sex with a host of indicators. For example, in the male the palate and teeth are larger and the male skull is less rounded (Brothwell 1972: 59–60). A key element between the sexes is that the bones of the male are larger, longer and heavier than the female's, including the skull, pelvis and long bones, such as femur (thigh bone) (see below). Although the accuracy of sexing by long bones is only 80–5 per cent, they can still be a useful indicator of sex (Henderson 1989: 79).

The results of sexing can be very variable. At Taunton the skeletons were initially divided into definite males (25), possible males (17), definite females (26) and possible females (16). The definite and possible for each sex were then totalled, giving a sex total of 42 males, 42 females and 17 unknown. In most reports the number of definites and possibles are pooled together. Even where sexing is possible, it has been suggested that there is a 10 per cent bias in favour of males. In some cemeteries sexing is easier than in others, and where the differences are strong the population was said to be 'markedly sexually dimorphic', as at St Andrew's, York, where only three skeletons out of 312 adults were unsexed (Stroud and Kemp 1993: 167).

Once the individual skeletons have been aged and sexed, the group as a whole can be studied to answer general questions about the population. One question is whether there was a significant difference between male and female ages at death, which in turn might reflect different conditions of life. At Taunton it was found that females died earlier than males and no females survived to be 45 or over. The least likely age to die was between 15 and 20, and the most likely was between 25 and 30 (thirty-seven deaths) and then 30–5 (thirty-five deaths). The result may well be 'skewed', however, by the lack of infants and children's bones (see above). The 'normal' ratio of deaths of children to adults in pre-industrial societies is about 4 : 2 – at Taunton the ratio was only 1 : 30. The trend in adult deaths was different at St Andrew's, York: 42 per cent of adult females lived to between 40 and 50 in the tenth- to twelfth-century period, showing a much longer age span than those at Taunton. It has been argued that females were more likely to die younger, owing to the dangers of pregnancy and childbirth – a danger which is all too clearly seen by women with children in their womb, graphically shown at St Nicholas Shambles. It has also been argued that women had a lower status, not only socially, but also in the food they ate. Cases where women survived longer, as at St Andrew's, York, may be because females live naturally longer than males.

The mean estimated age at death can be determined for a group of sites from around the country, ranging in date from the tenth to the sixteenth century. (These figures normally exclude infant burials.)

(Figures in years)

	Male	Female	All
Hereford, Castle Green	34.5	24.5	30
Beckery Chapel, Glastonbury	33		–
North-East Bailey, Norwich	30.9	–	31.7
St Nicholas Shambles, London	–	–	30
Winchester	35.5	30.1	32.8
Wharram Percy, Yorkshire	35.3	31.3	33.3

The overall figure, of 30–1 years, is reasonably consistent and surprisingly low. However, this archaeological mean probably masks variation in the figures. A detailed study of English land-owners from historical records revealed that there were differences in life expectancy between centuries. Before the Black Death in 1348, the life expectancy figure for men had fallen from 35.3 years between 1200 and 1275 to 27.2 years for men born between 1326 and 1348. After the Black Death the figure fell further, to 17.3 years for men born between 1348 and 1375, but climbed once again in the fifteenth century to 32.8 years. If people survived past 50 they were likely to live much longer. The percentage of nobles who died before 50 years old also fluctuated: from 18 per cent pre-1325, to 66 per cent between 1350 and 1370, which then decreased to 34 per cent in the first half of the fifteenth century (Minois 1989: 212–13).

A further consideration is that of stature or height of the individual. The key element is that of the long bones, especially the femur (thigh bone). Unsurprisingly in most studies adult males are taller than adult females with varying levels of overlap. At York adult females ranged in height from 145cm to 170cm, with a mean of 158cm, and males ranged from 155cm to 190cm with a mean of 172cm (Stroud and Kemp 1993: 174), whilst at Taunton females ranged from 146cm to 171cm (mean of 156cm) and males ranged from 165cm to 180cm (mean of 171cm). A mean average can be worked out for a group of sites, which include friaries, priories and parish churches: the mean average male height is 171.26cm, and from 11 sites the mean average female stature is 157.55 (figures from White 1988: 31, Stroud and Kemp 1993: 174, and Rogers 1984: 195). Some anomalies are apparent, such as the group of larger males (average 177.80cm) from the Austin friars, Leicester, or a group of smaller males (average 165.00cm) from Rothwell Charnel House (White 1988: 31). The heights do not obviously reveal patterns, for example the larger males are not always from burials found at religious houses (monasteries or friaries), so that a correlation cannot be made between potentially a better diet or living conditions and an average height of the community. Whilst it is interesting to compare average statures from sites, it is difficult to know what the figures reveal, or what environmental conditions, if any, cause the height to fluctuate. Modern studies of twins have revealed that 90 per cent of a person's height is inherited, and 10 per cent is from environmental causes (Brothwell 1972: 100).

One environmental aspect which does show up is that of long-term famine or very severe under-nourishment, which may have stunted growth for a while. These, or other, types of trauma show up in the long bones, such as the femur, as transverse lines across the bone. These lines have several names such as transverse lines, lines of radiopacity, lines of arrested growth, bone scars or Harris lines. There are two processes: first, the long bone stops growing, and a thin layer of cartilage is laid down instead, forming a barrier to further growth. When the cause of the stunted growth is removed, the bone starts to grow but leaves a line around the bone. Unfortunately these rings cannot be matched between skeletons (as can tree-rings) to show periods of famine. Not only do they differ in severity between people, they are age-specific (only affecting males between 0 and 14 and females between 0 and 12), and the single biggest problem is that they are reabsorbed into the bone within ten years, so it is impossible to know how many lines have been lost (Higgins 1989: 188–9).

One element which might be revealed over a longer-time scale is height ranges between different periods, for example comparing Iron Age, Roman, Anglo-Saxon and Medieval. Although patterns might emerge, the results need to be treated with caution. Indeed, the medieval figures are broadly consistent with height ranges in a modern population where the average height of a modern British population is 173.8cm for males and 160.9cm for females, based on national figures for 1981 (White 1988: 30, 52). These figures do of course reveal that – contrary to widespread popular belief – the medieval population was not significantly shorter than the modern population.

One further factor needs to be mentioned, that of ethnic affinity. These characteristics are especially important after an invasion, whether Roman, Anglo-Saxon or Norman, and skull measurements have been analysed to determine patterns of ethnicity. Victorian excavators were keen on this analysis and at Durham, Fowler recognised 'a difference between the "long-headed" skulls of the occupants of the [Anglo-Saxon] cemetery and the "round-headed" [skulls] of the interments which followed them" (Carver 1980: 13). One large-scale modern experiment was conducted on the skulls from St Helen-on-the-Walls, York, which tried to assign classifications to populations as diverse as the Yorkshire Bronze Age and Norse Medieval (Dawes and Magilton 1980: 80–1). These population results are very controversial and such studies are rarely carried out, although they have not been completely abandoned (pers. comm. D. Brothwell). Criticisms have included a lack of understanding about the environmental and genetic influences upon the skull shape (Stroud and Kemp 1993: 175), and the fact that invasions included only a small number of people in comparison with the total population. In certain exceptional cases ethnic distinction does seem possible: in the Roman cemetery of Trentholme Drive, York, one skull had exceptional characteristics and it has been assumed to be negroid. A further skull was interpreted at first as negroid in the late Anglo-Saxon cemetery at the north-east Bailey, Norwich (Stirland 1985: 53, 57), but was later reclassified as from the local Anglo-Saxon population.

Genetic influences may highlight sub-groups within a cemetery, especially family connections. At St Nicholas Church, Thanington, Kent, two bodies were found in one coffin (the second one having been moved into the coffin after partially decomposing) and both skulls displayed metopism, where the suture persisted in the frontal bone, which normally disappears within the first two years after birth. This condition has an incidence of only 9–11 per cent in British material and is considered a hereditary character (Bennett and Anderson 1991: 311). Genetic features are most noticeable on the skull, such as wormian bones which are extra, sutural, bones. At the Austin friars at Leicester the presence of wormian bones in six burials led to speculation that the bodies 'could indicate a related population drawing on a restricted gene pool' (Mellor and Pearce 1981: 168). However, there is some debate about how much environmental, rather than genetic, influence there is upon bones, and it is by no means certain that the wormian bones or metopic suture are a genetic feature. The environmental argument seems to be in evidence at Rivenhall where the majority of skulls had wormian bones and it was argued that the sutural anomalies 'might be linked to low life expectancy and poor nutrition' (O'Connor 1993: 101).

There is one technique that is rapidly developing which might be the most useful in genetic studies of skeletons: DNA analysis. As yet, DNA analysis of archaeological material is in its early stages, but DNA may be extracted from bones up to 1,000 years old. At Hulton Abbey, samples from the femurs and ribs were taken from eight skeletons, which indicated that three were related. The key determinant is only passed through the female line, so the relatives could not be three generations of men, but could be one family of one generation (male or female) or up to three generations of women. As has been noted, this opens up interesting possibilities for the study of burial practices (were all members of one family buried near to each other?). Spatial distribution maps of where members of one family were buried should be made possible (Klemperer 1992: 87). Even though there are still some problems, the potential of DNA analysis is rapidly becoming apparent. Other chemical analysis of bone has also produced a reliable and scientifically simple process to determine whether a bone is human or not by testing for human albumin (Cattaneo *et al.* 1992). In medieval cemeteries this distinction is less problematic than pagan or pre-historic sites where animals may have been interred with a body.

Another way to get close to the previously living person is by facial modelling. The techniques have developed from surgery and police forensic work and they are now increasingly used by archaeologists to bring a skull 'to life'. Although some aspects will always remain unknown, such as the length and colour of a person's hair, the reconstructed skulls can have a dramatic impact on the presentation of the past to the general public, for example at the Jorvik Viking Centre in York where seven skulls have been modelled (Briggs 1995).

When comparisons between sites are correlated, the general population features of age, sex and stature help to throw light upon a population in general, but as well as the general population characteristics, the skeletons are still important in their own right. Details of injury, diet and disease may be discovered through an individual's pathology.

Given the amount of potential violence with bladed or pointed weapons (such as daggers, swords or arrows), either through street fights or full-scale battles, it is often assumed that many skeletons show signs of blade injuries. Death by blade injury can be determined when there is no evidence of the bone beginning to heal. In fact evidence for blade injuries is relatively rare, although some clusters in cemeteries do exist. At Rivenhall there were two skulls showing signs of cuts, both of which were not fatal (O'Connor 1993: 100). At Hereford a skull 'had clear evidence of being attacked with a sharp cutting instrument such as a sword which resulted in death' (Shoesmith 1980: 45) and at Stratford Langthorne a skull had clear evidence of blade wounds (Stuart-Macadam 1986: 71). One aspect which has been little considered is that of surgery, the processes of which are well known from medieval surgical guides (Jones 1984).

A large and unexpected cluster was discovered at St Andrew's, York, where a total of twenty-nine males had injuries caused by bladed or pointed weapons. Twenty-two had more than one injury. The most common areas of injury were the skull and torso and several had cuts front and back, possibly indicating that they had been surrounded and did not have any head cover. In one burial (number 1487) microscopic analysis showed the direction of the blow and the slight defect in the blade edge showed that the same blade had been used to cause another cut. After the skull, the spine and vertebrae were the most common areas of attack. Six had been decapitated, at least two by a blow from the front. This is a further indication of death in battle as medieval executioners seem to have struck from behind (see Chapter 3). An assumption that in a right-handed single combat the blows fall on the left-hand side may be borne out as there are more than twice the number of blows to the left-hand side of the body compared to the right. The spread of blows to back and sides may indicate less formalised fighting. One tactic in a fight may have been to attack the relatively unguarded legs to cripple the opponent and nine skeletons showed deep or piercing damage to the leg bone (Stroud and Kemp 1993: 232–7). It is of course possible to die in a fight which leaves no trace on the bone, so it could be that the number of deaths by combat was much greater. At Agincourt more men probably died by suffocation or by having their throats cut when lying on the ground than actually in battle (Hibbert 1964: 124).

Bone fractures, probably through accidental injury, may have led to death and instances of healed fractures are reasonably common. At York, St Andrew's, their ribs were the most fractured bone (20 cases) with the right and left sides being affected to the same degree. The next most common site was the vertebrae (10 cases), then the ankle and foot (9 cases) and ankle (9 cases) (Stroud and Kemp 1993: 225). Whilst individual cases may be of interest, of more potential use is to try to discover how the accident happened. All too often, all that can be noted is that the break was caused by a trauma of some kind. Most fractures may therefore be put down to a fall, crushing injury or a direct blow, the cause of which is unknown.

Occasionally a particular fracture can be related to a known work pattern or disease. One type of injury to the lower vertebrae is a lifting injury – the 'clay-shoveller's fracture'. This is caused by a sudden jerking motion which causes a severe muscle pull. Three cases were found at St Andrew's, York (Stroud and Kemp 1993: 226). At St Nicholas Shambles, London, a spinal disorder was four times more common in men than women, and was probably due to lifting activities (White 1988: 6). At the Austin friars in Leicester a group of eight strong males was found, all of whom were robust and were probably engaged in continual hard manual labour. The bones show that they habitually adopted the squatting posture and that the condition of the bones was a reaction to chronic trauma or strain. There were deformities to the spine, to the left side of the neck or girdle and damage to the lumbar vertebrae, which all suggests heavy continual manual work (Mellor and Pearce 1981: 168–9).

Changes in the vertebrae also occurred. At Colchester a middle-aged female had osteophytes (an osteophyte is a growth of a bony projection at a joint margin, or vertebrae) on the thoracic vertebrae, which in this case caused additional bone growth on the vertebrae. It is a common condition and has been related to obesity or work patterns. Osteophytes in general have been connected with degeneration of the skeleton with advancing age (Crummy et al. 1993: 231, 254).

Other indications of malformation of the bone have been discovered. At Hulton Abbey, extensive bone growth along the spine, which caused fusion of some of the vertebrae, indicated that the person had 'DISH' (Diffuse Idiopathic Skeletal Hyperostosis) which may be predisposed by diabetes or obesity (Klemperer 1992: 86). Other examples have been found at the Augustinian friary at Hull (pers. comm. D. Evans) and at St Andrew's, York. At St Andrew's, seven individuals were found with this condition, all from the period of the priory, one of whom was buried with chalice and paten. It was tentatively speculated 'to see this as evidence for obese monks and wealthy well-fed patrons' but it is possible that the males developed it as a result of age (Stroud and Kemp 1993: 213). Other indications of obesity are gall stones (which only survive in very alkaline soils) as found at St Nicholas Shambles (White 1988: 44) and a 'particular type of spinal fusion' which is observed in the skeletons of high-ranking clerics and the Saxon bishops of Wells. Such obesity is hardly surprising. It is estimated that a monk ate up to three pounds of red meat a day (Rogers cited in Musty 1995: 143).

Occasionally a complete surprise occurs for which it is difficult to give any explanation. At St Andrews, York, a knee had undergone considerable damage, so much so that the joint could not be extended. In modern times the two most common causes of this type of injury are being hit by a car (the bumper being close to knee level) or as a footballing injury (as with Paul Gascoigne). Whilst a definitive cause cannot be given for the burial, it is suggestive that monastic regulations against monks footballing were made in the Middle Ages (pers. comm. R. Kemp) although excessive genuflections might also cause the same result (pers. comm. T. O'Connor). To try and rectify the situation, two copper alloy plates were placed around the knee to try to give it support, or, with a herbal poultice, to try and heal the injury (Stroud and Kemp 1993: 217).

A further surprise was discovered in Norwich from a group of skeletons from the North-East Bailey. The group of skeletons were lacking in vitamin D, and also had damage to their pelvic girdles, probably through lifting. A lack of vitamin D causes rickets in children and osteomalacia in adults. Examples included children as young as 5, 4 and 2 (Stirland 1985: 54). It is speculated that some skeletons were those of miners (it is not clear from the report whether children are included), working either in the chalk or flint mines. Alternatively the burial ground was part of an early hospital where those with a certain illness came to die (Stirland 1985: 56). If the mining theory is true, then the burials show interesting links between the city and the hinterland industry.

Rickets is caused by a vitamin D deficiency – a deficiency which is normally countered by diet or exposure to sunlight. It is thought that there was a higher incidence of sunlight in the Middle Ages, which would have counter-acted a dietary lack of vitamin D. Rickets therefore should be almost unknown (White 1988: 41). To find the medieval group from Norwich with vitamin D deficiency is therefore remarkable, but this group is not unique and other cases of childhood rickets and adult osteomalacia are known. In the case of the Norwich group it is difficult to believe that children as young as 2 could play a useful role in the mines, unless they were being cared for there. An alternative is needed to explain the case of rickets from a child buried at St Helen-on-the-Walls, York (Dawes and Magilton 1980: plate XIIb), or the possible six cases discovered at Rivenhall (O'Connor 1993: 100). In these cases child-rearing techniques may explain the cause. At birth and for a time afterwards children were kept in the dark to symbolise the womb (pers. comm. J. Goldberg). There is one further, much more widely applicable, explanation – that heavy clothing resulted in sunlight not reaching the skin (pers. comm. D. Evans). This has far-reaching consequences. Children heavily wrapped up in cloth bands might have little skin exposed to sunlight, but also monks and nuns might experience an almost total covering and a lack of direct exposure to sunlight. Nuns in particular might be completely covered as even their face could be covered by a veil. This might explain the cases of osteomalacia found amongst the Augustinian canons during excavations at Hull (D. Evans pers. comm.). Despite these reasons, rickets is still a rare finding in the medieval population, and out of ninety-four Cistercian monks at Stratford Langthorne, none had rickets (Stuart-Macadam 1986: 69).

Work-related bone injury falls into the category of 'degenerative joint disease', a term which also covers changes in bones for reasons of age, sex and disease. These can include osteophytes, pitting or roughening of joint surfaces, and severe bone or cartilage damage can lead to a loss of cartilege between the bones, resulting in the bones moving against one another and producing a polished appearance (technically called 'eburnation of the articular surfaces'). Age is a key factor in the amount of joint disease. At St Andrew's, York, only 2 skeletons (out of 70) had any sign of bone disease in the age group 20–30, whereas 40 out of 42 skeletons had bone disease in the age group 50+ (Stroud and Kemp 1993: 209). The most common joint to be affected, and the earliest, is the knee followed thereafter by the foot, the hip, shoulder and elbow.

In some cases it is possible to determine attributes of the person's stature or behaviour from the bone changes. In burial number 2227 from St Andrew's, York, the curvature of the spine was severe and 'he would have had a stiff right leg, a slightly bent left knee, and walked on his toes' (Stroud and Kemp 1993: 217). Paget's disease is a physical disease which also affects the emotions. It is thought that the famous Icelandic warrior and poet Egil Skallagrimson had Paget's disease because of his emotional swings between poetic insight and violence (Byock 1993). Paget's disease in the archaeological record can be determined by a thickening of the bones, and its onset normally occurs after the age of 50 (Brothwell 1972: 55, 166; Byock 1993). The theory that Egil had Paget's disease is further reinforced because it was documented that it was impossible to crush his skull with an axe after it was dug up by his enemies. Medieval examples have been found at Winchester (Brothwell 1972: 166) and Carlisle (McCarthy 1990: 189). Interestingly the Carlisle example was wearing a belt, which might have been used as a cure (see Chapter 6).

Paget's disease is just one of a number of diseases which can affect bones, though the disease must be of sufficient duration for it to influence the growth of the bone. One type of disease is caused by inflammation or infection of the membrane covering the bone. This in turn aggravates the bone and results in new bone being deposited. This is called 'periosteal inflammatory reaction' and may result from trauma or infection. A further factor may be osteomyelitis where pus-producing bacteria penetrates the bone. Whilst the causes of the majority of cases remain a mystery, some are detectable, such as tuberculosis, where the main focus of infection is the ribs, resulting in build-up of new bone. Studies on a modern population have shown that in only approximately 16 per cent of cases is the bone affected, and that in over half the cases the ribs were affected (Stroud and Kemp 1993: 223). Tumours (technically called neoplasia) are not commonly found in archaeological contexts and, when they are, they are normally benign. Although interesting in themselves, there are few conclusions that can yet be drawn from them.

Whereas tumours can reveal little about external influences, diet can have a dramatic effect upon the skeleton and can show evidence of dietary trauma (such as famine) or nutritional deficiencies. Rickets (see above), is caused by a lack of vitamin D, and iron deficiency in the diet has been widely recognised. Iron deficiency causes pitting to certain bones (pitting of the orbit of the skull is called 'cribra orbitalia'; to the femur 'cribra femora'; to the vault of the skull 'parietal osteoporosis'). Documentary research has suggested that iron deficiency, leading to chronic anaemia, was widespread in the Middle Ages, as were parasitic infections which aggravated the conditions (White 1988: 41–2).

One of the most useful indicators of diet is the mouth, and especially the teeth. Differences in the coarseness of the food results in different rates of attrition – gritty bread causes the teeth to wear down whilst soft, refined food produces little attrition but may cause a build-up of calculus. Chewing harder or more sinewy meat or food also reduced the build-up of calculus. Sometimes different areas of one cemetery may highlight the differences in diet, either between social groups or through time. At St Andrew's, York, the tenth to twelfth-century burials were described as having 'a fairly coarse unvaried diet of sinewy meat and fibrous vegetables', whereas the twelfth to fifteenth-century burials – some of whom may have been monks – were described as having a softer diet with less sinewy meat and more variety of vegetables and cereals (Stroud and Kemp 1993: 247). In at least one case the teeth may also indicate that an ill child was cared for with a special diet for some time, as calculus built up on the teeth indicated that this child was fed with a soft diet for quite some time before death (Stroud and Kemp 1993: 247).

A long time-span can also highlight changes in diet. At Rivenhall there was a marked increase in caries and abscesses from the Saxon to medieval population, which, it was argued, showed a change in diet that caused a shift from alkaline mouth conditions to acid mouth conditions, probably as a result of increased carbohydrate intake (for example from sugars) or changing micro-organisms, or a combination of both (O'Connor 1993: 100). Erosion of tooth enamel may also indicate some aspects of health: stomach acid being vomited causes erosion, most commonly seen in modern times through bulimia. At St Andrew's, York, one burial produced evidence for this which may have been caused either by a hiatus hernia or some digestive problem (Stroud and Kemp 1993: 244). Some degree of pain can be determined from the state of the teeth. When cystic cavities (sacs containing fluid, gas or tooth) press on nerves, tingling, numbness or pain may result. Sometimes a more serious development occurs where an abscess breaks through into the sinus of the upper jaw (maxillary antrum) which could lead to severe pain, infection or possibly death (Stroud and Kemp 1993: 244).

The information that can be acquired from the body is now immense, and a far cry from the position cited in the 1960s. New scientific techniques are rapidly developing which allow a greater understanding of decomposition and trauma. The long-term aim of this research must be to bring out general points about life and conditions in the past. At the moment only about thirty excavations have taken place in English medieval cemeteries, of which about ten have more than a hundred bodies. Fewer still have been comprehensively published. The results are of great interest but as yet only allow a preliminary local picture to be built up. Further publication of the results from large cemetery excavations is awaited with interest, but for the vast majority of cemeteries across England the raw data will remain below ground, perhaps forever.

Plate 1 Crucified Christ, West Tanfield, North Yorkshire
(copyright of Dr A Finch, by permission of the Warden of
West Tanfield)

Plate 2 Chantry chapel, Holy Trinity, Goodramgate, York (copyright of Dr A Finch, by permission of the Friends of Holy Trinity, Goodramgate)

Plate 3 Detail of angel from the Marmion tomb, West Tanfield,
North Yorkshire
(copyright of Dr A Finch, by permission of the Warden of
West Tanfield)

Plate 4 The Marmion tomb and hearse, West Tanfield, North Yorkshire
(copyright of Dr A Finch, by permission of the Warden of
West Tanfield)

Plate 5 Group of skeletons, showing the compact nature of Christian churchyard burial, St Helen-on-the-Walls, York
(copyright of York Archaeological Trust)

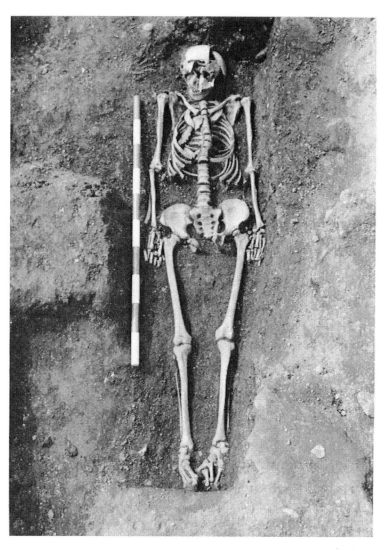

Plate 6 Skeleton of a woman, St Helen-on-the-Walls, York
(copyright of York Archaeological Trust)

Plate 7 Charnel pit, St Helen-on-the-Walls, York
(copyright of York Archaeological Trust)

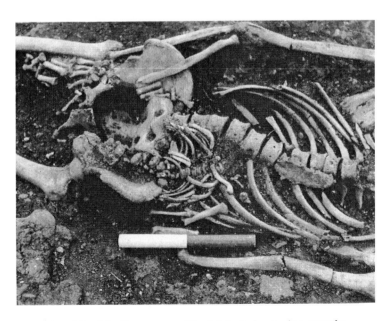

Plate 8 Burial of a woman with child of about nine months,
St Helen-on-the-Walls, York
(copyright of York Archaeological Trust)

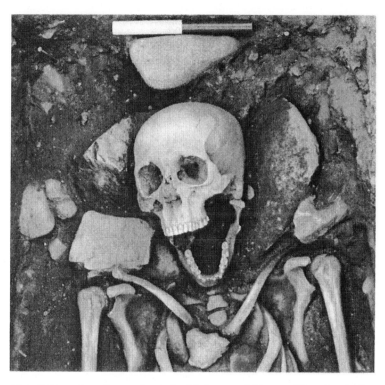

Plate 9 Decapitated man, buried with large cobbles cradling the skull,
St Andrew's Priory, Fishergate, York
(copyright of York Archaeological Trust)

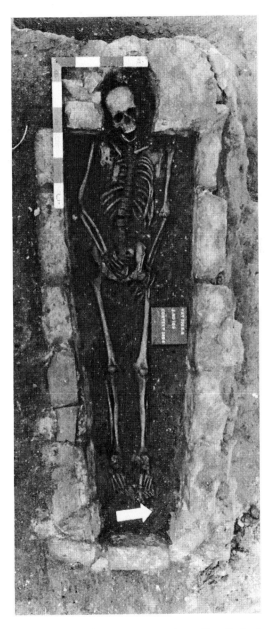

Plate 10 Skeleton of a man, buried in a cist coffin, St Andrew's Priory, Fishergate, York
(copyright of York Archaeological Trust)

Plate 11 (Left) The Archangel Michael weighing souls, West Tanfield, North Yorkshire

Plate 12 (Below) Detail of head, showing chain mail and double 'S' collar of the Lancastrians, West Tanfield, North Yorkshire (copyright of Dr A Finch, by permission of the Warden of West Tanfield)

Plate 13 Tomb stone with cauldron and fish (salamander?) design, Holy
Trinity, Goodramgate, York
(copyright of Dr A Finch, by permission of the Friends of Holy Trinity,
Goodramgate)

6

CEMETERIES AND GRAVE GOODS

In exceptional circumstances a cemetery could be consecrated and filled within a few months. The best documented examples were those opened in London during the Black Death. At Spittle Croft a plaque was erected on the site, which the Tudor antiquarian Stow recorded:

A great plague raging in the year of our Lord 1349, this church was consecrated; wherein, and within the bounds of the present monastery, were buried more than 50,000 bodies of the dead, besides many others from thence to the present time, whose souls God have mercy upon. Amen.
(Ziegler 1982: 163, Horrox 1994: 267)

The plague cemeteries were exceptional to the normal evolution of cemeteries over time. The initial foundation of a cemetery could take several different forms: continuing a previous tradition, whether Iron Age, Roman, Anglo-Saxon or Viking; the foundation of a new church in an area; or an outlying chapel being granted its own burial rights from the parish church. Once permission had been granted, the wholesale clearance of the land might then take place. At Mitre Street, in London, the Roman remains were completely cleared in the tenth century to make space for a Saxon graveyard. The same cemetery was clearly divided between the crowded and intercutting burials in the earlier western half, and those in the eastern half, which were carefully laid out to avoid each other (Riviere 1986: 37). The division of the graveyard into east and west sections was also visible in an early Christian cemetery (possibly ninth century) at Capel Maelog in Wales (Jones 1988: 27). At Raunds a new church was built, with five times the capacity of the old one, and the cemetery was cleared at the time of the Norman Conquest.

> At the same time the graveyard was cleared for a new generation of burial. Crosses were broken up, markers uprooted and mounds cleared. Stone coffins were smashed, and their occupants dumped unceremoniously in pits north of the church ...
>
> (Boddington 1987)

The obvious link is with the Norman Conquest, though other explanations are possible, and it has been argued that it is not possible to give an 'archaeology of ownership' (Boddington 1987).

Once the graveyard was in existence the position of the burials became an issue. The physical placing of bodies depended on the marking of other graves and how much space remained in the cemetery. At Kellington it was discovered that a major shift in the care of burial took place in the twelfth century: before that date, bodies were carefully laid out and any bones which were discovered were treated with reverence. After that date less care was taken about cutting through existing graves and many bones were incorporated into the backfill without any reverence shown (Mytum 1994). If this trend was discovered in other twelfth-century cemeteries, it could be argued that it reflected the change in belief from the Day of Judgement to Purgatory (see Chapter 7). When other cemeteries are compared the shift seems to be more a function of space. At Mitre Street intercutting occurred during the Saxon period. At the Augustinian priory in Taunton, the bodies in the lay graveyard, which started c.1350–1400, were carefully laid out in rows, and then pressure of space resulted in the insertion of later bodies and subsequent cutting of earlier graves.

Within the cemetery itself graves were often marked. (The most important graves were usually placed within the church and had large and elaborate tombs.) The marking of graves was not a universal habit: in the leper hospital cemetery at Chichester no grave markers were found (Magilton and Lee 1989: 256). One indicator of the lack of grave-makers is the degree to which bodies were disturbed when new graves were cut. There could be short-term markers, such as the mound itself, a hearse cloth over the grave, or possibly flowers. The intercutting of graves at the Dominican friary at Carlisle suggested that there were no long-term grave-markers (McCarthy 1990: 78) and the conclusion can be replicated across many cemeteries. A logical way to lay out a group of burials was in straight rows, usually shoulder-to-shoulder. This pattern was common when the land had not been used for burial before. The original layout can easily be masked, however, by later rows being cut into earlier rows; giving the appearance of a random placing of graves. Such a situation occurred at Whithorn within a relatively brief period between the thirteenth and fifteenth centuries. The initially chaotic burial pattern discovered during excavation proved to be an illusion. An analysis discovered that the graveyard had been reorganised at least nine times; each time the previous graveyard had been levelled and new graves had been laid out in regular or irregular rows. Once these had been filled, new rows were inserted until a new levelling was needed. The levelling took place probably every twenty or thirty years, and shows that in order to solve the number of burials needed in a restricted space, careful but ruthless measures had to be taken (Cardy and Hill 1992: 96–97). It would not have been possible to trace the location of one's ancestors in the cemetery over any length of time.

For the wealthy, more permanent markers were an option. These could be part of the grave itself, such as a marble statue or a memorial brass, and could either lie flat on the floor or slightly raised. An alternative was to have a marker on a wall nearby, a practice which was popular in the later Middle Ages with the increasing use of brass wall memorials. These were most often used in the church itself, but it is possible that the unmarked graves found occasionally in the cloisters would also have had wall markers, either nearby or elsewhere in the church: in Gloucester Cathedral chapter house eight names were painted on the wall as memorials (Payne and Payne 1994). The likelihood of wall markers in the cloister is increased as the cloister floor at Westminster had mats on (Harvey 1993: 131) and weeds could be a common feature in some cloisters (Graham 1929: 379). If the cloister floor burials were marked, then the monks, head bowed as they walked, would have seen the grave as they passed over. Not only would they have seen it, but they would also have been in direct touch with the dead as they trod on the marked grave itself. Other types of grave-markers are also possible: wooden crosses are shown in pictures of cemeteries from the

Netherlands, along with depictions of Christ's Crucifixion (Chatelet 1988: 38). At Bordesley a grave had a piece of wood with brass on (Astill and Wright 1993: 134) and Mirk described a marker as 'a cross of tree set at his head, showing that he hath full "leue" to been said [*sic*] by Christ's passion, that died for him on the cross of tree' (Erbe 1905: 295).

An associated issue is that of the orientation of the grave and the body within it. There are numerous possibilities as to what controls orientation, even in a Christian context: some event of religious significance (in Christian belief the Last Judgement and the Resurrection of the body), paths or roads (so that the memorial or grave could be seen) or holy buildings, such as the alignment of a church (Rahtz 1978: 2). By the Middle Ages the orientation of graves was consistent: the heads point west, the feet east. The explanations for the orientation given in medieval texts include: that Christ would appear from the east on the Day of Judgement; the cross of Cavalry faced west, so those looking at Christ faced east; the west is the region of shadows and darkness and the east is the region of goodness and light (Rahtz 1978: 4). All these reasons, and others, were probably attempts to explain the existing practice and no reason is given before the ninth century.

Various analyses have been made to see if the orientation was originally defined by either sunrise or sunset through the seasons, especially concerning Roman and the early medieval graves of pagan Anglo-Saxon. If this was successful, seasonal patterns of mortality could be worked out, allowing for unusual instances such as plague or battle. Despite studies of different cemeteries, such as Poundbury and Cannington, seasonal orientation was statistically not proven. Some trends were established in different parts of a cemetery, such as at Lankhills, but the explanation is still obscure (Kendall 1982: 115–16). Work on the medieval cemetery of St Andrew's, York, has shown that the majority of graves were consistently aligned within 10 per cent of each other on a 'roughly east–west alignment' which may have been in part determined by existing features such as the boundaries of the cemetery (Stroud and Kemp 1993: 145). Analysis of grave orientation on post-medieval cemeteries which still have standing headstones, such as Deerhurst, has shown that the major influence was the church, but other factors such as walls and pathways also contributed to the orientation (Rahtz 1978: 11).

Perhaps the best-known example of a different orientation in a Christian context is that of the priest who had his head pointing west, the theory being that when he was resurrected he would rise up facing his flock. However, this seems to be a post-medieval custom (possibly after 1600), as priests found with patens or chalices in medieval graves are facing the same way as their flock (Rahtz 1978: 4–5). Medieval priestly burials, assumed from the graves containing a chalice and/or paten, found at Deerhurst and St Andrew's, York, face the same way as the rest of the burials.

Whereas the grave may be east–west, the body may be reversed, that is the head may point east instead of west. One explanation given for the reverse orientation of some burials is that the bodies were buried in a hurry and at the time, probably because of plague, the coffin or shrouded body was put in the wrong way round (Magilton and Lee 1989: 256). In one group, seven bodies were buried in the same grave, but the grave had not been dug widely enough, so the bodies were buried head-to-toe (Ayres 1990: 58). There may also have been more sinister reasons. In the cemetery of St Andrew's, York, the only skeleton facing west had been decapitated (Stroud and Kemp 1993: 145). The reason for the decapitation and reversal of orientation is unknown. However, light may be shed by the cemetery of St Margaret in Combusto in Norwich, which was the churchyard 'where those who have been hanged are buried' (*ubi sepeliuntur suspensi*). The cemetery has recently been excavated, revealing the criminal dead: some were buried east–west, and ten were even buried north–south or south–north. Not only was the orientation wrong, but some had their wrists tied behind their backs and had been buried, or thrown, into the grave face first in the prone position. They also had not been prepared for burial or wrapped in a shroud, but had been thrown in fully clothed (Ayres 1990: 58).

The lack of concern with the burial of criminals explains the surviving clothes, but the burial of objects in graves in the Middle Ages is a problem. The situation should be straight forward for the vast majority of graves have no grave-goods, or occasionally a simple pin to hold the shroud together. For example, at excavations in Taunton of the Augustinian priory of St Peter and St Paul, out of 162 burials (many of which were not complete) the only finds apart from iron coffin nails were 2 pieces of pottery and some metal-working debris from the site's former use (Leach

1984: 109). A similar situation was evident in Carlisle, where from over 100 burials the only finds were 2 brooches and 2 lace tags from a single grave (McCarthy 1990: 77). This lack of finds can be replicated across the country in medieval cemeteries. This absence of grave-goods is hardly surprising, as England was nominally Christian and Christians were not expected to be buried with objects. Dire examples were given of people who were buried with money. An example from a fourteenth-century preacher's manual concerns a usurer who was unafraid of death because he believed that if he had money on him he could make a 'good and careful bargain' – presumably with God or the Devil. He was buried with his money, but a papal legate arrived and ordered the priest to dig up the body, cast it into the open field and then burn the corpse. When the body was dug up they found 'ugly toads that gnawed at his miserable decomposing body and countless worms instead of an armband of money'. The buried money had been a disadvantage. The body was then burned and 'many died of the stench'. A further example from the same manual is given of a usurer who was dug up and it was found that a toad 'held burning coins to the dead man's mouth and fed him these' (Wenzel 1989: 352–5).

The horror of Christian writers against placing coins in the grave may be a reaction against pagan burials. Roman burial practice occasionally included coins as grave-goods, either in the mouth of the person or near them, in a container. These have been related to pagan practices, and one early Christian writer wrote 'certain sorcerers, acting against the Faith, place five *solidi* on the chest of the dead, thus imitating the gentiles who put a *denarius* in the mouth of the dead' (quoted in Alcock 1980: 59, original author not given). The custom continued into Anglo-Saxon England and in this context it may be relevant that the famous ship burial at Sutton Hoo contained a purse full of coins. The Vikings were also occasionally buried with coins in their mouths. Whether this custom continued is debatable, but it was certainly recorded in the nineteenth and twentieth centuries (Alcock 1980: 57). (A famous literary example from Hardy's *The Mayor of Casterbridge* occurred when Susan Henchard was buried and had coins placed on her eyes.) It is possible that the payment of mortuary to the Church was a Christianisation of the burial of coins with the dead (Alcock 1980: 59). This idea seems to be strengthened because it is usurers who are singled out as the people who want to keep the money to themselves so that they could make a 'good and careful bargain' rather than paying it to the only authority who could make the bargain: the Church.

There is a further lack of medieval evidence which is a common factor in other burial practices – that of broken objects placed in the graves to symbolise death. Broken items in Roman and Celtic (Alcock 1980: 62), Anglo-Saxon and Viking graves have been found. The practice of putting broken objects into graves continued, or restarted, in the Tudor era. In 1502 the Comptroller and Steward of Prince Arthur's household broke their staffs and threw them into Arthur's grave (the former broke the staff over his own head) and the gentlemen ushers threw in their broken rods (Kipling 1990: 93). Also in 1509 the Lord Treasurer and Lord Steward broke their staves and threw them into the burial vault of Henry VII (Cherry 1992: 25). It is possible that the practice of placing broken seals in the grave occurred throughout the Middle Ages, but only exceptional pieces of evidence point towards this view. In the cemetery of St Andrew's, York, a 'cancelled seal matrix' with a 'secular image on' was associated with disturbance close to a grave (Stroud and Kemp 1993: 137). However, there does seem to be a continuation of the practice of bending, folding or breaking objects throughout the Middle Ages to signify death, even though they were not placed in the graves. Personal seals were sometimes broken after the owner's death. The seals of the Abbots of St Albans were broken with a hammer in front of all the people after High Mass, the day after their death (Cherry 1992: 24). The seal was perhaps the most identifiably personal object that could be broken to symbolise death, but other more enigmatic objects were bent and folded. One large group was the numerous pilgrim badges which have been found in rivers, often at major crossing points. The reason for these is difficult to determine, and may be connected with acquiring good luck or in gratitude for a safe homecoming. There does not seem to be a specific funerary motive behind them. Another group of bent objects included a sixteenth-century group of swords or daggers from the Thames. This may have had no significance other than disposal of illegal or inferior swords and daggers by the Cutler's Company, but if this find is not unique it may signify superstition or the death of a person. It has also been pointed out that folded or cut coins may have had the same significance (Merrifield 1987: 108–15) and two folded silver coins and a jet pendant were found in a twelfth-century grave from the Benedictine priory in Bristol (Jackson 1995: 1).

The reason why broken objects were not put into the graves is problematical. One answer may be that they were, but have not been discovered yet, for example broken staffs or 'meteyards' (see below). Another possibility is that they were placed elsewhere. It has been noted that a large number of Viking swords have been found in rivers (thirty-five between 800 and 1100, the majority from the Thames or its tributaries) and it is possible that the reason was funerary in that objects so closely associated with their owners should not pass into other hands, nor could they be buried in a Christian context. They were therefore placed in rivers as an alternative way for them either not to be used, or for them to reach the dead (Merrifield 1987: 108). Broken objects were common symbols of pagan deaths and it may be for that reason that broken objects were *not* put into Christian graves in the Middle Ages. The objects buried with bishops or archbishops, such as croziers, staffs or rings, had not been damaged or destroyed, and neither had the pilgrim staffs. There seems to have been a fundamental shift in belief. It would be pleasing to equate this again with the rise of Purgatory in the twelfth and thirteenth centuries, except that Christian Anglo-Saxon graves do not contain broken objects either. The shift seems to be a Christian one – in England at least. (It would be interesting to see whether this was a Europe-wide phenomenon.)

A further answer may be that broken items held no power or influence for the soul. Indeed the reverse may have been true: it was whole objects which were helpful. A bishop or pilgrim could not use his staff in Purgatory if it was broken. Any breaking of objects that occurred tended to be a community gesture to signify the death of the person, as in the breaking of the seals of the Abbots of St Albans the day after their death. The soul had long since departed. Similarly, the breaking of their staves by the Lord Treasurer and Lord Steward was more a public act to show that their master had gone, rather than an attempt to free or help Henry VII's soul. As broken objects were not helpful to the soul in the afterlife, there was no point in including them in the grave at the time of burial.

The absence of grave-goods in Christian graves is a truism, and any items found are normally commented upon at length in archaeological reports. However, there is a massive problem with the general statement that there are no grave goods in Christian graves: it was the Christian hierarchy who were buried with the most elaborate grave goods. At the bottom of the scale were clerics who were buried with chalice and paten. At the top of the scale were the bishops and archbishops who were buried in full ceremonial robes. Pilgrims could also be included in this category, for some have been found dressed in their pilgrimage clothes, most notably at Worcester Cathedral. Royalty may also be included as being buried in robes, perhaps because of their divine right to rule. However, the tradition of grave goods for the Christian hierarchy sits oddly with the general no grave goods policy of other burials.

An explanation is not that easy to give. It was certainly an early custom, for Cuthbert was buried in his full robes and with many precious religious objects in the seventh century, a fact which, through his cult at Durham, was very well known. The only reason given for being dressed in this way is about his shoes, which he wore 'in readiness to meet Christ' (Colgrave 1985a: 131). Boots and shoes seem to have played a significant part in the cross-over between life and the afterlife, and if any material item could be taken with a person, shoes were the most probable. The French bishop Durandus stated that boots or shoes should be worn to meet Christ (Rowell 1977: 66). It is noticeable that the pilgrim at Worcester Cathedral had his boots deliberately cut so they would fit (Lubin 1990), and in the twelfth century when the boy martyr William was translated for the first time, a monk, Brother Thomas, acquired one of his shoes. In a vision William was adamant that it should not be kept in a shrine 'for that is not seemly enough' (Anderson 1964: 157). The same pattern of the importance of footwear was also common in Germany. A citizen of Cologne re-appeared to his granddaughter 'in a shining dress and all over him and especially on his boots was written in verse: "Hail Mary, full of grace etc" . . . seen written more often on his feet' because he prayed while walking about. This was explained as God rewarding good deeds by 'putting the mark of glory most of all on those members by which it was earned' (Scott and Bland 1929: 336–7). Another account by Caesarius of Heisterbach described how the mistress of a priest, when about to die, 'asked for new shoes of the best sort to be made for her, saying: "Bury me in them; they are very necessary for me" '. After her burial,

153

a knight was riding along a road and heard the shrieks of a woman clad only 'in a shift and those shoes', with a devilish hunter coming towards them. The knight defended her while she pleaded with the knight 'Let me run, let me run; see he approaches' (Scott and Bland 1929: 306). In this case the shoes are to flee the Devil, rather than to meet Christ. This story, and the one of the boots with verses on, come from Germany: without parallels being found in England it is difficult to know whether similar beliefs were held.

Bishops were also buried in robes. As they wore them in Heaven – as attested by visions – the robes were also probably worn 'in readiness to meet Christ'. In the *Life of St Anselm* by Eadmer, a monk had a vision of Anselm's death:

> and the room was filled with a host of people most wonderfully and beautifully arrayed in white apparel . . . The company was under the authority and direction of a bishop [St Dunstan] of outstanding splendour dressed in full pontifical robes . . .
>
> (Southern 1979: 155)

After Anselm's death a vision was seen of him 'wearing an alb of purest white and [he] was arrayed in his pontifical vestments' (Southern 1979: 162). In these cases the bishops were wearing their pontifical vestments to show that they were in Heaven, and in Dunstan's case to show that he was in authority. Bishop Herbert of Norwich was also the subject of a vision, and he was seen 'clothed in Episcopal robes that glistened with an incomparable whiteness. He rousing me with the Episcopal staff which he carried . . .' (Anderson 1964: 145). Durandus also believed that Christians should be buried in clothes of their rank, and those in holy orders with the *instrumenta* of their order (Rowell 1977: 66).

By extension, the same themes and ideas can be applied to archbishops and bishops and all the ecclesiastical hierarchy. Not only the spectators of the burial would expect them to be appropriately dressed, but Christ also. There are problems connected with the idea of meeting Christ in full robes. In accounts of Purgatory bishops are not depicted in ecclesiastical robes, but simply holding a cross or wearing a mitre. For example, when a bishop crossed a bridge in Purgatory, which was pulled down, an angel took from him his cross and mitre (Easting 1991: 104–5).

In the same account of Purgatory a bishop is also seen in Heaven, but supposedly without any distinguishing features: the only reason the witness, Owayne Miles, knows that it is a bishop is because he was told by St John of Bridlington.

The concept of important people being buried in the finest clothes could also be appropriate for holy pagans who died before the time of Christ. In the poem 'St Erkenwald', written about 1386, a description was given of a pagan judge who was found buried but undecayed under St Paul's Cathedral. After being brought back to life, the judge explains that the grieving people

> in their bounty they buried my body in gold:
> They clad me in the finest clothes the courts possessed
> [. . .]
> Robed me as if I were the richest ruler in Troy,
> Befurred me as befits one of flawless faith
>
> (Stone 1977: 38–9)

The reason why the judge was so dressed was that he was honoured by the people themselves (it was not his own wish or vainglory which accounted for the sumptuous clothes) to show his 'flawless faith' and their respect. It was also so that he was acceptable (*meet*) for Christ 'the most humane of judges'. The judge's body and clothes had been preserved in perfection by God so that he could be baptised at a later date. After baptism the judge physically disintegrated – presumably with his clothes – and his 'soul was established in bliss'.

As well as ecclesiastical or lay finery, the simple cowls of monks too had a spiritual power and significance. Caesarius of Heisterbach described how several people, both monks and laymen, were buried in a Cistercian cowl. This point was emphasised in several stories. In one account a monk threw off his cowl just before death because of terrible pain. That night, as psalms were being said round the body, the dead man came back to life – to the consternation of the other monks – and reported that St Bernard had refused to believe he was a Cistercian and asked 'If you are a monk, where is your habit? This is a place of rest, and are you going to enter in your working dress?'. The dead monk was allowed to return to life, put on the cowl, received a blessing and then expired again (Scott and Bland 1929: 267–9). From this it is obvious that in some cases dress was thought to play an important part in the afterlife. Although the cowl was important for entering Heaven, it was not a substitute for a pure soul. The tyrant Ludwig the Landgrave, who was buried in a Cistercian cowl after becoming a monk, was met by the Devil and taken to Hell (Scott and Bland 1929: 290–1). The burial of monks, or lay people in cowls, also occurred in England. Burials excavated in the Austin friars, Leicester, were probably lay people, wearing cowls and a burial possibly in a black habit or shroud was found at the Cluniac priory of St Mary, Thetford (Carter and Henshall 1957: 102–3). Documentary evidence for habits or cowls is limited. It is reputed that King John was buried in a monk's cowl in Worcester Cathedral (Gill 1936: 12), though when the tomb was opened up this was not reported (Welander 1991: 150). One definite example was of John Nyghtyngale, a former rector, who requested in 1474 to be buried in the habit of a monk and buried in Whitby Abbey.

Despite the commonplace medieval notion that the souls in Heaven were sexless and naked, huge numbers of works, paintings and stained glass showed that Heaven was not only populated by a hierarchy, but a clothed hierarchy. The English poem 'Purity' explained that the higher the heavenly rank, the costlier and better the clothes. The noblest were the 'best and brightest attired' (McDannell and Lang 1988: 77). The notion that Christians were not buried with grave-goods was obviously not a universal one and in some cases grave-goods were thought to make a difference to the soul in the afterlife, as testified by the monk who returned for his cowl. The reason for the dress and paraphernalia of the bishops may be a purely social one, but it is likely that they would not have hindered the soul on its way through Purgatory or to Heaven.

This emphasis upon the clothes worn was only appropriate for the highest ranks of society, presumably as their status in Heaven required. For the vast majority of the population, a simple shroud sufficed. The shroud was normally a piece of coarse cloth in which the body was wrapped for burial. The lack of clothing discovered archaeologically and depictions on memorial brasses indicate that the body was naked in the shroud. The shroud was sometimes sewn together, or tied at head and feet, or kept together by pins. There might be a difference between male and female shrouds, as linen shrouds were common for female burials, whereas men were sometimes buried in hair shirts woven from coarse two-ply yarn (White 1988: 20, quoting Hassall, 1971:

273). If the shroud was not sewn, the most common form of holding it together was either by tying it at head and feet, and therefore the lace or tag ends of the twine may survive, or by a metal or wooden shroud pin. At Whithorn one of the shrouds was held together with a fish hook (Hill 1988: 88). The shroud was used to wrap the body, but this did not exclude a coffin for in at least one case a fragment of a linen or flax shroud was found adhering to the skull of a woman in a coffin (White 1988: 18).

Alternative methods of wrapping or covering the body have also been found, and especially interesting are the organic remains. The use of plant material in graves has a variety of explanations, from the functional (to lessen the smell of the decaying corpse) to having religious significance. The custom is a very ancient one (going back to Bronze Age burials (Denison 1994a)) and in some rural districts has continued into this century. Medieval organic remains have been found under bodies or as grave linings. At Sandwell (Hodder 1991: 100), hay, straw, mosses and associated flowers were found in graves which in general was indicative of damp grassland, meadowland or wasteland. At Hulton Abbey, pollen analysis from the grave samples showed that all the graves were dominated by grass or rush pollen. It is possible that the pollen was included accidentally, perhaps from the rushes or flowers used in the adornment of the church (Klemperer 1992: 87–8). As well as these possible accidental inclusions there is evidence of the deliberate placing of plants within the graves. At Hull one grave contained box leaves (pers. comm. D. Evans) and at Hulton Abbey one burial in the chancel was wrapped up in rushes, which indicates a lost local custom (Klemperer 1992: 87–8). A burial in the south aisle of Winchester Cathedral lay on a bed of leaves, which was probably a mixture of oak and some sort of cereal plant (Ottaway 1982: 131). In the case of Prince Arthur, who died in 1502, his body was 'dressed with spices and other sweet stuff', although no reason was given (Kipling 1990: 81).

Inorganic linings were also used and at York a grave, probably dated to the thirteenth or fourteenth century, contained a lime lining. Though the significance of this is uncertain, its position in the middle of the presbytery and the unique status of the lining indicate that it was an important burial (Stroud and Kemp 1993: 157). Another grave containing lime, as a rubble foundation, was discovered at Norwich from '?eleventh century levels'.

At other sites, graves have been found with floors of crushed chalk or mortar, for example at St Nicholas Shambles, London, ten burials (seven female and three male), but they were not in particularly significant areas, lying (like the majority of the burials) to the north of the early church (White 1988: 18–20). An alternative flooring used was charcoal.

Charcoal burials, first documented in the fourth century by Sulpicius Severus in a letter about the burial of St Martin of Tours (pers. comm. D. Crouch), became common from the ninth to the twelfth century. Such burials have been found in a number of Saxon cathedral or abbey cemeteries, such as at Exeter, Hereford, Gloucester, Lincoln, Oxford, Repton, Worcester and York. Local parish churches could also have charcoal burials, for example St Nicholas Shambles, London, where an (unsexed) child was encased in charcoal (White 1988: 18–19) and a single example from St Helen-on-the-Walls, York, where a woman was encased in charcoal (Dawes and Magilton 1980: 16). Although these burials are mainly found in Anglo-Saxon areas, they have been found in Viking areas such as York. They are also found in Scandinavia, and the tradition there lasted until at least the twelfth century (Dawes and Magilton 1980: 16).

It is difficult to assess whether the plant material, chalk, lime and charcoal were all thought of in the same way; that is, whether it was the floor of the grave which was important, or whether it was the material that mattered. There are arguments possible for either case. One theory could be connected with the Resurrection of the body, where it would be kinder for the body to lie on material than on cold earth. This is a possibility, but no firm evidence has been found for this view. A potential piece of evidence (or at the least the view that the lying on chalk started with specific parts of the body and then developed for the whole body) occurs at Norwich, where several skeletons had patches of chalk either at their head or feet (Ayres 1985: 19). The crushed chalk at the feet gives the visualisation of the body rising so that it is standing on the patch of chalk.

There is some circumstantial evidence that colour was important, especially in the case of charcoal. Durandus wrote that coal should mark the spot of a burial so that it could no longer be used for secular purposes, and that the coal would last longer than any other substance. This is difficult to equate with the majority of charcoal burials because the charcoal was put under the body, which would hardly leave a lasting testimony, unless charcoal was sprinkled over the site of the grave on the floor. In two out of eight charcoal burials at Hereford Cathedral (burials S46 and S80), charcoal had been placed on top of the coffins (Shoesmith 1980: 27), which might indicate that it was acting as a marker. It is possible that similar views were held about other materials, or alternatively that the whiteness of the lime was contrasted with the black charcoal.

Charcoal is an enigmatic inclusion in a grave and several explanations are possible. One is that the charcoal soaked up bodily fluids in coffins which had been transported a long distance (P. Buckland, quoted in Dawes and Magilton 1980: 16). This may well explain the case from St Helen-on-the-Walls in York, where a female burial was encased in a thick layer of clean charcoal. At Kellington, Yorkshire, some interments were buried on charred planks probably dated to the tenth or eleventh century (Mytum 1993: 16). This generates a number of questions: were they burnt in situ? was the body carried on them? were the planks re-used? and what sort of wood were the planks made of? It is tempting to see the charcoal as a memory of pagan cremations, especially when it occurs in Viking areas, but this is unlikely because the tradition was first recorded for the burial of St Martin of Tours (see above) and remained common as a monastic ritual. If the use of charcoal can be associated with that of the well-documented penitential ashes on which a dying monk was placed, then it could be considered a sign of penance for one's sins. A further theory is that the use of charcoal was a status symbol. During the excavations at the Old Minster, several graves had charcoal packing and iron-bound packing, which were 'features most often associated with the burials of people of rank' (Fleming 1993: 26). The presence of charcoal does indicate that an additional effort had been made. It would be useful to discover more about the charcoal used. Was the wood all one type and fresh, or was it a mixture of woods embedded with nails, which would indicate it was being re-used? If it could be proved that the wood had been cut especially and that it was a one-off firing, it would be more likely to signify rank or social importance, along with other indicators, such as burial position.

At Hereford there does not seem to be any age or sex pattern to the ten charcoal burials: four are adult and the others are a combination of infant, juvenile or young adult. Similarly, some had coffins and some not, and some had a thin spread of charcoal and one had a 'large quantity' of charcoal. It is possible that the use of and reasons for charcoal in graves changed over time, for two different phases of charcoal burial were discovered during the Castle Green excavations, being probably dated to the tenth and eleventh centuries (Shoesmith 1980: 25–8). Whatever the reason for the grave linings, they are all found in Christian settings and only a minority of graves had them. Their significance is probably therefore a combination of social status and religious belief.

Another puzzling type of burial is that of the 'pillow-graves', where stones were placed around the head. The chronology is roughly the same as charcoal burials, being found within a date range of tenth/eleventh century to twelfth century, and, exceptionally, at St Mary's Church, Stow (Lincolnshire), into the thirteenth century (see Chapter 7). Different cemeteries seem to have different trends for pillow-graves: predominantly female burials at St Nicholas, Shambles, London, where 15 out of 22 pillow-graves were female; at Raunds predominantly male burials, coffined (Barton-on-Humber), or in uncoffined graves (St Andrew's, York; St Helen-on-the-Walls, York) (White 1988: 20–2). Three charcoal burials with 'pillows' were also found in the excavations at Hereford Cathedral. Reasons for the use of stone pillows are difficult to assess. They could be viewed as a form of 'punishment' – the head would feel the cold and uncomfortable stone packing at its resurrection. However, once consideration is given to the site of burial – often inside churches – the use of stones seems to suggest varying degrees of prestige rather than punishment. Another explanation might be that the stones were a sign of penitence or humility. In a particularly interesting example, Henry II's son, Prince Henry, was laid on a bed of sackcloth and ashes (known signs of penitence), with stones under his head and feet as well as the noose of a condemned criminal around his neck (pers. comm. D. Crouch). There may also have been regional or local trends. Two roughly contemporaneous cemeteries had different numbers of pillow graves: St Andrews, York had 1 male pillow grave out of 131 intact inhumations, whereas St Nicholas, Shambles, London had 22 out of 234 burials.

Several examples have been found of plant material, as well as plant material under the body. At Sandwell one body had plant material under the body and three graves had the head resting on a 'pillow' of plant material, which in one case was of moss (Hodder 1991: 100). A similar example of a grass-filled 'pillow' was found at Barton-on-Humber.

As not all graves had pillows, there was obviously some differentiation between burials, although on what basis is now difficult to determine. However, it is also valid to ask why there were two centuries (from the tenth to the twelfth) when both charcoal burials and 'pillow-graves' occurred. It could be argued that the pillows had a purely functional use in keeping the skull in position, and this is quite possibly the reason in the single York example where the head had been decapitated (Plate 9). However, the question then arises, 'functional for what purpose?' Between the tenth and the twelfth century, belief about the afterworld changed. During that time there was a greater emphasis upon bodily Resurrection and the Last Judgement when the dead would rise from their graves (see Chapter 7). With this belief it therefore becomes important for all the dead – or for those who could afford it – to rise facing the Risen Christ who would come from the east. Charcoal burials might have been thought to preserve the body so that it would rise in a better condition than other bodies. This of course leaves the question of the other bodies which do not have pillows. It is possible that a cradle of earth was placed around the head, rather than stone, or for some reason it was not considered necessary to support the head.

As well as the materials within the grave there are variations of the material used for the coffin itself. The most obvious were the stone coffins. At St Andrew's, York, eleven skeletons were found in monolithic (that is one block of stone) or composite stone coffins, although at least some of them probably had wooden rather than stone covers. The coffins were either sunk into the ground, or, in the nave, were standing on flat ground (Stroud and Kemp 1993: 153). Much more difficult to assess are the stone lined graves; the stones being either free-standing or mortared (Plate 10). These can be viewed in a number of ways. They may have been a less prestigious form of stone-coffin (White 1988: 23), but equally they may have been less prestigious than a wooden coffin, either because wood was scarce, or because the amount of work to line a grave with stone was possibly less than to collect and then make a wooden coffin. The variation between cemeteries can be great: in St Mark's Lincoln there was only one stone-lined ('cist') grave out of 202 early medieval graves (White 1988: 25), whereas in the late Saxon graveyard at Mitre Street, also in London, 'the majority' of the sixty-one burials were in a stone- or mortar-lined cist or tomb (Riviere 1986: 37). There is therefore a difference in emphasis between different cemeteries and at Winchester out of twenty priestly graves only nine were of cist type (Kjølbye-Biddle 1975: 89–91). However, it does seem that the stone cist graves were usually important in signifying status. At Capel Maelog, out of about 500 graves, the largest and most elaborate was an early Christian grave which had small upright slabs of stone which defined the upper edges of the grave (Jones 1988: 27). For this reason, and because the later church seems to have been positioned by the grave, this burial has been called the 'founder's grave'. On the Isle of Man, at Peel Castle, the range of grave types has been described as ranging from the 'deluxe well constructed "lintel graves" to simple uncoffined burials' (Freke 1988: 93). The extra care and effort, as well as the positioning of the graves lined with stone, do seem to indicate social status. This element of status is also reinforced in that in some cemeteries, for example Kellington, wooden coffins were designed to replicate the shape of stone coffins. One interesting, but unfortunately unprovable, idea is that the grave reflected the person's own house whilst living, for the grave-as-house was a common literary theme (see Chapter 3). This may explain the differences in materials and grave construction within, and between, cemeteries.

The survival of wooden coffins is extremely variable. Occasionally the excavator has to make a subjective decision as to whether a coffin had been used for the burial or not. More helpful in determining the presence or absence of a coffin is wood staining of the soil (generally leaving a brown stain), or metal nails which held the coffin together. (Coffins were also held together by wooden pins, so the lack of nails does not necessarily indicate there was no coffin.) The existence of coffins may be implied by the careful plotting of the nails, but at St Helen-on-the-Walls, York, some graves had fewer than six nails, which is not enough to hold the six sides of the coffin together (Dawes and Magilton 1980: 14). A combination of wooden pins and metal nails may have been used in these cases. Other attempts to identify coffined burials include recording the cases where the lower jaw had fallen away, the theory being that the coffin space would allow the jaw to drop more easily than a shrouded burial. Unfortunately there was no consistency in the result and the method was judged to be unreliable (Dawes and Magilton 1980: 14–15).

In exceptional cases the survival of part of the coffin is so good that the wood used can be identified, for example at Hulton Abbey coffins were made from oak, Scots pine and elm (Klemperer 1992: 88): at Hull coffins were made from imported Baltic Oak (pers. comm. D. Evans) and at Barton on Humber the coffins were made of oak (Panter 1994: 29). Henry IV's coffin was of elm 'very coarsely worked, about one inch and a half thick' (JHS 1872: 298). At York a coffin was made from boards no more than 20mm thick, on the evidence of the nails (Dawes and Magilton 1980: 14). Wooden coffins have been found on sites from at least the seventh century onwards into the present century (White 1988: 19–20). One remarkable example of a four-teenth-century coffin, complete with a skeleton – possibly a Carmelite – is on public display at St Peter Hungate, Norwich.

Rather than full coffins, sometimes simple wooden boards were placed over the grave which either rested on a lining (of wood or stone) or the earth sides of the grave. Such wooden grave covers have been deduced at York (Stroud and Kemp 1993: 153) and at Colchester (Crummy et al. 1993: 215–17). In the two Colchester examples the evidence for wooden grave covers was strengthened because some of the bones had been damaged or displaced, as if the wooden covers had decayed, and then col-lapsed into the grave hollow thereby displacing the right hand of one body whilst it was still attached and dislodging the knee-cap (patella) of the other body. A half-way between no-coffin and a full-coffin burial was discovered at Capel Maelog in Wales, where some coffins had a triangular cross section: two unjointed boards of wood had been rested on the ground and simply propped or tied against one another (Jones 1988: 28).

The role of the coffin is more or less defined by its function as something to bury the body in, but its manufacture is more problematical. Several coffins have been found to be reused either from earlier times or from other objects. The most obvious examples are the Roman coffins which were found and then reused: Bede recorded the reuse of a Roman coffin for the body of Abbess Aethelthryth (Colgrave and Mynors 1981: 395). Stone objects other than coffins do not seem to have been reused, but this is not so with wooden objects. At Whithorn three eighth- and ninth-century burials were buried in wooden coffins, but two had keys, one had a hinged lid, and the wooden coffin in the children's graveyard had a lock. These factors suggest that the coffins were in fact reused domestic chests (Cardy and Hill 1992: 95). This is not an isolated incident and similar conclusions have been drawn from finds at Dacre (Newman 1989: 233) and York (Rogers 1993). The majority range either side of the Norman Conquest from late Saxon to twelfth century. What the significance of these chests was is now difficult to determine, but that they held an importance can be seen from their widespread use. They might have been heirlooms or have had particular social meaning. Other reused objects have also been deduced: a bed and a wooden stool or bench at Barton upon Humber (Panter 1994: 30).

Structural timbers from previous buildings too seem to have been deliberately incorporated into graves. At Bordesley Abbey one of the earliest burials was covered with a reused structural timber. A further grave also had structural timber associated with it, which was not intended to be part of the grave nor was it a grave-marker. This was reminiscent of a French example where unused pieces of a new building were buried between the lay brother's dormitory and the mason's lodge. These three examples seem to be evidence that there was a religious or social significance to being buried with pieces of the church: that at Bordesley has been interpreted as the burial of a founding monk with part of the original church (Astill and Wright 1993: 126). It is possible, however, that the inclusion of the material was purely functional, either of disposal or reuse of unwanted material. More difficult to explain convincingly are the examples of a gaming board for nine-men's-morris incised on coffins. These have been discovered on the head niches at Sandwell (Hodder 1993: 191), on a reused piece of timber for a child's grave from St Benet's church, York (Panter 1994: 31), and on the side of a coffin at Deerhurst (pers. comm. P. Rahtz). At Chichester leper hospital, a chalk block for the head had an incised cross upon it (Magilton and Lee 1989: 256). The gaming boards may have been carved by labourers at the time of the making of the coffin (which conjures up the image of a mid-morning break pastime) or by those awaiting the body.

After the coffin and the shroud pins, the frequency of grave-goods rapidly declines. As a general rule, the earlier the burial (that is, pre, or just after the Norman Conquest), the more likely grave-goods are to be found. In France tools were sometimes buried in the grave as a symbol of trade. For example, a chisel and ball of lead were buried with a mason in the Grandmontine priory of Pinel (Hutchinson 1991: 278). The French author Jacobus also described how bodies arose from graves, each 'with the tool proper to his craft' (Ryan 1993b: 285). The burying of tools does not seem to have happened in England. Some grave-goods are very difficult to explain, especially the placing of pebbles in a grave. At St Nicholas Shambles a pebble had been placed in the mouth of four bodies (three elderly women, all around 40 years old and one elderly man of late 30s). At Raunds one skeleton, a youth of 17–25 who had poliomyelitis and then tuberculosis, also had a pebble placed in the mouth (White 1988: 25). It is difficult to tell whether it is the stone that is important, or its placing. If its being placed in the mouth was important, perhaps it was supposed to prevent talking at Resurrection, as gossip and 'back-biting' were condemned by the Church. An alternative is that the stones acted as a weight to stop the person rising up. At Raunds, stones were laid over parts of the body, especially the head and face (White 1988: 25). The placing of stones does not seem to be equated with any one particular type of burial.

One indication that it was the stone which was important rather than its placing was that at Kellington Church several skeletons were buried with quartz pebbles (Mytum 1993: 16). Burial with quartz pebbles has been found on other excavations. At Capel Maelog, Wales, a particularly elaborate early medieval grave contained a scatter of large white quartz pebbles (Jones, 1988: 27). At Whithorn 'almost all the graves have produced white quartz pebbles and cattle teeth which seem to have been included as symbols of purity or lucky charms' (Freke 1988: 90). No explanation has yet been given as to what the significance of the pebbles was, though it is possible that the whiteness of the quartz was important. However, one possible piece of evidence is the 1384 decree by William of Wykeham, Bishop of Winchester, which condemns 'stone-castings' in cemeteries (Chambers 1971: 72). Whether this is relevant to being buried with stones is impossible to tell without more evidence.

Tile may also have a significance. At St Nicholas Shambles, Roman tile or stones were placed on the body of three burials, as also happened in a single grave of St Bride's, London. The use of tile, rather than stone, may, or may not, be significant. Unused ceramic roofing tiles were also found lining two graves of St Andrew's, York, in the cloister alley, and also at Clementhorpe Priory, York (Stroud and Kemp 1993: 153). If the tile is a symbol (rather than just a straight alternative to stone) then it is possible that it marks some enhanced Christian devotion because Durandus, in a symbolic explanation of a church, described the tiles on the roof as the 'soldiers of Christ' (Scott and Bland 1929: 32).

The stone and tile placed in the grave are only made into Christian symbols by guesswork, but there are many objects which can easily and more explicably be classed as Christian gravegoods, such as crosses, pilgrim garb, papal bulls, chalice, paten, 'wands', mitres, croziers and ecclesiastical vestments. A mortuary cross within the grave is a relatively common feature and at least fifteen lead crosses were found at the Greyfriars cemetery in London (Platt 1978: plate 86). A cross could be a very simple pair of crossed twigs. Under the elm board coffin of Henry IV was a 'very rude small cross, formed by merely tying two twigs together, thus +. They fell to pieces on being moved' (JHS 1872: 298). More substantial mortuary crosses made of wood were found at Sandwell Priory, both in the 'Latin' and 'Greek' styles (Hodder 1991: 114). The presence of mortuary crosses in graves may also illuminate the case of the Glastonbury cross. In the 'grave [of Arthur] was a cross of lead, placed under a stone, and not above it, but fixed on the under side' (Rahtz 1993: 43). This cross is usually considered to be a twelfth-century forgery, but it is interesting that it was actually in the grave, for it might be that it represented a particularly elaborate, indeed royal, mortuary cross. Simpler crosses of lead have also been found in the 'Latin' and, less commonly, 'Greek' types, a Greek example coming from Bury St Edmunds (Goodall and Christie 1980: 260). Mortuary crosses could also be made from wax: 'Than is there another cross [after the wooden grave-marker] of a wax candle laid on his breast, in token that he died in burning charity to God and man' (Erbe 1905: 294). As far as is known, no such candle has been found archaeologically.

At the other end of the scale from the simple lead crosses were the fully clothed burials. The most impressive outside the Christian hierarchy (if kings can be taken to be God's secular representative on earth) are the pilgrim burials. One particularly impressive pilgrim burial was discovered at Worcester Cathedral (Lubin 1990). The significance is that the man was discovered in full pilgrim attire: leather boots, leather coat, pilgrim staff and a scallop shell. Unfortunately the head and hat were removed in the last century in the construction of a pipe trench and it is likely that the head would have had on it pilgrim badges from places the pilgrim had visited. This particular burial is interesting because the body had been dressed after death. The boots had to be split to allow the feet to be put in, so it seems that either his attire was a social comment and he would be seen during the funeral ceremonies, or that his clothes were important in the afterlife. Other symbols of pilgrimage have been discovered. A grave at Hulton Abbey had in it a wax seal with the impression of the hospital of San-Spirito in Rome. The body had also been buried with leather shoes on (Klemperer 1992: 88).

A potential pilgrim symbol is that of the 'pilgrim staff', which has been found at Worcester (Lubin 1990), Sandwell (Hodder 1993: 190), Hulton Abbey (Klemperer 1992), Hull (pers. comm. D. Evans; O'Connor 1994: 19) and further afield at Lund in Sweden. However, these 'staffs' are variable in strength and functionality. The only undisputed pilgrim staff was found at Worcester (Lubin 1990). The staff was very sturdy and had a metal spike at the end. This was a functional staff which could support and carry a heavy weight. More normally flimsy rods – interpreted as pilgrim staffs – are found in graves. It is possible that the rods symbolically represent a pilgrim staff, but this is unlikely. The second functional possibility is that they may have been stretcher poles or crutches (pers. comm. D. Evans), but the Hull examples at least were not strong enough. The third possibility is that they were used as beating rods, and as such were a symbol of office. References to wand- or rod-bearers (*virgatarii* and *virgatores*) occur at Westminster Abbey and they were probably responsible for 'medieval methods of crowd control' (Harvey 1993: 29). They were not necessarily servants of the abbey, as they were paid in money, and were possibly called upon when needed. Their position was such that it was unlikely they would have been buried with their wands or in important positions within the church. However, that the wands may have denoted an office holder or particular group may be indicated by the Hull examples, where six of the seven instances were 'found within one small area of the nave'.

It is much more likely that the staffs were symbolic grave-goods, possibly to represent the Resurrection or the power of Christ. A very late example occurred in 1615 when 'a man was presented at the Archbishop of York's visitation for "putting the metwand into the winding sheet in a superstitious manner" ' (Gittings 1984: 45). A metewand, also known as a 'meteyard', was a measuring stick and several instances of the word are known from fifteenth- and sixteenth-century literature. The reason for the inclusion of a wand into the grave was enigmatically given by Mirk in his fifteenth-century burial sermon: 'There is also a meteyard [*met-yorde*] laid by him [in the grave] instead of a staff, in token that he goeth to his long home [*sic*]; but his staff is broken, in token that there is no defence; but must need take better and worse, as he hath deserveth' (Erbe 1905: 295). The meteyard was possibly therefore a sign that he was about to enter eternity and appear at the Day of Judgement. Meteyards that have been discovered archaeologically have been made out of wood, symbolising the Resurrection: willow at Bordesley, hazel at Barton on Humber and Hulton, and a combination of both types at Hull. It is unfortunate that Mirk's description leaves certain questions unanswered: what the definition of the 'long home' was, the difference between a meteyard and a staff, and whether both, or only the staff, were broken? It is possible that both the meteyard and the staff changed their meaning over the centuries, for the discovered examples were not broken and the majority have been found mainly at abbeys or priories.

A possible pilgrim symbol (or amulet – see below), and certainly a Christian one, is the lead seal (called a papal bull) attached to papal documents, which may have been buried with the body. Papal bulls are a small but significant group of finds buried with the body: they have been found in graves or cemeteries; for example in the hand of a skeleton from All Saints Peasholme Green, York (Brinklow 1987: 6) and Hulton Abbey (bull of Innocent IV, 1352–62 from a grave in the chancel). Bulls presumed to have been originally buried in graves, but then disturbed, have been discovered at Chester, Beverley (pers. comm. D. Evans) and York (Daniell 1994: 11). Unfortunately a bull is made of lead, which easily corrodes, so bulls may have been more commonly placed in graves than the surviving evidence indicates. In size, a bull is usually about 3 cm in diameter and on one side has a picture of St Peter and Paul, with their names above. Interestingly the figures of St Peter and Paul are reversed on earlier bulls (pers. comm. D. Tweddle). On the reverse of the bull is the name and number of the pope who granted it, for example Urban IV. Despite the possibility of a document, with bull, being included in the grave, this is unlikely: first, because the document would have been useful to the living family or community, and second, because many skeletons are holding the bull itself, rather than the bull being apparently attached to a document. From the tenth and the eleventh century onwards, the papal court in Rome became increasingly central-ised and the official written grants or court decisions that came from it all carried the papal bull. These actions affected laymen as much as clerics so that it is possible that a skeleton holding a lead bull is a lay person; for example, the founder of a church holds its foundation charter. The inclusion of charters or docu-ments in graves was rarely mentioned in medieval texts, but one story does show this process in action. During a famine, a rich man gave £20 to help feed the poor. He then died and was buried, and Bishop Odo and the man's wife – who held a promiss-ory note from the Bishop for the £20 – opened the grave:

> There the dead man was lying, with a peaceful face as if asleep, and held a beautiful charter in his hand sealed with a golden seal. [The Bishop and wife opened the charter.] In it they found the following written with gold letters: 'Let all present and future know that the money I gave to Bishop Odo to be distributed for the use of the poor I have received a hundredfold return before my death in this world, namely full remission of my sins, and in future, as he had promised, eternal life.
>
> (Wenzel 1989: 555)

There are several particularly interesting points about this account. The document is called a charter (*cartam*) and has the same introduction as a charter, with a charter's standard opening 'Let all present and future know...' Second, it is a layman who holds it, and third, the charter is in the grave. No examples of bishop's charters or notifications have been discovered in English graves, but papal bulls probably performed the same function.

The most common status and belief symbol to be buried in the grave was that of the priest's chalice and/or paten (Rodwell 1981). They are found on many sites around the country, such

169

as St Andrew's, York, where one burial was found holding a lead chalice and paten, whilst another held a lead paten (Stroud and Kemp 1993: 156–7). At Lincoln Cathedral eight out of nine thirteenth-century graves in the Chapter House had pewter chalices in them (Bruce-Mitford 1976). At least in one case, at Monk Bretton Priory, the depiction of a chalice on a grave slab cover matched a chalice in the grave (Ryder 1991: 63). Whether this correspondence between art and grave-goods always holds true is debatable.

The role of the chalice and the paten in the grave is not clear. In some instances they may have held consecrated wine or bread. When the tomb of Archbishop Hubert Walter was opened in 1890 it was thought to contain wine (Stratford 1982: 88, 92). In the twelfth and thirteenth centuries various ordinances made a distinction between chalices to hold the consecrated wine (made of precious metals), and those of base metals, such as tin, pewter or lead, to bury with the priest, or to be used for drinking unconsecrated wine after communion. Chalices of base metals were common in churches, and eight churches of the fourteen in the patronage of St Paul's had pewter chalices in 1297. In 1229 William of Blois, Bishop of Worcester, specified that every church should have two chalices, one of silver for the Mass and the other of tin for burial with a priest (Tweddle 1986: 208–9). It is possible, especially for earlier graves, that the chalice and paten were consecrated and when buried contained wine or bread. The change – if indeed there was one – from chalices containing wine to base-metal chalices may have come about as a result in the increasing belief in Purgatory, with the associated lessening in importance of the Day of Judgement and the bodily Resurrection.

The chalice and paten also held other symbolism. The paten found in Archbishop Walter Hubert's grave had the inscription: 'The altar represents the cross, and the chalice the tomb, and the paten the stone, and the white *corporale* the winding-sheet' (Stratford 1982: 91). This inscription gave the symbolic reasons why the chalice and paten might be buried in the tomb. Not only were they a symbol of office, they also symbolised Christ's tomb and the stone before it. A precursor to the inscription from a paten in the grave of Sicardus, the Bishop of Cremona, who died in 1215, increases the symbolism by adding 'also the chalice (signifies) the body, because wine is in the chalice, blood is in the body' (Stratford 1982: 91). This adds weight to the belief that the chalice did in fact contain wine when buried.

Higher up the ecclesiastical hierarchy were the deans, abbots, bishops and archbishops. Graves of archbishops and bishops have been discovered which contain fully robed bodies with various accoutrements, such as croziers and rings. The most famous example is St Cuthbert whose remains still survive at Durham Cathedral. Other later examples include Thomas Becket (a drawing exists of c.1200, showing his burial wearing the pallium (Backhouse and de Hamel 1988: 19)), and archbishops Walter (died 1205), de Grey (died 1255) and de Ludham (died 1265) (Ramm et al. 1971). Many of these graves were opened in previous centuries but enough remains for a detailed description to be given of the vestments. Over forty silk fragments remain from Walter's vestments, although only the mitre, stole, buskins and shoes have survived well. These and other fragments show designs of birds (including eagles), trees, leaves, scrolling and patterning, and animals such as lions and dragons. Some of the silks have been identified as being made in Spanish workshops in the late twelfth century (Muthesius 1982: 80–7). Other objects in the grave include a gold ring, crozier and a matching chalice and paten. Also in the grave were antique gems, possibly Etruscan or Roman, which had been set within the crozier, and an antique gem inscribed with Greek set into a ring. Stylistically the silver-gilt chalice was made in the middle years of the twelfth century (possibly with its matching paten), so it was over half a century old when buried, having been commissioned in Walter's early life.

The chalice and ring highlight the inclusion of deliberately old material into the grave. It could be argued that these gems were part of existing items which were buried with Walter, but in the case of the ring the situation is not so clear-cut. Later bishops often had large numbers of rings. Bishop Stapledon of Exeter had ninety-one rings listed on his death in 1328 and Bishop Grandisson's will in 1368 mentions seven individual rings and, in addition, rings for any bishop attending his burial (Cherry 1991: 205–6). There may well have been an element of choice as to which ring Walter chose to have buried with him, and the idea of burying pagan antique rings in graves goes back to the Anglo-Saxon period, for example at the royal grave at Sutton Hoo.

As well as antique items, old clothes were sometimes included. Cardinal Wolsey in the sixteenth century was buried in 'all such vestures and ornaments as he had been professed in' (Lockyer 1962: 228). This idea of wearing the garments professed in is interesting as it implies the garments travelled with Wolsey and related back to a significant point in his life. A very clear example also occurred in the thirteenth century. William Marshal, one of the most powerful men in England, died in 1219. As he lay dying he called for the 'rich silken pall' which he had bought in the East to be brought to him from one of his Welsh castles or monasteries, where it had lain untouched for thirty years (Crouch 1990: 187). Similarly Becket was buried in the clothes he wore at his consecration (Backhouse and de Hamel 1988: 19). Clothes and items were therefore deliberately kept throughout life for use at the moment of death or burial. These cases might also explain the items (or 'achievements') of the Black Prince, such as the coat-armour, which hang over his tomb and are original rather than being newly made for the funeral (Arnold 1993: 12–24). This tradition fits oddly with people being buried with newly made objects. In a case cited by Caesarius in Germany, a woman specifically asks to be buried in new shoes (Scott and Bland 1929: 306).

The position of royal burials regarding grave-goods is unclear because few royal burials have been analysed in detail. In 1771 the tomb of Edward I was opened at Westminster. The tomb

> was opened in the presence of the Society of Antiquaries and the King was found in his royal robes, wrapped in a large waxed linen cloth . . . [his] shanks . . . were concealed in the cloth of gold . . . Pitch was poured in upon the corpse, and, as Walpole comically laments, in deploring the final disappearance of the crown, robes and sceptre, 'They boast now of having enclosed him so effectively "that his ashes cannot be violated again" '
>
> (Stanley 1869: 144–5)

Although detailed medieval accounts, both financial and descriptive, exist for the burial ceremonies of royalty, the whole opening of Edward I's tomb seems to be unique for an English king. A partial attempt was made in 1832 to expose the body of Henry IV which was encased in lead. An oval piece of lead was cut out.

> Under this we found wrappers, which seemed to be of leather, and afterwards proved to have been folded five

times around the body . . . These wrappers were cut through
and lifted off, when, to the astonishment of all present, the
face of the deceased King was seen in complete preservation

(JHS 1872: 298)

Unfortunately the face sank away 'on the admission of the air' but
the surveyor had 'distinctly felt the orbits of the eyes prominent in
their sockets'.

The high royal and ecclesiastical burials are oddities in that,
although well documented, they are a tiny proportion of the
population as a whole. In large-scale cemeteries very few grave-
goods are found. One class, which is occasionally found, consists
of metal buckles or leather objects, for example shoes or belts.
Fragments of leather belts, with associated buckles, were found
in graves at the Austin friary in Leicester. Three different types
of belt were found and it is known that the Austin friars wore a
black leather belt ('black leathern thong'). The archaeological
evidence of the buckles (which were either bronze or iron) indicates that the buckle was worn low down at the front as the
buckles were generally found low down on the pelvis. In one
example, an annular brooch form was discovered, which might
indicate the use of a codpiece or belt (Mellor and Pearce 1981:
133). If the former, the body was certainly not buried in the habit
of a friar. Similar finds are of two brooches on a lay skeleton
from the Dominican friary in Carlisle. The brooches, directly
analogous to a series of brooches found in mass graves from the
battle of Visby in 1361, were found on the thighs of the skeleton
and were probably used for belts or hose (McCarthy 1990: 189).

The Carlisle case is a particularly interesting one because the
man wearing the belt was suffering from Paget's disease. This
highlights the possibility that the belt was being worn as a cure.
In Eadmer's *Life of St Anselm* an example of a miracle was given
of the knight Humphrey who was cured of dropsy by Anselm's
belt (Southern 1979: 158–60). Eadmer gave Humphrey the belt,
whereupon he kissed it and put it round his body: the swelling
disappeared. Eadmer asked for Anselm's belt back, but agreed to
let Humphrey have a rather narrow strip of it from the whole
length of the belt. A much earlier, but comparable, example of
the healing power of a saint's belt is that of St Cuthbert's girdle
which healed an abbess and a nun (Colgrave 1985a: 231–3). The
archaeological, and provable, instances of medical treatment are

very rare and it has been suggested that papal bulls found in graves were 'amulets' and were 'considered worthy of pious worshipping' (Madsen 1994: 68). It is possible they were thought to cure illness as well. One certain and one possible identification of medical treatment have been found. The positive identification comes from a monastic cemetery in York where a skeleton was found with two copper alloy plates attached to a man's knee (Stroud and Kemp 1993: 217; see Chapter 5). More debatable cases have been found elsewhere. At the leper hospital excavated at Chichester, the western end contained many coffins (Magilton and Lee 1989: 256) – possibly in an attempt to confine the disease. An alternative medical practice, this time discovered during archaeological excavations at Llandough monastery in Wales, was the wearing of iron bands around the stomach, interpreted as a surgical truss (Denison 1995b: 4). There may be other explanations, however, for iron bands were used as a punishment. Caesarius of Heisterbach wrote two accounts of sinful women who wore iron bands. The first, Clementina, 'committed a sin of the flesh' and when she died 'there were found round her body nine iron bands'. The second account concerned a nun; grieving for her sins 'she had bound herself with bands of iron. But as she stood at prayer with these upon her, they all burst asunder' (Scott and Bland 1929: 262, 263).

The rare 'medical' grave-goods may be described as functional, but the reasons for inclusion of grave-goods in general in the Middle Ages is problematic. It is possible to explain the grave-goods of the Church hierarchy in terms of their role in Heaven, but Heaven was not only filled with churchmen and it is surprising that lay people did not follow the example. The lack of legislation about burial practices indicates that the Church was not particularly concerned, and elsewhere on the Continent, for example France, people were buried with objects of their trade or status – such as the master mason with his chisel and ball of lead from the highly religious Grandmontine Priory of Pinel (Hutchinson 1991: 277). The role in Heaven may be one answer, but others undoubtedly wait to be found.

7

DEATH FROM THE CONQUEST TO THE REFORMATION

The history of death and burial in England between 1066 and 1600 may be divided into three broad sections: the eleventh to mid-fourteenth century, the period between the Black Death and the Reformation (1348 to mid-sixteenth century), and the Reformation. The importance of these divisions is that they allow analysis of important themes concerning death and burial, of which the most important is theological change. In the twelfth century Purgatory was, for the first time, clearly defined, which led to a change in burial practice. The second major theological change was the Reformation, when many of the medieval religious beliefs were swept away and the emphasis was on the individual, the Bible and his or her faith. Almost exactly half-way between these changes was the Black Death, which arrived in England in 1348. The Black Death was possibly the worst catastrophe that the human population has ever suffered, and from then on mortality was given a much more prominent role in art and the population's consciousness. Although the sources are very different for each period, some sort of understanding can be attempted as to what were the driving forces behind changes in death and burial.

The period of the late eleventh, twelfth and early thirteenth centuries (a period sometimes described as the twelfth-century renaissance) had a profound effect upon attitudes to death and burial. At the beginning of the twelfth century the Church's attitude towards the dead was, broadly, as follows: at the Last Judgement souls would be judged and then divided into the saved and the damned, depending on their life on earth. If a person had done good works, then in all probability salvation would follow: if a person had led an evil life, then the soul would be condemned to Hell. By the twelfth century this imagery was changing to signify a more judgemental, legalistic, attitude. God was depicted as a fearsome judge passing sentence on the soul. Intercessors on the soul's behalf included Christ or the saints, whilst the Devil was the prosecutor and attempted to get the soul damned. The image of the courtroom can be taken further, with Christ or God sitting on a judge's throne; the souls being judged by being weighed, often by the Archangel Michael (Plate 11). (Evidence of sin weighing the soul down.) Throughout the twelfth and thirteenth centuries the imagery of the courtroom as the Last Judgement grew in strength (Ariès 1987: 99–102). After the decision the souls would be divided: the blessed to Heaven, and the damned to Hell. One other significant change occurred in the twelfth century: the evidence used to determine the soul's fate became linked to the actions of the soul whilst on earth. Not only was the evidence directly linked, it was also physically recorded into a book. Previously, books in heaven had recorded the names of the elect, but now the books used in the heavenly court recorded the sins of the souls. The written sins could not be forgotten. The book of sins was to be used only once, but at the crucial moment to determine the final destination of the soul (Ariès 1987: 103–6). The importance of writing sins in a book led to the belief that they could be wiped clean by pilgrimage. In *The Golden Legend* a man committed a sin so terrible that the bishop could not absolve him. The sin was written down and laid on the altar of St James. The man prayed and on opening the paper the ink and sin had been erased (Ryan 1993b: 6).

What happened between death and the Last Judgement was a matter of debate. Some authors believed the soul would rest in the grave, and others believed the soul might rest in one of a number of places. One of the most popular was the bosom of Abraham, the authority for which ultimately came from the Bible (Luke 16: 23). The bosom of Abraham, whilst not being Heaven, was, nevertheless, a place of rest and peace in darkness and with no material suffering (Le Goff 1984: 133). The image which has been connected with the notion of Abraham's bosom is the naked and sexless soul being carried to Heaven in a napkin or sheet, usually standing or kneeling (the lower half of the body is covered by the sheet) and praying. The image was a popular one all over Europe and appears on tombstones – such as at Ely (possibly that of Bishop Nigel 1133–69) – and manuscripts – such as the mid-twelfth-century Shaftesbury Psalter. Although the belief declined in theological importance from the twelfth century onwards, the idea of Abraham's bosom was continued as an under-current: in 1459 it was painted on a retable for the church of Saint-Bertin at Saint-Omer. The biblical authority for Abraham's bosom meant that the theme remained in popular usage throughout the Middle Ages and beyond into Protestant theology. Shakespeare wrote of Abraham's bosom in several of his plays; in *Richard III* (IV. iii. 38) Richard commented on the murdered princes: 'The sons of Edward sleep in Abraham's bosom' (Boase 1972: 53).

The alternative was that the soul had to be cleansed, or 'purged', of its sins before it could reach Heaven: only the blessed passed straight to Heaven. This purgation normally consisted of some sort of fire, a belief given authority by the biblical passage in 1 Corinthians 3 : 10–15. Fortunately, following the biblical reference of 2 Maccabees 12 : 46, the souls could be helped by the living. Bede, in the eighth century, described in detail the vision of Drythelm who not only saw the horrors of Hell and the pleasures of Heaven, but also saw the souls who had repented and confessed. These souls were being horribly tortured (implying that they were being cleansed), but 'the prayers of those who are still alive, their alms and fastings and specially the celebration of masses, help many of them to get free even before the day of judgement' (Colgrave and Mynors 1981: 495, McGuire 1989: 73).

Throughout the Middle Ages, and especially until the thirteenth century when Purgatory was formalised, the living and the dead were in close contact with each other. (Warnings were given by important liturgists, however, that the living should not communicate with the dead: a departure from common practice (McLaughlin 1991)). Whilst the living prayed, the dead warned the living of the horrors awaiting unless they led a more Christian life. There was little consensus, however, as to who would undergo purgation, when or where. Some believed, following Augustine, that earthly tribulations were the first stages of purgation of the soul (Le Goff 1984: 134). These could be inflicted from above, but could also be chosen. Honorius of Autun, a twelfth-century writer believed that purgation, wholly or partially, could be accomplished on earth by a series of self-inflicted penances or fasts, or loss of worldly goods (Boase 1972: 46).

It was a logical step for the idea of Purgatory as a place, rather than just a concept, to develop at a time when there was increasing interest in what happened to the soul after death and before the Last Judgement. The date that purgatory was 'born' as a place in Christian theology was, according to Le Goff, between 1170 and 1180 (Le Goff 1984). Furthermore, it was 'born' at the 'school' of Notre-Dame in Paris. Between these dates, Peter Comestor used the noun *purgatorium* to denote the place of Purgatory, and not some abstract idea of purgatorial fire acting on souls. This defining of Purgatory as a place caused a revolution in the geography of the other world (Le Goff 1984: 154–9). The popularity of Purgatory as a place quickly grew and in 1254 Pope Innocent IV gave the first papal definition of Purgatory (in response to the Greek Church) which is still authoritative:

> since the Greeks themselves, it is said, believe and profess truly and without hesitation that the souls of those who die after receiving penance but without having had the time to complete it, or who die without mortal sin but guilty of venial (sins) or minor faults, are purged after death and may be helped by the suffrages of the Church; we, considering that the Greeks assert that they cannot find in the works of their doctors any certain and proper name to designate the place of this purgation, and that, moreover, according to the traditions and authority of the Holy Fathers, this name is Purgatory, we wish that in the future this expression be also accepted by them. For, in this temporary fire, sins, not of course crimes or capital errors, which could not have been forgiven through penance, but slight and minor sins, are purged; if they had not been forgiven during existence, they weigh down the soul after death.
>
> (Le Goff 1984: 283–4)

Purgatory had been officially defined and the introduction of Purgatory as doctrine can hardly be over-emphasised in importance for the Middle Ages. Three hundred years later the belief in Purgatory was abolished in England, but its impact on the beliefs of people in the intervening time was immense.

Until the twelfth and thirteenth centuries the commemoration of the dead was almost entirely based in the monasteries. This emphasis grew with the monastic reforms of the tenth and the eleventh centuries. The new and spiritually pure orders of the Cluniacs and Cistercians vied with each other over the number and quality of prayers, which in turn attracted different political and social groups around them. The Cistercians emphasised the benefits of their prayers – William of Malmesbury wrote in the twelfth century, 'the Cistercian order, ... is now both believed and asserted to be the surest road to heaven' (Stevenson 1991: section 334), whilst the monastery of Cluny 'can at times be seen as something of a prayer factory'. Increasingly the emphasis was that 'prayers for the dead [made] a decisive difference' for the souls of the departed, and without them 'the pain of the dead would be much worse' (McGuire 1989: 69, 75, 77).

The most powerful weapon of remembrance, and therefore prayer, was the written word. This was exemplified by the Bible itself, for Christ was remembered via a book. Once written down, the chances of being forgotten were far less than through oral memory. The book in which souls were recorded was significantly called 'the Book of Life' (*Liber Vitae*). If a name was listed, the soul would be prayed for. There were problems connected with this approach. The Order of Cluny in the early years recorded a huge number of names – in some registers into the thousands – of royalty and benefactors down to individual monks and laity. As part of this process Abbot Odilo of Cluny introduced the feast of All Souls in 997, which was intended to embrace all the faithful departed. Not only did each abbey or priory celebrate the anniversaries, but lists were swapped between abbeys or priories in reciprocal prayers. As well as prayers, food was consumed after the event. The situation became so bad that by the middle of the twelfth century the Abbot of Cluny, Peter the Venerable, declared 'the dead would drive out the living'. The Cistercians, who had the same problem, reacted by restricting the number of services and in 1225 the general chapter of the order agreed that only one Mass a year should be said for a specific soul. An even more stringent measure was passed in 1270 – that all separate anniversaries should stop and twelve general services should take place instead (Colvin 1991: 153). This was a remarkable admission that the role of memory had become too much for the living – especially as it was at a time when Purgatory had only recently been officially defined and sanctioned, and the wealth and prestige of the monasteries were at their height.

Fortunately for individual souls there was an alternative. Chantries developed in Europe in the late twelfth century and early

English examples were the chantry at Wells Cathedral (no date) (Barrow 1988: 94) and those for the bishops of Lincoln and Lichfield in the 1230s (Cook 1947: 17). There were several important advantages of a chantry over an anniversary. The anniversary, which had predominated in the previous centuries and remained relatively popular throughout the Middle Ages, not only involved a service but also food. Furthermore, from the benefactor's view, the service commemorating the death was only once a year (therefore helping the soul in Heaven only once a year). A chantry, however, gave a daily Mass (or in the earliest period a weekly Mass) for the soul. The heavenly benefits were therefore much greater. There were also benefits on earth. First, a degree of spiritual privacy could be given as a Mass was said for a specific soul, and second, a chantry allowed a priest to say Mass for a family. Instead of anniversaries being spread throughout the year, the family could be grouped together as a unit for prayers (Barrow 1988: 94).

As well as a theological change from great emphasis on the Day of Judgement to the increasing prominence of Purgatory, burial practices changed. Distinctive burial practices, which had become common in the ninth century, included a range of materials within the graves: charcoal, chalk, tiles and ashes, or stones placed as 'ear-muffs' (Plate 9). During the twelfth century these were replaced by graves which had no distinguishing features. The chalk and charcoal may have been purely functional (to soak up the body fluids) or they may have had a theological reason, for example to help preserve the body until Judgement Day. During the same period, sack-cloth and 'ashes' (which could equate with charcoal) were used to lay the monk on for his last moments. No literary reference has yet been found to indicate whether the monks were buried with the sack-cloth and ashes, but even if such references exist the lay charcoal burials still have to be explained.

During the period between the ninth and twelfth century, the position and condition of the body, and especially the head, became important. 'Head niches' became more common in coffins chiselled out of solid pieces of stone. At the other extreme two large pebbles (commonly known in archaeology as 'ear-muffs') were placed at the ears to stop the head rolling sideways. A further possibility is that earth was built up around the head to stop movement, a possibility which can be explored archaeologically. (If it could be established that earth had never been used, then the stone itself may have had a symbolic meaning.) An important function of the head niche or ear-muffs seems to have been to keep the head upright – an importance highlighted by the raising of the dead at Judgement Day. If the head was facing upwards the person would have a direct line of sight to the risen Christ.

Judgement Day was important – theologically, spiritually and practically. In ways that are not yet fully understood the burial customs and practices seem to mirror this belief. The theory of the importance of Judgement Day is considerably strengthened by the time-scale within which these burial practices took place. The charcoal burials, 'ashes' and the 'ear-muff' burials all fade out in the late twelfth and early thirteenth centuries, exactly at the same time that the role of Purgatory was being emphasised.

Although a case has been made for burial customs reflecting a change in religious views, alternative reasons for change apart from Purgatory have been suggested, mainly by French scholars (D'Avray 1994: 177–84). One powerful argument against the role of Purgatory is that it had been discussed, albeit in general and rather undefined ways, for centuries before the twelfth-century formalisation. This can be countered, however, by the fact that it was just one of several views and did not come to pre-eminence until the late twelfth century. Another alternative was changing perceptions of the nature of the corpse. Previous to the eleventh century, the dead (excepting saints) were regarded as 'passive, even pathetic figures' whose visions were plaintive. From the eleventh century the angry, aggressive ghost became more frequent, occasionally physically assaulting wrongdoers. The ordinary corpse, too, gained power in popular belief, and teeth from a corpse were thought to cure toothache (McLaughlin 1991: 31).

In the longer term, change in funeral practices may have come about through increasing urbanisation and individualism. The joint processes of migrations into towns and plague led to a separating of people from their ancestral graveyards, a subsequent dislocation and isolation. To reassert their own identity within towns a new flamboyant and more macabre funeral ceremony developed which emphasised the role of the individual (D'Avray 1994: 182 Chiffolean 1980). This theory can be argued against on several counts: that people continued to migrate to towns throughout the Middle Ages, but it was only at certain times that changes to funeral and burial customs occurred; that migration was not necessarily one way as people often returned home; that changes in burial practices, such as the decline of charcoal burials, can be seen in villages as well as towns (people returning home?); and that 'ancestral graveyards' could equally occur in towns as well as in rural areas. However, before dismissing the role of urbanisation there are two aspects which can be considered further. The first is that of the idea of the 'Heavenly City'. This image became increasingly strong in the eleventh and twelfth centuries, and churches themselves were seen to evoke the heavenly Jerusalem on earth (McDannell and Lang 1988: 72–7). Whilst no evidence has been found for tying burial or graves into this image, the idea of urbanisation was a common motif across a wide spectrum and maybe burial in church represented burial within the Heavenly City. The grave itself was frequently depicted as a house, an image which became popular in the twelfth century (see Chapter 3). These themes, and competition (see below) might have been particularly strong within an urban setting. The second, and later, piece of evidence comes from wills. In a study of fourteenth and fifteenth-century wills from Bury St Edmunds and a small village called Blackbourne Deanery, a difference was noticed between prayer bequests (Dinn 1995: 158). The wills from the town have many more requests for the testator's soul alone (50 per cent), compared with only 10 per cent in the village. In the village, however, 55 per cent of bequests mentioned friends, compared with only 15 per cent in the town. These figures indicate a difference in perception between town and country and it is possible that the emphasis on the 'self' within towns meant more extravagant funerals and competitiveness than in the villages.

A connected argument runs that the Church deliberately set out to promote what has been called 'The Cult of Death' and the 'Catechism of Fear' from the twelfth century onwards because it realised that 'the socioeconomic process of change and the individualisation of death could threaten its leading role in contemporary society' (Menache 1990: 82–3). This theory is based upon a perception of the Church seeking to enforce its own power by 'manipulation' of the population, and that the most effective way to bring people back from the 'anonymous social structures' of the city was by the Catechism of Fear by which the

Church turned this world into a ' "house in ruins" and a "mass of sin" ' (Menache 1990: 82–3). Whilst it is true that the Church sought to emphasise sin and death, the population embraced it more than a cynical Church-led 'manipulation' of death might imply. Ultimately both the Church and the individual were concerned with the fate of individual souls and they both worked together to bring about the best result possible.

French scholars have also suggested that there were remnants of ancient pre-Christian beliefs which filtered down and became incorporated into medieval burial practice (Chaunu 1978, Volvelle 1976, D'Avray 1994: 178). One potential example is that the 'charcoal' burials in England reflected pagan cremations, or that shoes in the graves followed Roman customs. The problem is proving these links to the past as there are many alternative explanations or long gaps when no examples exist. However, occasional pieces of evidence demand attention. In the twelfth century the practice of calming a restless spirit was to disinter the body and cremate it – an action reminiscent of pagan cremation and rejected by Saint Hugh of Lincoln (Clayton 1931: 137). A fourteenth-century tale, about an exhumation of a body for burning, described how the money in the grave had turned into 'countless worms instead of an arm-band of money' (Wenzel 1989: 352–5). The correspondence between burning and an arm-band of money – a method of carrying silver well attested in the Viking Age – might also indicate echoes of an earlier tradition.

From an archaeological perspective there are alternative ways of looking at burial customs, whether through competition, group identity, processes of burial, and the material remains. Competition certainly existed at times between the powerful lay and ecclesiastical communities (for example Thomas Becket and Henry II) or between the churches and saints (York trying in vain to match the prestige of Canterbury's St Thomas Becket). The movement of relics provided an excellent occasion for a powerful statement, and the spectacle when St AElfheah's relics were moved before the Conquest included 'a dragon prowed ship, rows of armed housecarls and a gaggle of chanting monks' (Fleming 1993: 30). The supreme example was that of the medieval kings of Europe who vied with one another for prestige and influence, and aimed to impress their own followers. Both the kings of England and France developed their funeral ceremonies from 'relatively unceremonial, low-key affairs' in the eleventh century to magnificence by the thirteenth century (Hallam 1982). This change can be exemplified by the treatment of William the Conqueror, and that of Henry III. When William died in 1087, his attendants stripped him and left him 'almost naked on the floor of the house'. He was then refused burial in a plot of land and when he was stuffed into a coffin the corpse disintegrated – the ensuing stench was so bad that the service had to be rapidly ended (Hallam 1982: 359). In 1272 Henry III died and was buried in Westminster Abbey. His body was fittingly decked out with the richest clothes and the royal crown and his body 'shone with greater splendour than it had in life' (Hallam 1987: 104). Henry III had modelled himself on, and competed with, the French King Louis IX: 'The patterns of their religious foundations, their pious benefactions and almsgiving were very similar, and there was almost certainly a conscious element in this [since when they met in 1262] they indulged in piety contests' (Hallam 1982: 372). At a more local and parochial level it is difficult to detect the competition or group identity in the burial record although individuals – whether marked by grave-goods (for example charcoal or 'ear-muffs') – or grave stones marked by design or inscriptions may have been competing for attention. It is noticeable that the great lords in eleventh- and twelfth-century England favoured urban burials (Fleming 1993: 25) which may be a combination of competitiveness, urbanism and individualism. Future studies of the differences between competitive groups will undoubtedly reveal group identity in tomb design and it was not uncommon for tombs to portray worldly allegiance, for example Sir John Marmion was portrayed wearing a Lancastrian double 'S' collar (Plate 12).

Cadaver tombs may be a case in point. Cadaver tombs originated from the Continent and were first incorporated as a grave design in England in 1420. The 'cadaver' was a sculpture or depiction of the corpse decomposing, which was sometimes heightened by the inclusion of worms or toads on, or in, the body. Although there were many such tombs or brasses, those made between 1465 and 1480 seem to show distinctive differences between Lancastrian and Yorkist designs and allegiance. Such tombs reflect

a select trend passing amongst members of a discernible group, to be picked up later by lesser persons living in the

184

same area or owing a debt of allegiance or admiration [to Margaret of Anjou, whereas] . . . none of the supporters of Humphrey, Duke of Gloucester seems to have had a cadaver tomb . . . nor do any die-hard Yorkists favour the design.

(King 1984: 54)

The cadaver tombs between 1465 and 1480 seem to be part of a dynamic process of defining the group both by the testators and their relatives – the living reinforcing their own allegiances through the burial of the dead. The Lancastrian identity was heightened around John Baret's cadaver tomb for the Lancastrian motto and livery badge were painted around it and on the ceiling (Tymms 1850: 15, 234–7). These were not requested in his will, so the living probably played a part in the decoration. More cases of group identity will undoubtedly come to light through the combination of the textual and material record. In the case of John Baret at least the questions 'Why are these patterns being created, who is creating them, and what is their purpose?' (Lucy 1992: 94) can be answered with some certainty, whereas normally there is a void of evidence into which theory can be poured.

Cadaver tombs in general, however, are interesting but puzzling depictions of the dead. Many explanations have been given for their existence: the Black Death (unlikely, as they first appeared in England seventy years afterwards); the nature of the perfect soul (the unsullied body) and the mortal sinful body (the decomposing effigy underneath) (pers. comm. V. Thompson); the desire for prayers; representations of the dead; moralistic writing; *memento mori* imagery; and the conflict between the possible luxury of life and self-abasement, such as wearing hair shirts under fabulous clothes (Cohen 1973: 4–5). It has been suggested that the meanings of cadaver tombs changed over time: at first they were a sign of anxiety (Cohen 1973: 8), then for group identity – either for Lancastrian supporters (see above) (King 1984) or favoured by the 'trading middle classes' and especially the engravers in Norwich (Norris 1995: 195) – and in the sixteenth century changing 'to express the greater security of the period' (Cohen 1973: 8). Some of these theories can be challenged. The East Anglian cadaver images probably derived from the popular images of the Low Countries and were equally applicable to priests as merchants. The same images can also be made to represent both 'anxiety' and 'security' at different times.

They were principally, however, powerful images of mortality – reminding the onlooker that life and all worldly pomp was transient (pers. comm. C. Kightly).

Theoretically, if group identity was a strong factor in burial practice, then invasions should be marked by a change in elements of burial. The Viking invasions in the ninth to eleventh centuries brought new burial practices: 'hog-back' grave markers and an increase in grave stones outside a monastic setting (Bailey 1980). The Norman Conquest also had a profound impact in some localities. At Raunds the graveyard was cleared, crosses broken up and coffins smashed (Boddington 1987). Anglo-Saxon saints too, or those of doubted worth, were literally uprooted and thrown out of their shrines and cathedrals. A particularly spectacular example occurred at Malmesbury when Warin, the second Norman abbot, threw out the remains of Saint Meindulf (Sumption 1975: 147). These were dramatic instances, but to use the Conquest as a vehicle for change (in whatever area of society) can be a standard excuse for ignoring other issues, for example the change in the belief system.

One tradition which started before the Conquest and continued after it was the burial of lay people within the church itself. This caused concern, and was forbidden by church synods and councils across Europe. At Ravenna the founder of the church of Saint Vitale had the bronze doors engraved with an inscription to the effect that only bishops could be buried there. At the Council of Mainz in 813 the decree was repeated that 'no dead body was to be buried within a church, except those of bishops and abbots, or worthy priests or faithful laity' (which included royalty) (Colvin 1991: 125). In England too there was a reluctance to bury lay people in churches, but there is at least one firmly chronicled pre-Norman example from the Anglo-Saxon Chronicle. In 1055 Earl Siward died and his body was buried in the church of St Olaf in York (Garmonsway 1982: 185). The Chronicle is clear that the body was buried 'in' the church, which is not that surprising as Earl Siward was thought of as the founder. Gradually the prohibitions against lay burials were relaxed: by 1292 the Statutes of Chichester stated that there must be no indiscriminate lay burials in the church or chancel, with the honourable exceptions of the lords of the village, patrons of the church, and their wives. These burials would add to the honour and nobility of the church (Powicke and Cheney 1964:

117). By the fifteenth century, burials of lay people in the nave and aisles of the church were common, and the laity (including citizens, tradesmen, burgesses, gentlemen and sometimes wealthy tradesmen) were increasingly buried in the chancel – the most holy part of the church.

The process of the secular encroachment upon the religious space within monasteries was shown by different sets of Cistercian legislation. In 1157 lay founders were allowed to be buried within the confines of the monastery and at some point before 1217 founders and their descendants could be buried in the cloister walks. From the mid-thirteenth century, burial took place more frequently in the precincts, cloister and church, and by 1322, anyone who had contributed to the construction of the church could be buried in these areas (Astill and Wright 1993: 125). The secular world had encroached upon the religious ground. As well as the bodies in the ground, religious space was also invaded in the stained glass, or by secular objects of the deceased, such as shields, hanging above or near the grave. Heraldry was also very popular as a private and personal statement within the confines of the holy space.

The introduction of Purgatory as official doctrine probably gave a great momentum to high-status lay burials in church as it became more important that lay people should be remembered. During the thirteenth century the presence of lay effigies in churches became increasingly common. The beliefs concerning the effigies themselves are difficult to gauge, but there is a strong case that they represented the person as though they were still living, with some contracts specifying that the effigies should be 'lively' representations or 'as he appeared in life' (pers. comm. C. Kightly). Indeed, they may have been thought of as a living part of the community. An early example is the effigy of Queen Eleanor at Fontevrault who is lying down and reading a book (Martindale 1992: 155–6). Most medieval effigies also have their eyes open, although this may reflect the words from the Book of Job, 'I shall see God; whom I shall see for myself, and mine eyes shall behold him, and not another' (Harvey and Mortimer 1994: 4). The presence of the 'living' and ever watchful effigy was a powerful incentive to pray for the person's soul.

The effigy also became more three-dimensional – as if arising out of the grave, or resting on it. The same process can be seen with grave-goods. In the Anglo-Saxon period personal objects or status symbols were buried with the body but this trend died out at the same time as the arrival of Christianity. (Christianity did not necessarily cause this change and it is remarkable how little concerned the Anglo-Saxon church authorities were about burial practice.) By the later Middle Ages sermon writers were vehement against the burial of money in graves. Instead of physical burial there were two alternatives. The first was as an artistic representation, either as an effigy, or a symbol carved into the grave cover, a particularly odd combination occurring in York (Plate 13). Across the country there is a marked variation in the number of symbols on grave slabs, and north of the rivers Trent and Dee (that is, in formerly pagan Viking areas) they are more numerous and have a more varied range of symbols (Butler 1987). The second alternative was to physically place the objects near the tomb: the Black Prince's own coat-armour ('jupon'), sword, helmet and gloves were all hung above his tomb in Canterbury Cathedral (Arnold 1993).

The objects also played a part in the funeral service as well. One of the most bizarre objects, used only for royalty in the Middle Ages, was that of a funeral effigy (Harvey and Mortimer 1994). From the Norman Conquest the body of the king was normally on open display, but the three months between Edward II's death and burial in 1327 probably rendered it impossible to display. Edward's funeral was the first recorded instance of the use of an effigy and at the funeral it was clothed in robes of state from the Great Wardrobe. Funeral effigies, fully clothed, lay above the coffined body and formed the focal point for the obsequies. The effigies were placed on the hearse and were important from the initial funeral procession until the trental Mass had been said (usually thirty days after the funeral, but see Chapter 2). Women too could have effigies: the first being that for Richard II's wife, Anne of Bohemia, in 1394. The purpose of the effigy was linked into the belief that the kings were 'divine' because they had been anointed at their coronation. The king therefore had two bodies: spiritual and temporal; or, alternatively, natural and politic. The normally visible mortal body was hidden in the coffin, whilst the usually invisible body politic was represented by the effigy (Kantorowicz 1985: 421). The effigies were exceptional, but a 'custom' at noble burials was that 'the most noble lord and closest relative will present the first offerings for him and offer his shield at the altar' (Wenzel 1989: 235). Better-known examples included horses. For Henry V's funeral four horses pulled the coffin up the nave of Westminster Abbey. These horses, with their bridles, were then given to the lord abbot (St John Hope 1915: 139).

The reasons for the 'movement' of personal objects from the grave to above-ground may have been influenced by the introduction of 'soul-scot' or 'mortuary', which was the gift of the deceased to the church. This was ostensibly for forgotten tithes, but it had the effect of bringing items previously buried into the possession of the church. An alternative explanation may be that, with the introduction of Purgatory, individuals gave objects in return for prayers, whereas burial would have rendered them useless. The process of 'using' the objects may be seen by a comparison of a preacher's sermon, describing an event at about the same time as the Conquest, and a fifteenth-century example. The preacher's sermon described how a rich man had given money to the poor and when his grave was opened a 'beautiful charter' sealed with a golden seal was found in his hand (see Chapter 6). The buried charter can be compared with the wishes of John Baret of Bury, who, in 1463, requested in his will that the 'bull and bishop's seal' should be on display so that 'it may be read and known to exhort people rather to pray for me' (Tymms 1850: 19).

By the middle of the fourteenth century many theological beliefs and burial practices had changed radically since the twelfth century. How these would have developed is unknown for in the mid-fourteenth century a sudden catastrophe further changed people's perception of death. The Black Death arrived in England in 1348 and killed between one-third and a half of the entire population. There is general agreement (though it is not universal) that the Black Death first arrived in England at the small Dorset port of Melcombe at the end of June 1348: 'two ships, one of them from Bristol, came alongside. One of the sailors had brought with him from Gascony the seeds of the terrible pestilence, and, through him, the men of the town of Melcombe were the first in England to be infected' (Ziegler 1982:122). From Dorset it spread with frightening speed across the country reaching Lincoln by April 1349 and Scotland by 1350.

The surviving evidence for the impact of the Black Death is sporadic. Scotland has little quantitative material surviving (Ziegler 1982: 205), but much fuller records survive for England

(Horrox 1994). The most impressionistic and subjective records are the chronicles. William of Dene, a monk of Rochester, wrote:

> the plague carried off so vast a multitude of people of both sexes that nobody could be found who would bear the corpses to the grave. Men and women carried their own children on their shoulders to the church and threw them into the common pit. From these pits such an appalling stench was given off that scarcely anyone dared even to walk beside the cemeteries.
>
> (Ziegler 1982: 168)

A Latin graffito on the north wall of the church tower at Ashwell, Hertfordshire, from 1350 records 'Wretched, terrible, violent. Only the remnants of the people are left to tell the tale' (Ziegler 1982: 171). Although no serious statistical study can be based on such accounts, they give a flavour of the horror and personal anguish that many people went through. In cold statistics one-third or a half might not seem devastating, until known names are struck off a list. It is all too easy to get wrapped up in the statistics and forget the grief, misery and pain (both physical and spiritual) that was caused to people who lost husbands, wives, brothers and sisters.

However, statistics do allow some sort of objective analysis of the impact of the Black Death, and England is fortunate in having a large number of documents highlighting the local situation. One such set of records is the ecclesiastical appointments, which show how many priests were appointed to parishes. There are various problems in using the exact numbers – for example, a priest might have died naturally, or fled the region – but they do indicate in general terms the social upheaval. The appointments to benefices have been studied in the diocese of Bath and Wells. From 9 appointments in November 1348, the figure rose to 32 in December, 47 in January 1349, 43 in February, 36 in March, 40 in April, 21 in May and returned to a more normal level of 7 in June (Ziegler 1982: 129–30). How far these figures can be directly correlated with lay deaths is problematic, for on the one hand priests may have had better living conditions and diet, but on the other the nature of their work (especially visiting the sick) made them very susceptible to the plague.

The second class of documents are the manorial records which in some areas survive well enough to be studied in detail. One remarkable set, which contains the names of tenants and payments of rents from the estates of Durham Cathedral in County Durham, has been analysed (Lomas 1989). During the Black Death the mean death rate was just over 50 per cent in one year (362 died in 1349, from a total of 718 in 1347). This was not a uniform spread across all townships, and even neighbouring places could have very different rates: in Over Heworth 36 per cent of the population died, whilst in Nether Heworth 72 per cent died. The extremes of death were at Jarrow, where 78 per cent of people died, and Monkton where only 21 per cent died. From scarce evidence it also seems that men and women were affected equally (Lomas 1989: 130). Elsewhere in England the statistics were similarly bleak. It has been estimated that about 42 per cent of the Bishop of Worcester's tenants died in 1348–9, but the figures ranged from 80 per cent at Aston to 19 per cent at Hartlebury and Henbury (Dyer 1980: 238). At Climsland in Cornwall 'only' 40 per cent of people died whilst 55 per cent from manors belonging to Glastonbury Abbey died and about 66 per cent on the bishop of Winchester's estates (Lomas 1989: 130–1). There seems little logical explanation as to why places were differently affected, except for the medieval reason that it was God's will.

There is no doubt that the Black Death was a human disaster. Across Europe, and in England, half the people died (Hatcher 1977). Such a calamity inevitably caused a demographic decline, but by what percentage has been fiercely debated. In some areas total collapse did occur and in the leper hospital of St James in Westminster all but one of the brothers and sisters died of plague (Rosser 1989: 306). Once firmly held beliefs, however, have been rigorously challenged, especially that the Black Death caused the numerous deserted medieval villages which can be found scattered across the countryside. This all-embracing theory has now been overturned, for it has become clear that the villages were losing population before the arrival of the Black Death: in Gloucestershire, north-west Oxfordshire and the Stroud Valley there were reports of abandoned holdings and uncultivated arable land in 1341, seven years before the arrival of the Black Death (Dyer 1987: 176). In urban centres the same pattern emerges. Westminster experienced 'a contraction of population ... two or three decades before ... 1348' (Rosser 1989: 169). Whilst the Black Death may have worsened the situation, it was not the primary cause of depopulation as this had already started in the earlier part of the fourteenth century.

This example highlights a problem concerning the impact of the Black Death: how much did it exaggerate existing trends, and what, if any, trends did it begin? In terms of death and burial this problem can be illustrated from wills. It is unfortunate that sufficient English wills have not survived which cover the period before, during and after the Black Death. Whilst the French culture cannot be equated with the English, the problems of using wills can be shown in both cultures. A short run of wills survives from Montpellier in France for 1347 (38 wills) and 1348 (28 wills) which can be compared to a fragmented longer run from 1293 to 1345 (72 wills) (Reyerson 1978: 254). From these wills there is evidence that the Black Death increased a trend, started only shortly beforehand, of friaries being the preferred burial place rather than the cathedral. In a situation where documentary material is very patchy, and a single year's worth of documents can be the difference between a trend and start of the process, it is unsurprising that there are so many disputes concerning the impact of the Black Death.

One impact the Black Death did have was extreme social dislocation. Normally death and burial were communal events, the living being part of the process, whether around the bedside or at the funeral and burial. The communal nature was important to help the soul on its journey and the prayers of the living would help fight the forces of evil which attacked the soul as it left the body. During plague this social system could collapse: at the height of the Black Death the Bishop of Bath and Wells issued a remarkable letter to his clergy, which stated that not enough priests could be found and that others 'perhaps for fear of infection and contagion' were not visiting the sick, and so people 'are dying without the Sacrament of Penance' (Ziegler 1982: 128–9). In such cases the Bishop allowed the extreme measure that a layman could hear another's confession, and 'if no man is present, then even to a woman'. Even more remarkable are the Bishop's comments about the giving of the Eucharist at death: 'The Sacrament of the Eucharist, when no priest is available, may be administered by a deacon. If, however, there is no priest to administer the Sacrament of Extreme Unction, then, as in other matters, faith must suffice.' This is interesting for two points. The first is that for an unordained deacon to administer the Eucharist is exceptional in the extreme. The second is that the Bishop seems to make a distinction between the Eucharist and Extreme Unction, with Extreme Unction being the more holy as not even a deacon could administer it. The normal social and religious systems connected with the death-bed and burial simply collapsed. The living were overwhelmed by the dead. Instead of being surrounded by people, a person might die alone and be thrown into a burial pit without any burial ceremony. This lack of a communal death and the way that bodies were buried without ceremony was one of the aspects that chroniclers commented upon. The same concerns were also raised in other extreme situations, such as sieges where the dead could be left in the streets without burial.

The Black Death was but the first of a series of plagues which swept across the country for the next three hundred years. If this had been the only major plague, the population and economy may have rapidly recovered. Immediately after the Black Death there were signs of stability returning. At Roel, a village in Gloucestershire, the Black Death 'shook [it] more than other Cotswold villages' but the 1380–1 poll tax suggests 'that Roel experienced not continuous decline, but a generation of relative stability after the Black Death' (Aldred and Dyer 1991: 156). This same situation seems to have happened in Westminster where 'by 1370 the house-building ... indicates that the depredations had been checked. Further evidence of this kind testifies to a population which was actually expanding for forty years' (Rosser 1989: 170).

This stability did not last as further plagues swept through the country. Between 1430 and 1480 there were eleven outbreaks and eighteen years of national epidemics, and when local outbreaks are included, some places such as London had twenty-seven years of epidemics in a fifty-year period (Gottfried 1978: 63). From the wills of the Exchequer Court at York, and some documentary evidence, plague and disease probably caused the high mortality rates within the York diocese in the years 1391, 1429, 1436, 1438, 1459, 1467, 1471–2, 1474, 1483, 1505–6 and 1508–9 (Goldberg 1988: 41). At the other end of the country, and within the restricted population of monks at Westminster, there were nine crisis years of mortality between 1390 and 1530: 1399–1400, 1419–20, 1420–1, 1433–4, 1457–8, 1463–4, 1478–9, 1490–1 and 1529–30. The years 1419–20 and 1478–9 were especially bad (Harvey 1993:

122). These deaths were probably the result of plague or disease, although the cause of death was not specified. Comparison of the years of high deaths between the York diocese and the monastery at Westminster shows remarkably little overlap. This may be because a whole diocese is being compared to one monastery (although the rate at Christ Church Canterbury is remarkably similar to that of Westminster (Harvey 1993: 122)), or because plague took time to travel across the country. The alternative explanation is that high mortality could be confined to localised areas or regions, and especially to towns or cities. If this is correct, generalisations about the impact of plague are much more difficult to make. However, it was this continual wave upon wave of plagues that has been seen by many to have kept the population so low, for a population can recover remarkably fast after one calamity, but not if there are many occurrences.

The Black Death was often called the 'great pestilence' by the chroniclers, but other plagues also seem to have been given this title – presumably if the initial plague had passed by a particular place. In 1440 an inquiry was set up to examine the relationship between Templeton Church and Witheridge Church. During this inquiry the 72-year-old John Palfryman remembered back to the 'first great pestilence' (which, if John was, say, 15 at the time would have been 1387). The detail he gives is graphic:

> at the time of the first great pestilence the servants (of whom he was one) of William Wyngrave, then rector, went with a cart to Templeton to bring back the bodies of the dead by night for burial at Witheridge; and at Belbyford, so full was the cart, one body fell off; and William atte Heyne was given a penny to go and fetch it next day.
>
> (Dunstan 1966: 211)

Occasionally the parishioners refused to carry the dead to burial, as in 1450 at Plympton when the bishop had to grant an exceptional licence 'for the burial of parishioners at Plymstock in this time of severe pestilence, during which the parishioners utterly refuse to carry their dead to Plympton for burial' (Dunstan 1967: 272).

The plagues of the fourteenth and fifteenth centuries emphasised the inevitability of death and the frailty of human flesh. Death received unprecedented attention and interest (Fiero 1984: 271). One manifestation was the growth in the number of chantries and the associated increase in prayers. Chantries were not a new phenomenon and they had been growing steadily since the beginning of the fourteenth century (in York thirty-nine were founded in the first half of the century (Morris 1989: 371)). The subsequent plagues, however, increased the foundations: in London alone 280 private chantries were founded in the fourteenth century. In the fifteenth century there was a decline in foundations in both York and London, but sweeping generalisations are dangerous – in Norwich, chantries continued to be founded in reasonable numbers until the eve of the Reformation (Litten 1991: 8; Morris 1989: 371). New themes connected with death and burial also appeared in art and literature. Continental themes and images became popular in England: the Dance of Death, the Three Living and the Three Dead (see Chapter 3) and cadaver tombs (see above). These were constant reminders of the unpredictability of death and were seen as reminders of death – the *memento mori*. The associated theme, often implied, was that of repentance before it was too late. Another category were the realistic depictions of funeral services in Books of Hours. The focus of the pictures was the living, thereby demonstrating that society still existed with 'a new sense of confidence and security' (Fiero 1984).

Changes in the meaning and appearance of funerary monuments have also been seen after *c.*1400. The importance of status symbols diminished; whilst kneeling and the portrayal of children became more common (Martindale 1992: 169–70, Page-Phillips 1970). The kneeling probably represented supplication to God, whilst the children were a way of looking to the future and perhaps to emphasise lineage – a theme found on the Continent (Cohn, 1988). Memorial brasses in England during the fifteenth century also recorded the merits and achievements of the person commemorated (Martindale 1990: 175). Why these changes occurred is difficult to assess, unless they are a symbolic way of defeating death: a full life was led despite death and the children will (hopefully) outlive the parents.

If these changes can be equated with the Black Death and subsequent plagues they show how an overwhelming number of deaths can influence the artistic and cultural mind-set of a population (although see Appendix 2: 'The Living'). One important point, however, was that such a huge number of deaths did not change the core of traditional theology or religion. This can be contrasted with the Reformation, where a major change in theology and religion was introduced, without a huge number of deaths. Ultimately belief had a far greater impact on burial practices than large numbers of dead. The story of the Reformation in political and social terms is well known and need not be detailed here, but one of the key areas of protest by the growing band of Protestants concerned the fate of the soul.

In the period immediately before the Reformation (the late fifteenth century to the 1540s) some shifts in popular belief about the afterlife and ways of helping souls have been discerned. The number of chantry foundations dropped dramatically (only thirteen between 1503 and 1547). This does not necessarily represent a dissatisfaction with religious beliefs: rather a shift in emphasis. From an analysis of 2,000 Cambridgeshire wills of the 1530s a trend was noticed where money for prayers, masses and anniversaries was entrusted to the family or executors, instead of to the public guilds or parish. Furthermore, some anniversary doles were requested near Christmas, Easter or Lent, rather than the testator's date of death (Bainbridge 1994: 202). Another growing trend in the early sixteenth century was for testators to have a greater involvement in their own funeral arrangements. In wills from Bury St Edmunds as a mean average, 11 per cent of wills mentioned funerals between 1439 and 1482, whereas between 1491 and 1530, 27 per cent of wills mentioned funerals (Dinn 1995: 152). The idea of a greater personal involvement in religion was also noted with the gentry and their 'withdrawal into their private chapels, into their books of devotion and into their own heads'(Richmond 1984: 203). These shifts of emphasis and changing attitudes have not yet been fully explored, but they led to the greatest religious change within Christian thought with the dramatic and revolutionary changes in social life and theological thought brought about by the Reformation.

The Protestant reformers based their ideas and beliefs solely on the Bible, rather than on a combination of the Bible and 'tradition' which had built up over the centuries. One of the most important questions was on the fate of the soul immediately after death. In 1531 the reformer John Frith wrote *A Disputacion of Purgatorye*. Frith rejected the idea that prayers for the dead could have any beneficial effect. The only way to purge sin was by the blood of Christ, who stood between God and mankind. It was Christ, and Christ alone, who could save: priests, prayers, alms or the other traditional methods were of no consequence to the soul's salvation. The importance of Christ in salvation was the key to the Reformers' ideas – and it was only through the Scriptures, and most importantly the New Testament, that Christ could be studied. The New Testament, and much of the Old Testament, was translated from the Greek and Hebrew for the first time by William Tyndale who gave an accurate and popular reading of the Bible in English to a mass market (Daniell 1994).

The insistence on biblical authority struck at the heart of Catholic beliefs based on tradition which had evolved over the centuries. As well as religious reasons, political reasons played their part, as Henry VIII's divorce of Catherine of Aragon resulted in a political break with the papal authority in Rome. This break also had serious consequences for the notion of Purgatory, for the only person who could 'bind or loose' souls in Purgatory was the Pope by indulgences. (The Pope took his authority from Christ's statement to Peter (seen as the first Pope) that Peter could bind or loose souls (Matthew 16: 19)). Attacks on the Pope therefore led to attacks on Purgatory, which was found not to be in the Bible. During the 1530s the role of Purgatory diminished in the emerging Anglican theology. In the *King's Book* of 1543, which laid out the articles of religion, there is no mention of souls being in pain, or that their state was uncertain. The notion of Purgatory as painful and 'cleansing' had disappeared (Kreider 1979: 151–2). Purgatory had officially existed in England as a belief from its formal acceptance by Pope Innocent IV in 1254, to the *King's Book* of 1543: a total of 289 years.

With Purgatory no longer in existence, the systems of belief built up upon it collapsed. The theological reasons for the continual stream of prayers supplied by monasteries, friaries and chantries were destroyed. They therefore became much more vulnerable to attack by the Crown, which was desperate for money and land. Political expediency and financial desperation were as much behind the English abolition of Purgatory as the fact that there was only circumstantial evidence of Purgatory in the apocryphal scriptures.

The process of the dissolution of the monasteries was systematic and total. The monasteries, nunneries and friaries were dissolved with their lands and incomes passing to the Crown. Under severe pressure, and with no strong theological argument to back them up, the monastic system collapsed like a house of cards. The requested ceaseless rounds of prayers for the founders and bene-factors stopped.

In the parish churches too, fundamental changes took place as the chantries were dissolved. 'Voluntary' surrenders, initiated by the Crown, of chantries, chantry colleges, hospitals and free chapels took place in an increasing stream from 1540, the total number having been dissolved by 1545 being 60. Although not very high numerically, they were some of the largest and wealth-iest institutions in the country (Kreider 1979: 160). This piece-meal dissolution changed with Henry VIII's death and Edward VI's new government. The new Chantries Act of 1547 was more thorough. It also had a theological rationale. Purgatory was no longer just forgotten, it was openly attacked. In such a theological climate the institutions which interceded for the dead by prayers no longer had a place in the theological scheme. All institutions which had been founded to pray for the dead were to be dis-solved. There were to be no exceptions. The framework support-ing the institutions was systematically attacked and confiscated, as in the compulsory sale of chantry lands in 1548 and the seizure of their goods, jewels, plate and ornaments (Kreider 1979: 197, 202). The theological and political results of this change had a profound impact across England. Within twenty years the medi-eval structure of the Church, and its reason for surviving, had been dismantled and effectively destroyed. The monasteries and friaries had gone, and the concept of afterlife had changed for ever. Purgatory had disappeared from England (it was still alive in Catholic European countries) and many Reformers now believed that the soul went straight to Heaven or Hell, although a few advocated a third place, Abraham's bosom, which was given authority by the Bible (Luke 16: 22). At the parish level, the long term-results of loss of income through the ancillary services and priests, the destruction of church assets and the different theolog-ies which emerged all contributed to a fragmentation of ideas about religion, and in some cases apathy (Burgess 1987b: 858). The income of parish churches decreased as the financial foun-dation of Purgatory was destroyed, most clearly seen in the almost complete cessation of church-building.

With the theological framework smashed, a radical change in burial practice might be envisaged. The archaeological evidence for late sixteenth-century and seventeenth-century burials is negli-gible, partly because the churches which were dissolved at the

Reformation had no more burials in them, and those which remained have often survived to the present day. One minor trend continued the theme of the privatisation of a communal space, as after the Reformation it was not unusual for the charnels to be cleared and taken over by prominent local families as their burial vault, an event which occurred at Saffron Walden and Thaxted (Litten 1991: 8). Fortunately a large amount of historical data survives to fill the archaeological gap.

Despite an official line in the sixteenth century which wavered between the extremes of Protestantism and Catholicism, many people were conservative in their beliefs. This was unsurprising as events were moving very fast and largely depended on the monarch on the throne. There were four changes of theological direction between 1540 and 1560, which left the mass of the population unsure of what lay ahead. This process is well shown by the changes of formula connected with the burial of the dead. In the 1549 Book of Common Prayer the traditional four-stage ritual was used – the procession to the church or grave, the burial (where the priest would commend the soul and cast earth upon the body with the words 'earth to earth, ashes to ashes, dust to dust'), a brief office for the dead and the funeral Eucharist. The 1552 version was more Protestant and simply committed the body to the ground. Queen Mary reversed the trend and many Catholic traditions flourished, but in Elizabeth's reign the 1552 Prayer Book was used and although the burial service was supposedly not about the passage of souls, traditional services were permitted to some degree (Cressy 1989: 102).

These theological changes produced different patterns of behaviour. At one extreme were the Puritans, who, in terms of burial, were more concerned with the functional disposal of the body than with the welfare of the soul. In 1589 Mistress Quarles ordered 'a maidservant to be interred in the orchard "without any ceremony"' (Gittings 1984: 50). At the other extreme were the people who held tenaciously on to their beliefs and could pray for souls and include symbolic objects into the graves: in 1615 a man was brought before Archbishop Grindal of York for 'putting the metwand into the winding sheet in a suspicious manner' (Gittings 1984: 45) (see Chapter 5). One way that has been attempted to gauge the impact of the Reformation upon individuals is to analyse the thousands of wills that remain. The most important passage is the preamble of the will where the person commends his or her soul to God, Christ or saints, which has been seen as indicating whether a person was a Catholic traditionalist or a Protestant. As is often the case in such debates, there are very clear examples of the extremes of belief, but a huge grey area in the middle. From a study of Gloucestershire wills, the difference between will preambles was found to be dependent on the clergymen who wrote them (Litzenberger 1993).

An alternative is to study the funerals themselves, which, even in the supposedly Protestant Essex, seem to continue along traditional lines, though with a change in emphasis. The emphasis was on social status rather than religious desire to help the soul. Many wills used the formula that the funeral should be 'without pomp'. This could be ambiguous, either meaning that excessive expense should not be used (but even so the funeral should mirror the social status of the person), or it could signify a Puritan attitude that burial was a functional act of disposing of the body with little, or no, religious overtone (Cressy 1989: 105). It is difficult to determine numbers but a majority of burials seem to have involved showing social status but using pre-Reformation traditions.

Whereas many traditions survived, official attitude could be a strong force for change. One area of particular concern was the design of tombs. Following the Second Commandment – 'Thou shalt not make unto thee any graven image, or any likeness of anything that is in Heaven above' – many Reformers and Puritans included the making of human figures for tombs within this category. This was not universally accepted and many Anglicans argued that sculpture of lay people on tombs acted as examples to good behaviour (Howard and Llewellyn 1989: 238). Pre-Reformation biblical narratives or religious scenes were replaced with secular imagery which was occasionally satirised. The character Bosola in the Jacobean play *The Duchess of Malfi* described the new style of tombs:

> Princes images on their tombs
> Do not lie, as they are wont, seeming to pray
> Up to heaven: but with their hands under their cheeks
> (As if they died of tooth-ache) – they are not carved
> With their eyes fixed upon the stars; but as
> Their minds were wholly bent upon the world,

The self-same way they seem to turn their faces
(*The Duchess of Malfi* IV. ii. 153–9, quoted in Tristram 1983: 196)

Pre-Reformation tombs were also officially ordered to be destroyed in 1550 (Loades 1994: 214) and Edward VI's government 'abandoned to destruction' all the tombs of the earls and dukes of Lancaster at Leicester and the dukes of York at Fotheringhay (Colvin 1991: 255). Petitions from the nobility or gentry to save ancestors' tombs were occasionally submitted, and even less frequently granted. One petition was written by Lord La Warr to Thomas Cromwell, and he specifically mentioned the importance of his ancestors: 'I have a poor house called Boxgrove [Sussex] . . . whereof I am founder, and there lieth many of my ancestors and also my wife's mother: and because it is of my foundation . . . [may the King] forbear the suppressing of the same' (Baskerville 1937: 157). A further petition by Lord La Warr to save the tomb was successful, but many other nobles were not so fortunate. One of the surprising aspects of the destruction is that the fate of the tombs of ancestors did not become a major issue during the 1540s and 1550s. Some families were embittered, such as the Pole family (Baskerville 1937: 158), but for the majority their ancestors seem to have been quietly forgotten. There may be two reasons for this. The first was that royal tombs did not always escape either: Henry I's tomb at Reading Abbey, and Stephen's at Faversham Abbey, were both completely destroyed. The nobility may therefore have thought resistance useless. The second was that the religious atmosphere dictated that once the soul had departed, the body was lifeless and useless, so there was no reason to remove it. Attacks on monuments of the aristocracy, however, were seen as highly subversive to the political order and in 1563 a royal proclamation was issued expressly forbidding the destruction, breaking or defacing of any memorial (Colvin 1991: 255; Loades 1994: 214; Howard 1995: 11). Even so it is puzzling why there was no outcry about the destruction of ancestors' tombs on such a wide scale earlier in the century.

As well as the official large-scale destruction, there also appears to have been widespread rifling of graves. At Oxford in 1536 Christopher Tredar was denounced to Cromwell 'for encouraging people to dig for money, the result of which was that "Divers crosses have lately been cast down". The rifling of graves was evidenced in the excavations (Lambrick 1985: 201). Despite all the churches' dire warnings there was obviously a popular belief that money or precious objects had been placed in the graves. Digging for them may not have been pleasant.

The Reformation marked a fundamental and very rapid shift in religious attitude. Theologically, the abolition of Purgatory led to the Anglican belief that the soul after death would not have to suffer torments or become the centre of a battle between angels and devils, but have a 'short period of happy relaxation' before the Resurrection. With the soul in contentment (albeit partial) there was no need for intercessory prayers, or a bond between the living and the dead (Loades 1994: 215). It is therefore not surprising that funerals increasingly emphasised the social role, whilst still using many of the pre-Reformation traditions. From an archaeological perspective the change in religious belief is powerfully manifested in the material record by the wholesale national destruction of the monasteries and the institutions for intercessory prayer. It is perhaps ironic that the most obvious impact of the Reformation today – the ruined monasteries – had become relatively insignificant nationally by the 1530s.

By exploring medieval attitudes and theology towards death, burial and the afterlife it is possible to argue that burial rites fundamentally changed twice, and possibly three times. In the late twelfth and thirteenth century a major theological shift took place with the formal acceptance of Purgatory. Many of the old reasons for burial practices, such as the importance of the head facing upwards in readiness for the Resurrection, ceased to play such a prominent part. As prayers became more important, so burial rites became more focused on the idea of long-term memory and prayers. The higher the tomb, the more visible and memorable it was, resulting in tombs rising from the floor. The role of Purgatory was a key target for the Reformers and in the Reformation its theological basis was swept away. Whilst traditional customs may have continued, the emphasis had changed from prayers to social status.

Appendix 1: Jews and Lepers

There are two groups in the Middle Ages who have the advantages of a plethora of historical and archaeological data, but are discrete enough entities to form separate and visible groups: Jews and lepers.

The Jewish community was highly visible within Christian England, not only being a race apart with different culture and beliefs, but also visibly distinguished by being forced to wear two strips of yellow cloth, six inches long and three inches wide (Hallam 1987: 131). They had arrived with the Norman Conquest. As long as they were beneficial to the Crown, they were tolerated and given protection, but in 1290 they were expelled from England by Edward I. In a medieval Christian context, Jewish burials are particularly interesting because they reveal how differences in religious belief can be reflected in the burial record. There were ten Jewish cemeteries in England, but only three have been archaeologically examined: 7 graves at London, 10 at Winchester, and 482 graves from Jewbury in York (Lilley *et al.* 1994). The Jewbury report forms the basis of discussion about Jewish burial practices.

It is rare that a precise estimate of population size can be obtained from a burial record, but an accurate estimation can be given from Jewbury. The equation is: ((number of burials times life expectancy) divided by time period), all of which can be reasonably ascertained. The final figure is 254 (900 times 24, divided by 85), although taking highest and lowest values the range is 196 and 362. Potential complicating factors are that Jewbury was also the burial place for the Jews of Lincoln and Stamford (Lilley *et al.* 1994: 538).

The burials themselves were distinctive. Intercutting of graves was carefully avoided (Lilley *et al.* 1994: 332) because of the Jewish belief that the body supposedly will literally rise up in its condition from the grave. Some clustering of burials by sex occurred, and the absence of children was suggestive that the area reserved for them had not been dug.

The general characteristics of the population have also been compared to two medieval Christian cemeteries from York: the parish church of St Helen-on-the-Walls, and the Gilbertine priory of St Andrew's. The basic conclusion was that there was little ethnic difference between the populations, although there were some unusual features which differentiate the Jewish population: the curvature of the back of the skull, the morphology of the palate and nasal aperture, and adults, especially men, were slightly shorter than their Christian contemporaries. Dietary differences were shown by fine banding on the teeth, produced by sudden changes in the oral environment. This may have been caused by routinely eating different types of food on a daily basis. Genetic features, to be expected from such a self-reliant and closed community, were evident. For example, there was a very high proportion of females (21.8 per cent) with a metopic suture (suture of the frontal bone of the skull). There was also evidence of blade injuries to six individuals, five of whom had head injuries, and one of whom may have had surgery. One conclusion is that the individuals were attacked by Christians, but this is going beyond the evidence: bladed trauma is not uncommon in Christian cemeteries.

Jews in medieval art and literature were often depicted as ugly, with warts, or long noses or generally distorted. The supposedly distorted soul within was reflected by the exterior appearance (see Chapter 2). This was especially true of leprosy. The treatment of lepers was given authority by a biblical passage in Leviticus (13: 44–6):

> he is a leprous man, he is unclean; the priest must pronounce him unclean; his disease is on his head. The leper who has the disease shall wear torn clothes and let the hair on his head hang loose, and he shall cover his upper lip and cry 'Unclean, unclean'. He shall remain unclean as long as he has the disease; he is unclean; he shall dwell alone in habitation outside the camp.

As the exterior body was seen to be a reflection of the interior state of the soul, leprosy was seen as a sign of a sinner. One of the sins that leprosy punished was lust, especially as it was considered to be a sexually transmitted disease (Gilchrist 1995: 114). Leprosy was also a punishment for other sins and in one miracle collection men who were stricken with leprosy for false allegation were healed after their confession (Vitz 1992: 988).

The physical deformities caused by leprosy are horrible and in the Middle Ages were uncurable. A particularly nasty variety is 'lepromatous leprosy' which damages the nerves in the hands, feet and face, which in turn causes sores. In the face the bone in the nose disappears, the front teeth may fall out and palate and larynx may become affected, thus affecting speech. The hands become paralysed and claw-like and fingers and toes may be lost, thereby giving a 'clubbed' appearance. It is a nasty disease which led to a slow death.

To modern thought the treatment of lepers was as cruel as the disease itself. By various processes lepers were pronounced dead to the world, either literally, or legally. The most extreme form took place in France. During the ceremony to declare them dead they were required to stand in an open grave. In England the ceremony was just as symbolic. Although the Office for the Seclusion of a Leper varied from one diocese to another, the rites used at Salisbury (known as the Sarum use) were widely adopted. In this rite the lepers were led to the church and made to kneel under two trestles and beneath a black cloth in the 'manner of a dead man'. A Mass was then said. Afterwards the lepers were led outside and had earth cast upon their feet by the priest who said 'Be thou dead to the world, but alive again unto God'. They were then led to the leper hospital or where they were to live.

Not only were they dead to the Church, they were also dead legally and socially. In 1200, at the Council of Westminster, lepers were forbidden to make a will or plead in court. Furthermore, once they had been excluded they had to avoid churches or other crowded places. Other injunctions stressed that they must never touch a child, must avoid contaminating water sources or food, must go about in their leper-dress, must wear their gloves, must only eat or drink with other lepers, and could only talk with others if the leper was down-wind. Secluded religiously, socially and legally from everyone apart from other lepers, they lived a living death.

A few leper hospitals have been excavated: St Margaret's, High Wycombe, with twelve burials (Farley and Manchester 1989); Ilford; South Acre (Wells 1967) and St James and St Mary Magdalene Leper Hospital in Chichester, the largest cemetery discovered to date (Magilton and Lee 1989). The remains of 351 individuals were recovered, revealing the organisation of the cemetery during its use from the twelfth to the seventeenth century. The earliest phase, in the western part of the cemetery, had the highest concentration of leprous males (women were technically excluded from the hospital until the sixteenth century). The second area was the most disorganised, with graves most often bisecting one another. The third was the most organised; and children and women were admitted. 'Over eighty three' skeletons exhibited some form of leprosy. As there was a very low number of immature individuals, this indicates that individuals were not admitted until some mutilation through leprosy had occurred.

The importance of Jews and lepers within medieval society is that both groups were liminal to Christian society: socially and spiritually. The leper hospitals were placed on the outskirts of towns, marking the beginning of a 'no-mans land', and lepers themselves were spiritually cut off from society by a symbolic burial (Gilchrist 1995: 115). Jews too were physically cut off from Christian society in death by their own graveyards beyond the confines of the town. Jews were also literally the property of the king, who had complete control over them. Comparisons between main-stream Christian societies and these liminal groups throw both into sharper contrast.

Appendix 2: The Living

Two matters concerned the living: whether the funeral and actions were for the benefit of the living or the dead, and how much the ethos of torment and damnation of the soul in the afterlife was believed.

Theologically the soul of the deceased was the most important aspect of funerals (which has been emphasised in this work), but there was a consistent sub-theme of the role that funerals had for the living. This was summed up in a statement by St Augustine, which was well known to medieval theologians, that funerals were 'rather comforts to the living than helps to the dead' (Gittings 1995: 170). This sentiment was occasionally picked up and stated in instructions for funerals: in 1425, Bishop Wakeryng described elaborate ceremonies and processions as a 'solace for the living':

> I want the vigils of the dead to be performed in the ordinary way immediately after my death, without elaborate ceremonies and processions, which solace the living, according to the blessed Augustine, rather than help the dead.
>
> (Tanner 1984: 99)

When taken to extremes, the living could totally dominate the funeral with hardly any reference to the recently deceased at all. The heraldic funeral, run by the College of Heralds, was the supreme example. The first such funeral was in 1463. Throughout the sixteenth century they gained in number. Anyone who had the right to a coat of arms was required to have the heralds to control the funeral – even down to which mourners could be present. A rule stated that the chief mourner should be of the same sex as the deceased, so the spouse could not even be the principal mourner (Gittings 1995: 177). The heraldic funeral was concerned with the legitimate transfer of status and property from the dead to the living. The whole performance therefore revolved around the living, with the dead person playing little part. Thomas More complained:

> Much superfluous charge used for boast and ostentation, namely devised by the dead before his death, is of God greatly disliked; . . .
> as how we might be solemnly borne out to burying, have gay and

206

goodly funerals, with heralds [*herawdes*] at our hearses, and offering up our helmets, setting up our escutcheons and coat armours
on the wall ...

(More 1557: 335, Owst 1926: 266)

In her excellent summary of these funerals, Gittings poses the question,
which of the living were these funerals for? She makes a very strong case
that the funerals were 'part of the crown's control over its subjects'
(Gittings 1995: 178) as the heralds were crown servants. Elizabeth I took
a personal interest in many of the funerals. Only in the seventeenth
century did the heralds lose their power over funerals (James I took less
interest). As a reaction against the heraldic funerals a new fashion
appeared of burial at night (Gittings 1995: 180).

The second matter is the frequent assumption that death pervaded
every sphere of life in the Middle Ages, and that the whole mentality of
the time focused upon it. There is a large amount of material to support
this view and much of this book is based upon that assumption. As a
corrective, however, to a potentially unnecessarily bleak view, it is worth
reflecting evidence to the contrary. In the thirteenth century, Aquinas
stated: 'It is not necessary for one always to be thinking of one's ultimate
end whenever one desires or does something: any more than a traveller
needs to think of his destination at every step' (quoted by Tristram 1976:
159). At the gentry level there was also a lack of dread about death.
One of the best-documented fifteenth-century gentry families, the Pas-
tons, lived life to the full. They

were not prone to morbidity, being about as opposite as one could
readily imagine to those psychological wrecks with whom some
historians populate the Middle Ages ... [they were] not oppressed
by the so-called burdens of late Medieval religion. Anxiety ... is
not to be detected in them.

(Richmond 1984: 195)

This lack of anxiety manifested itself in various ways, such as *not* founding
the required perpetual chantry, and *not* founding the college of priests
and poor men at Caister specified by Sir John Fastolft, and *not* hurrying
to build a magnificent tomb for John Paston (it took over twelve years:
the money eventually left for it by the son was ungenerous and it may
never have been built) (Richmond 1984: 195-6). A similar lack of *angst*
was detected after an analysis of 355 fifteenth- and early sixteenth-century
wills from Hull. They give a broad overview of the religious consensus
of the will-making population.

In very few wills indeed are there any signs of that torment about
the fate of the soul and none of that morbid anxiety so long
regarded as the late-medieval norm. The assumption that most
medieval people were anguished by the prospect of the horrors
awaiting them in the next world rests particularly upon the frequent and vivid portrayals of purgatory and hell in literature,
sermons, paintings and stained glass of the period; yet may not

their frequency and intensity . . . simply testify to their futility and neglect?

(Heath 1984: 228)

In the heavily religious atmosphere of the Middle Ages it is all too easy to forget that during their soul's transitory life on earth medieval people were human, had fun and enjoyed living.

BIBLIOGRAPHY

MANUSCRIPT SOURCES

BIHR = Borthwick Institute of Historical Research, York.

Chapter 3

John Beisby	1535	BIHR Probate vol. 11, 147v
John Chambelleyne	1516	BIHR Probate vol. 9, 32v
Bartram Dawson	1515	BIHR Probate vol. 9, 39v
Robert de Crosse	1395	BIHR Probate vol. 1, 83v
Thomas Glasyn	1531	BIHR Probate vol. 11, 9r
William Huby	1531	BIHR Probate vol. 11, 9r
Robert Lee	1513	BIHR Probate vol. 11, 250v
John Mason	1537	BIHR Probate vol. 9, 16r
Richard Olyver	1535	BIHR RI vol. 28, 168
Ralf Pullan	1540	BIHR Probate vol. 11, 529r
John Shaw	1515	BIHR Probate vol. 9, 26r
John Shawe	1538	BIHR Probate vol. 11, 276r
John Wirrall	1517	BIHR Probate vol. 9, 74r
William Wylson	1517	BIHR Probate vol. 9, 52r

Chapter 4

Thomas Catlynson	1498	BIHR Probate vol. 3, 331r

Chapter 5

Numbers of male and female burials from parish churches:

	Male	Female
Rivenhall	31	40
Barton Bendish	33	14
All Saints, Norfolk	13	5

St Nicholas Shambles	90	71
St Helen-on-the-Walls	338	394
North-East Bailey, Norwich	39	22

PUBLISHED SOURCES

Alcock, Joan P. (1980) 'Classical religious belief and burial practice in Roman Britain', *Archaeological Journal* 137: 50–83.

Aldred, David and Dyer, Christopher (1991) 'A medieval Cotswold village: Roel, Gloucestershire', *Transactions of the Bristol and Gloucestershire Archaeological Society* 109: 139–170.

Anderson, M. D. (1964) *A Saint at Stake: The Strange Death of William of Norwich, 1144*, London: Faber.

Ariès, Philippe (1974) *Western Attitudes Towards Death*, trans. P. N. Ranum, Baltimore: Johns Hopkins University Press.

—— (1987) *The Hour of Our Death*, trans. H. Weaver, Harmondsworth: Penguin.

Arnold, Janet (1993) 'The jupon or coat-armour of the Black Prince in Canterbury Cathedral', *The Journal of the Church Monuments Society* VIII: 12–24.

Astill, Grenville G. and Wright, Susan M. (1993) 'Perceiving patronage in the archaeological record: Bordesley Abbey', in Martin Carver (ed.) *In Search of Cult: Archaeological Investigations in Honour of Philip Rahtz*, Woodbridge: Boydell Press.

Aston, M. (1994) 'Death', in R. Horrox (ed.) *Fifteenth-Century Attitudes: Perceptions of Society in Late Medieval England*, Cambridge: Cambridge University Press.

Ayres, Brian (1985) *Excavations within the North-East Bailey of Norwich Castle, 1979*, East Anglian Archaeology Report 28.

—— (1990) 'Norwich', *Current Archaeology* 122: 56–9.

Backhouse, Janet (1989) *The Luttrell Psalter*, London: The British Library.

—— and de Hamel, Christopher (1988) *The Becket Leaves*, London: The British Library.

Baildon, William Paley (ed.) (1890) *Select Civil Pleas*, vol. I: *1200–1203*, Selden Society 3.

Bailey, Richard (1980) *Viking Age Sculpture in Northern England*, London: Collins.

Bainbridge, Virginia R. (1994) 'The medieval way of death: commemoration and the afterlife in Pre-Reformation Cambridgeshire', *Prophecy and Eschatology, Studies in Church History* 10: 183–204.

Banker, James R. (1988) *Death in the Community: Memorialization and Confraternities in an Italian Commune in the Late Middle Ages*, London: University of Georgia Press.

Bannister, A. T. (ed.) (1929a) 'Visitation returns of the Diocese of Hereford in 1397, I', *English Historical Review* XLIV: 279–89.

—— (1929b) 'Visitation returns of the Diocese of Hereford in 1397, II', *English Historical Review* XLIV: 444–53.

Barber, Paul (1988) *Vampires, Burial and Death*, London: Yale University Press.

Barber, Richard (1974) *The Knight and Chivalry*, London: Cardinal.

—— and Barker, Juliet (1989) *Tournaments, Jousts, Chivalry and Pageants in the Middle Ages*, Woodbridge: Boydell Press.

Barker, Eric E. (ed.) (1976) *The Register of Thomas Rotherham, Archbishop of York 1480–1500*, vol. I, Canterbury and York Society 69.

Barlow, Frank (1968) *Thomas Becket*, London: Methuen.

Barrett, John C. (1992) 'Comment', *Archaeological Review from Cambridge* ('*In the Midst of Life*') 11 (1): 157–62.

Barron, W. R. J. (1981) 'The penalties for treason in medieval life and literature', *Journal for Medieval History* 7: 187–202.

Barrow, Julia (1988) 'Vicars choral and chaplains in northern European cathedrals 1100–1250', *Studies in Church History (The ministry: clerical and lay)* 26: 87–98.

—— (1995) 'Urban cemetery location in the high Middle Ages', in Steven Bassett (ed.) *Death in Towns: Urban Responses to the Dying and the Dead, 100–1600*, Leicester: Leicester University Press.

Baskerville, Geoffrey (1937) *English Monks and the Suppression of the Monasteries*, London: Jonathan Cape.

Bassett, Steven (ed.) (1995) *Death in Towns: Urban Responses to the Dying and the Dead, 100–1600*, Leicester: Leicester University Press.

Bennett, Paul and Anderson, Trevor (1991) 'St Nicholas Church, Thanington, 1991 Interim Report', *Archaeologia Cantiana* CIX: 308–11.

Bethnall, Philip (1989) 'Chemical analysis of shadow burials', in Charlotte A. Roberts, F. Lee and J. Bintliff (eds) *Burial Archaeology Current Research, Methods and Developments*, British Archaeological Reports – British Series 211, 205–14.

Biddle, Martin (1979) *St Albans Abbey Chapter House Excavations 1978*, The Alban Link Occasional Paper 1.

Binski, Paul (1996) *Medieval Death: Ritual and Representation*, London: British Museum Press.

Bland, Olivia (1986) *The Royal Way of Death*, London: Constable.

Boase, T. S. R. (1972) *Death in the Middle Ages: Mortality, Judgment and Remembrance*, London: McGraw-Hill.

—— (1985) 'King death: mortality, judgment and remembrance', in Joan Evans (ed.) *The Flowering of the Middle Ages*, London: Thames & Hudson.

Boddington, Andy (1987) 'Raunds', *Current Archaeology* 107: 380.

Bond, Ronald B. (1987) *Certain Sermons or Homilies (1547) and A Homily against Disobedience and Wilful Rebellion (1570)*, Toronto: University of Toronto Press.

Bossy, J. (1983) 'The mass as a social institution 1200–1700', *Past and Present* 100: 29–61.

—— (1985) *Christianity in the West 1400–1700*, Oxford: Oxford University Press.

—— (1991) 'Christian life in the Middle Ages: 1) Prayers', *Transactions of the Royal Historical Society*, Series 6, 1: 137–50.

Boyd, Brian (1992) 'The transformation of knowledge: Natufian mortu-

211

ary practices at Hayonim, western Galilee', *Archaeological Review from Cambridge ('In the Midst of Life')* 11 (1): 19–38.

Bradley S. A. J. (ed.) (1982) *Anglo-Saxon Poetry*, London: Dent.

Brereton, Geoffrey (1968) *Froissart's Chronicles*, Harmondsworth: Penguin.

Brigden, Susan (1991) *London and the Reformation*, Oxford: Clarendon Press.

Briggs, Richard (1995) 'Facing the past', *Archaeology in York (York Archaeological Trust) Interim* 20 (2): 23–7.

Brinklow, David (1987) 'Bulls in the church', *The Archaeology of York (York Archaeological Trust) Interim* 12 (1): 1–7.

Brothwell, Donald (1971) 'Forensic aspects of the so-called Neolithic skeleton Q1 from Maiden Castle, Dorset', *World Archaeology* 3 (II): 233–41.

—— (1972) *Digging up Bones*, Oxford: Oxford University Press.

Brown, Elizabeth A. R. (1981) 'Death and the human body in the later Middle Ages: the legislation of Boniface VIII on the division of the corpse', *Viator* 12: 221–70.

Brown, M. A. (1983) 'Grave orientation: a further view', *Archaeological Journal* 140: 322–8.

Brown, Peter (1981) *The Cult of Saints*, London: SCM Press.

Bruce-Mitford, Rupert L. (1976) 'Chapter House vestible graves at Lincoln and the body of St Hugh of Avalon', in F. Emmison and R. Stephens (eds) *Tribute to an Antiquary: Essays Presented to Marc Fitch*, London: Leopard Head.

Bruintjes, Tj. D. (1990) 'The auditory ossicles in human skeletal remains from a leper cemetery in Chichester, England', *Journal of Archaeological Science* 17: 627–33.

Burgess, Clive (1987a) 'A service for the dead: the form and function of the anniversary in late medieval Bristol', *Transactions of the Bristol and Gloucestershire Archaeological Society* 105: 183–211.

—— (1987b) ' "By quick and by dead": wills and pious provision in late medieval Bristol', *English Historical Review* CCCCV: 837–58.

Butler, H. E. (1949) *The Chronicle of Jocelin of Brakelond*, London: Thomas Nelson.

Butler, Lawrence (1987) 'Symbols on medieval memorials', *Archaeological Journal* 144: 246–55.

Byock, Jesse (1993) 'The skull and bones in Egil's saga: a Viking, a grave and Paget's disease', *Viator* 24: 23–50.

Byrne, M. St Clare (1981) *The Lisle Letters*, vols 1–6, London: The University of Chicago Press.

Camporesi, P. (1988) *The Incorruptible Flesh: Bodily Mutation and Mortification in Religion and Folklore*, trans. Tania Croft-Murray, Cambridge Studies in Oral and Literate Culture 17.

Capes, William W. (ed.) (1916) *Registrum Johannis Trefnant Episcopi Herefordensis*, The Canterbury and York Society 20.

Cardy, Amanda H. and Hill, Peter H. (1992) 'In the shadow of St Ninian: life and death in medieval Whithorn', *Death and Burial*, Pre-printed papers of a conference on medieval archaeology in Europe 21–24 September 1992 at York 4, 93–8.

Carelli, Peter (1995) *We Are not All Equal in the Face of Death: Profane Graves in Medieval Lund*, Papers of the Archaeological Institute, University of Lund 1993–1994, New Series, 10: 43–59.

Carter, H. B. and Henshall, Audrey S. (1957) 'The fabric from burial Q', in Reay Robertson-MacKay (ed.) *Recent Excavations at the Cluniac Priory of St Mary, Thetford, Norfolk, Medieval Archaeology* 1: 102–3.

Carver, Martin O. H. (1980) 'Early medieval Durham: the archaeological evidence', in Nicola Coldstream and Peter Draper (eds) *Medieval Art and Architecture at Durham Cathedral*, British Archaeological Association 3, 11–19.

—— (1993) *Arguments in Stone, Archaeological Research and the European Town in the First Millennium*, Oxbow Monograph 29.

—— (ed.) (1995) *The Age of Sutton Hoo: The Seventh Century in North-Western Europe*, Woodbridge: Boydell Press.

Cattaneo, C., Gelsthorpe, K., Phillips, P. and Sokol, R. J. (1992) 'Reliable identification of human albumin in ancient bone using ELISA and monoclonal antibodies', *American Journal of Physical Anthropology* 87: 365–72.

Cawley, A. C. (1990) *Everyman and Medieval Miracle Plays*, London: Dent.

Chambers, E. K. (1971) *English Literature at the Close of the Middle Ages*, Oxford: Oxford University Press.

Chatelet, Albert (1988) *Early Dutch Painting: Painting in the Northern Netherlands in the Fifteenth Century*, trans. Christopher Brown and Anthony Turner, Lausanne: Montreux.

Chaunu, Pierre (1976) 'Mourir à Paris (XVI–XVII–XVIII siècles)', *Annales E. S. C.* 21: 29–50.

—— (1978) *La mort à Paris*, Paris: Fayard.

Cheney, C. R. (1966) 'A recent view of the general interdict on England 1208–1214', *Studies in Church History* III: 159–68.

Cherry, John (1991) 'The ring of Bishop Grandisson', in Francis Kelly (ed.) *Medieval Art and Architecture at Exeter Cathedral*, British Archaeological Association XI, 80–7.

—— (1992) 'The breaking of seals', *Art and Symbolism*, Pre-printed papers of a conference on medieval archaeology in Europe 21–24 September 1992 at York 7, 23–7.

Chiffoleau, Jacques (1976) *'Pratiques funéraires et images de la mort à Marseille, en Avignon et dans le Comtat Venaissin (vers 1280–vers 1350)'*, Cahiers de Fanjeux 11.

—— (1980) *La Compatabilité de l'au-delà: les hommes, la mort et la religion dans la région d'Avignon à la fin du moyen âge (vers 1320–vers 1480)*, Collection de l'École française de Rome 47.

Christie, Patricia M. and Coad, J. G. (1980) 'Excavations at Denny Abbey', *Archaeological Journal* 137: 138–279.

Clanchy, M. T. (1985) 'England in the thirteenth century: power and knowledge', in W. M. Ormrod (ed.) *Symposium on England in the Thirteenth Century: Harlaxton Conference Proceedings*, Nottingham: University of Nottingham.

Clarke, David T.-D. (1962) *Painted Glass from Leicester*, Leicester: Leicester Museums.

Clayton, Joseph (1931) *Saint Hugh of Lincoln*, London: Burns & Oates and Washbourne Ltd.

Coales, John (ed.) (1987) *The Earliest English Brasses: Patronage Style, and Workshops 1270–1350*, London: Monumental Brass Society.

Cohen, Kathleen (1973) *Metamorphosis of a Death Symbol: The Transi Tomb in the Late Middle Ages and Renaissance*, Berkeley: University of California Press.

Cohn, Samuel K. (1988) 'Death and property in Sienna, 1205–1800: strategies for the afterlife', *The Johns Hopkins University Studies in Historical and Political Science* 106(2).

Colgrave, B. (ed.) (1985a) *Two Lives of Saint Cuthbert*, Cambridge: Cambridge University Press.

—— (ed.) (1985b) *The Earliest Life of Gregory the Great*, Cambridge: Cambridge University Press.

—— and Mynors, R. A. B. (eds) (1981) *Bede's Ecclesiastical History of the English People*, Oxford: Oxford University Press.

Collier, J. Payne (ed.) (1857) *Trevelyan Papers, Prior to A.D. 1558*, Cambden Society, First Series 67.

Colvin, Howard (1991) *Architecture and the After-Life*, London: Yale University Press.

Cook, G. H. (1947) *Medieval Chantries and Chantry Chapels*, London: Phoenix House.

Cook, R. B. (1915) *Some Early Civic Wills of York*, Yorkshire Philosophical Society Annual Report.

—— (1916) *Some Early Civic Wills of York*, Yorkshire Philosophical Society Annual Report.

—— (1918) *Some Early Civic Wills of York*, Yorkshire Philosophical Society Annual Report.

Cooper, William (1996) 'Richard Hunne', *Reformation* 1: 221–51.

Cox, J. Charles (1889) 'Receipt roll of the Peak jurisdiction of the Dean and Chapter of Lichfield', *Journal of the Derbyshire Archaeological and Natural History Society* XI: 142–56.

—— (1910) *The Parish Registers of England*, London: Methuen.

Craik, T. W. (1979) 'I know when one is dead, and when one lives', *Proceedings of the British Academy* LXV: 171–89.

Crawford, Sally (1993) 'Children, death and the afterlife in Anglo-Saxon England', in William Filmer-Sankey (ed.) *Anglo-Saxon Studies in History and Archaeology* 6: 83–92.

Cressy, David (1989) 'Death and the social order: the funerary preferences of Elizabethan gentlemen', *Continuity and Change* 5: 99–119.

Crouch, David (1990) *William Marshal: Court, Career and Chivalry in the Angevin Empire 1147–1219*, London: Longman.

Crummy, N., Crummy, P. and Crossan C. (1993) *Excavations of Roman and Later Cemeteries, Churches and Monastic Sites in Colchester, 1971–88*, Colchester Archaeological Report 9.

Cruwys, Elizabeth (1989) 'Tooth wear and the archaeologist: the role of human tooth wear in archaeological research', in Charlotte A. Roberts, Frances Lee and John Bintliff (eds) *Burial Archaeology Current Research,*

Methods and Developments, British Archaeological Reports – British Series 211, 151–61.

Cullum, Patricia H. (1994) 'Leper-houses and leprosy during the medieval period', *Archaeology of York (York Archaeological Trust) Interim* 19 (2): 24–31.

—— and Goldberg, P. J. P. (1993) 'Charitable provision in late medieval York: "To the praise of God and the use of the poor" ', *Northern History* XXIX: 24–39.

Dahmus, Joseph (1966) *William Courtenay, Archbishop of Canterbury, 1381–1396*, London: Pennsylvania State University Press.

Daniell, Christopher (1994) 'Traders and skeletons', *The Archaeology of York (York Archaeological Trust) Interim* 20 (1): 9–12.

Daniell, David J. (1994) *William Tyndale: A Biography*, London: Yale University Press.

Davis, F. N. (ed.) (1968) *The Register of John Pecham, Archbishop of Canterbury 1279–1292*, vol. I, The Canterbury and York Society 64.

D'Avray David L. (1994) *Death and the Prince: Memorial Preaching before 1350*, Oxford: Clarendon Press.

Dawes, Jean D. and Magilton, John R. (1980) *The Cemetery of St Helen-on-the-Walls, Aldwark, The Archaeology of York: The Medieval Cemeteries* 12/1, York: Council for British Archaeology.

Denholm-Young, N. (1957) *The Life of Edward the Second by the So-Called Monk of Malmesbury*, London: Thomas Nelson.

Denison, Simon (1994a) 'Floral tributes "go back to Bronze Age" ', *British Archaeological News* 17: 3.

—— (1994b) 'Stomach bug found in Lindow man's gut', *British Archaeological News* 18: 3.

—— (1995a) 'Brains found in medieval skulls', *British Archaeology* 1: 4.

—— (1995b) 'Welsh monastery found to have Roman origins', *British Archaeology* 2: 4.

Dent, J. S. (1983) 'Weapons, wounds and war in the Iron Age', *Archaeological Journal* 140: 120–8.

Devlin, Mary Aquinas (1954) *The Sermons of Thomas Brinton, Bishop of Rochester (1373–1389)*, vol. 1, Camden Society Third Series LXXXV.

Dinn, Robert (1995) 'Death and rebirth in late medieval Bury St Edmunds', in Steven Bassett (ed.) *Death in Towns, Urban Responses to the Dying and the Dead, 100–1600*, Leicester: Leicester University Press.

Donatelli, Joseph M. P. (ed.) (1989) *Death and Liffe*, Speculum Anniversary Monographs 15.

Douie, Decima (ed.) (1969) 'The register of John Pecham, Archbishop of Canterbury 1279–1292 Vol II', *The Canterbury and York Society* 65.

Duffy, Eamon (1992) *The Stripping of the Altars*, London: Yale University Press.

Dugmore, C. W. (1958) *The Mass and the English Reformers*, London: Macmillan.

Dunstan, G. R. (ed.) (1963) *The Register of Edmund Lacy Bishop of Exeter, 1420–1455*, vol. I, The Canterbury and York Society 60.

—— (ed.) (1966) *The Register of Edmund Lacy Bishop of Exeter, 1420–1455*, vol. II, The Canterbury and York Society 61.

—— (ed.) (1967) *The Register of Edmund Lacy Bishop of Exeter, 1420–1455,* vol. III, The Canterbury and York Society 62.

—— (ed.) (1971) *The Register of Edmund Lacy Bishop of Exeter, 1420–1455,* vol. IV, The Canterbury and York Society 63.

Durandus, Guillelmus (1671) *Tractatus de Modo Generalis Concilii Celebrandi,* Paris.

Dyer, Christopher (1980) *Lords and Peasants in a Changing Society: The Estates of the Bishopric of Worcester 680–1540,* Cambridge: Cambridge University Press.

—— (1987) 'The rise and fall of a medieval village: Little Aston (in Aston Blank), Gloucestershire', *Transactions of the Bristol and Gloucestershire Archaeological Society* 105: 165–82.

Easting, Robert (ed.) (1991) *St Patrick's Purgatory,* Early English Text Society Original Series 298.

Ellis, Henry (ed.) (1844) *Three Books of Polydore Vergil's English History, Comprising the Reigns of Henry VI, Edward IV and Richard III,* Cambden Society 29.

Erbe, Theodor (ed.) (1905) *Mirk's* Festial, Early English Text Society Extra Series 96.

Every, George (1978) *The Mass,* Dublin: Gill and Macmillan.

Farley, Michael and Manchester, Keith (1989) 'The cemetery of the leper hospital of St Margaret, High Wycombe, Buckinghamshire', *Medieval Archaeology* XXXIII: 82–9.

Fiero, Gloria K. (1984) 'Death ritual in fifteenth-century manuscript illumination', *Journal of Medieval History* 10: 271–94.

Fleming, Robin (1993) 'Rural elites and urban communities in late Saxon England', *Past and Present* 141: 3–37.

Freke, David (1988) 'Peel Castle', *Current Archaeology* 110: 92–7.

Frith, Brian (1990) 'Some aspects of the history of medicine in Gloucestershire, 1500–1800', *Transactions of the Bristol and Gloucestershire Archaeological Society* 108: 5–16.

Furnivall, Frederick J. (1882) *The Fifty Earliest English Wills in the Court of Probate, London,* The Early English Text Society Original Series 78.

Garland, A. N. (1989) 'The taphonomy of inhumation burials', in Charlotte A. Roberts, Frances Lee and John Bintliff (eds) *Burial Archaeology Current Research, Methods and Developments.* British Archaeological Reports – British Series 211, 15–37.

Garmonsway, G. N. (1982) *The Anglo-Saxon Chronicle,* London: Everyman.

Gasquet, F. A. (1907) *Parish Life in Mediaeval England,* London: Methuen.

Geary, Patrick J. (1994) *Living with the Dead in the Middle Ages,* Ithaca: Cornell University Press.

Gilchrist, Roberta (1995) 'Christian bodies and souls: the archaeology of life and death in later medieval hospitals', in Steven Bassett (ed.) *Death in Towns: Urban Responses to the Dying and the Dead, 100–1600,* Leicester: Leicester University Press.

Gill, A. R. (1936) 'Heart burials', *Proceedings of the Yorkshire Architectural and York Archaeological Society* II (4): 3–18.

Gittings, Clare (1995) *Death, Burial and the Individual in Early Modern England,* London: Routledge.

—— (1992) 'Urban funerals in late medieval and Reformation England', in Steven Bassett (ed.) *Death in Towns: Urban Responses to the Dying and the Dead, 100–1600,* Leicester: Leicester University Press.

Goldberg, P. J. P. (1988) 'Mortality and economic change in the diocese of York, 1390–1514', *Northern History* XXIV: 38–55.

Golding, Brian (1985) 'Burials and benefactions: an aspect of monastic patronage in thirteenth-century England', in W. M. Ormrod (ed.) *Symposium on England in the Thirteenth Century: Harlaxton Conference Proceedings,* Nottingham: University of Nottingham.

Goodall, I. H. and Christie, P. M. (1980) 'Lead and pewter objects', in Patricia M. Christie and J. G. Coad *Excavations at Denny Abbey, Archaeological Journal* 137: 138–279.

Gottfried, Robert S. (1978) *Epidemic Disease in Fifteenth Century England: The Medical Response and the Demographic Consequences,* Leicester: Leicester University Press.

—— (1986) *The Black Death,* London: Macmillan.

Graham, Rose (1929) 'The Great Schism and the English monasteries of the Cistercian order', *English Historical Review* 173: 373–87.

Grauer, Anne L. (1991) 'Patterns of life and death: the paleodemography of medieval York', in Helen Bush and Marek Zvelebil (eds) *Health in Past Societies: Biocultural Interpretations of Human Skeletal Remains in Archaeological Contexts,* British Archaeological Reports – International Series 567, 57–80.

Haines, Roy Martin (1986) *Archbishop John Stratford: Political Revolutionary and Champion of the Liberties of the English Church ca. 1275/80–1348,* Toronto Pontifical Institute of Mediaeval Studies, Studies and Texts 76.

Hallam, Elizabeth M. (1982) 'Royal burial and the cult of kingship in France and England, 1060–1330', *Journal of Medieval History* 8: 359–80.

—— (ed.) 1987 *Chronicles of the Age of Chivalry,* London: Book Club Associates.

Hamerow, Helena (1993) 'An Anglo-Saxon cemetery near West Hendred, Oxon', in William Filmer-Sankey (ed.) *Anglo-Saxon Studies in History and Archaeology* 6: 113–24.

Hamilton, Bernard (1986) *Religion in the Medieval West,* London: Arnold.

Hanham, A. (ed.) (1970) *Churchwardens' Accounts of Ashburton 1479–1580,* Devon and Cornwall Record Society New Series XV.

—— (1975) *Richard III and His Early Historians 1483–1535,* Oxford: Oxford University Press.

Harding, Vanessa (1992) 'Burial choice and burial location in later medieval London', in Steven Bassett (ed.) *Death in Towns: Urban Responses to the Dying and the Dead, 100–1600,* Leicester: Leicester University Press.

Harman, Mary (1985) 'The human remains', in George Lambrick (ed.) *Further Excavations on the Second Site of the Dominican Priory, Oxford,* Oxoniensia L: 131–208.

Harrison, F. (1952) *Life in a Medieval College: the Story of the Vicars-Choral of York Minster,* London: John Murray.

Harthan, John (1978) *Books of Hours* London: Thames & Hudson.

Harvey, Anthony and Mortimer, Richard (eds) (1994) *The Funeral Effigies of Westminster Abbey*, Woodbridge: Boydell Press.

Harvey, Barbara (1993) *Living and Dying in England 1100–1540: The Monastic Experience*, Oxford: Oxford University Press.

Hassall, T. G. (1971) 'Excavations at Oxford Castle', *Oxoniensia* XLI: 232–308.

Hatcher, John (1977) *Plague, Population and the English Economy 1348–1540*, London: Macmillan.

Hawkins, Duncan (1990) 'The Black Death and the new London cemeteries of 1348', *Antiquity* 64: 637–42.

Heath, Peter (1969) *The English Parish Clergy on the Eve of the Reformation*, London: Alan Sutton.

—— (1984) 'Urban piety in the later Middle Ages: the evidence of Hull wills', in Barrie Dobson (ed.) *The Church, Politics and Patronage in the Fifteenth Century*, Gloucester: Alan Sutton.

Henderson, Janet (1989) 'Pagan Saxon Cemeteries: A Study in the Problems of Sexing by Grave Goods and Bones', in Charlotte A. Roberts, Frances Lee and John Bintliff (eds) *Burial Archaeology Current Research, Methods and Developments*, British Archaeological Reports – British Series 211 77–84.

Henry, Avril (1985) *The Pilgrimage of the Lyfe of Manhode*, Early English Text Society, Original Series 288.

Hibbert, Christopher (1964) *Agincourt*, London: Pan.

Higgins, Valerie (1989) 'A model for assessing health patterns from skeletal remains', in Charlotte A. Roberts, Frances Lee and John Bintliff (eds) *Burial Archaeology Current Research, Methods and Developments*, British Archaeological Reports – British Series 211, 175–204.

Hill, Peter (1988) 'Whithorn', *Current Archaeology* 110: 85–91.

Hills, Catherine (1989) 'Spong Hill Anglo-Saxon cemetery', in Charlotte A. Roberts, Frances Lee and John Bintliff (eds) *Burial Archaeology Current Research, Methods and Developments*, British Archaeological Reports – British Series 211, 237–40.

Hillson, S. (1989) 'Teeth: some current developments in research', in Charlotte A. Roberts, Frances Lee and John Bintliff (eds) *Burial Archaeology Current Research, Methods and Developments*, British Archaeological Reports – British Series 211, 129–49.

Hirst, Susan M. (1993) 'Death and the archaeologist', in Martin Carver (ed.) *In Search of Cult: Archaeological Investigations in Honour of Philip Rahtz*, Woodbridge: Boydell Press.

Hitchcock, Elsie Vaughan (1921) *The Donet of Reginald Pecock*, Early English Text Society Original Series 156.

Hodder, M. A. (1991) *Excavations at Sandwell Priory and Hall 1982–88*, South Staffordshire Archaeological and Historical Society XXXI.

Hodder, M. A. (1993) 'Sandwell Priory', *Current Archaeology* 113: 187–92.

Horrox, Rosemary (trans. and ed.) (1994) *The Black Death*, Manchester Medieval Sources Series, Manchester: Manchester University Press.

Howard, Maurice (1987) *The Early Tudor Country House Architecture and Politics 1490–1550*, London: George Philip.

—— (1995) *The Tudor Image*, London: The Tate Gallery.

—— and Llewellyn, Nigel (1989) 'Painting and imagery', in Boris Ford (ed.) *The Cambridge Guide to the Arts: 3 Renaissance and Reformation*, Cambridge: Cambridge University Press.

Hughes, A. (1982) *Medieval Manuscripts for Mass and Office, A Guide to their Organisation and Terminology*, Toronto: Toronto University Press.

Hughes, J. (1988) *Pastors and Visionaries: Religion and Secular Life in Late Medieval Yorkshire*, Woodbridge: Boydell Press.

Huizinga, J. (1972) *The Waning of the Middle Ages*, Harmondsworth: Penguin.

Hutchinson, Carole (1991) 'Two Grandmontine priories: Pinel and Craswell', *Current Archaeology* 126: 274–9.

Jackson, Reg (1995) 'Rescuing Bristol's medieval past', *Rescue News* 66, 1–2.

JHS (1872) 'Tomb of King Henry IV in Canterbury Cathedral', *Archaeologia Cantiana* VIII: 294–9.

Jones, Nigel (1988) 'Capel Maelog', *Current Archaeology* 108: 26–9.

Jones, R. (1989) 'Cultural aspects of burial archaeology', in Charlotte A. Roberts, Frances Lee and John Bintliff (eds) *Burial Archaeology Current Research, Methods and Developments*, British Archaeological Reports – British Series 211, 284–5.

Jones, Peter Murray (1984) *Medieval Medical Miniatures*, London: British Library.

Jones, W. H. Rich (ed.) (1883) *The Register of S. Osmund*, vol. 1, Rolls Series.

Joyce, J. G. (1870) 'On the opening of a tomb in Winchester Cathedral reputed to be that of William Rufus', *Archaeologia* 42: 309–21.

Kantorowicz, Ernst H. (1985) *The King's Two Bodies: A Study in Medieval Political Theory*, Princeton: Princeton University Press.

Kendall, Giles (1982) 'A study of grave orientation in several Roman and post-Roman cemeteries from southern Britain', *Archaeological Journal* 139: 101–23.

Kenward, H. (1989) 'Inhumation insects: myths and maggots', in Charlotte A. Roberts, Frances Lee and John Bintliff (eds) *Burial Archaeology Current Research, Methods and Developments*, British Archaeological Reports – British Series 211, 285–6.

Key, C. A., Aiello, L. C. and Molleson, T. (1994) 'Cranial suture closure and its implications for age estimation', *International Journal of Osteoarchaeology* 4 (3): 193–208.

King, Edward (1979) *England 1175–1425*, London: Routledge.

King, Pamela (1984) 'The cadaver tomb in the late fifteenth century: some indications of a Lancastrian connection', in James H. M. Taylor (ed.) *Dies Illa, Death in the Middle Ages*, Liverpool: Francis Cairns.

Kingsford, Charles Lethbridge (1919a) *The Stonor Letters and Papers 1290–1483*, vol. I, Cambden Third Series XXIX.

—— (1919b) *The Stonor Letters and Papers 1290–1483*, vol. II, Cambden Third Series XXIX.

Kipling, Gordon (1990) *The Receyt of the Ladie Katheryne*, Early English Text Society, Original Series 90.

Kitchin, George William (1894) 'The burial-place of the Slavonians in North Stoneham church, Hants', *Archaeologia*, Second Series 54: 131–8.

Kjølbye-Biddle, Birthe (1975) 'A cathedral cemetery: problems in excavation and interpretation', *World Archaeology* 7 (1): 87–107.

—— (1995) 'Dispersal or concentration: the disposal of the Winchester dead over 2000 years', in Steven Bassett (ed.) *Death in Towns: Urban Responses to the Dying and the Dead, 100–1600*, Leicester: Leicester University Press.

Klemperer, W. D. (1992) 'The study of burials at Hulton Abbey', *Death and Burial*, Pre-printed papers of a conference on medieval archaeology in Europe 21–24 September 1992 at York 4, 85–91.

Kreider, Alan (1979) *English Chantries, the Road to Dissolution*, London: Harvard University Press.

Lambert, Malcolm (1992) *Medieval Heresy*, Oxford: Blackwell.

Lambrick, George (ed.) (1985) *Further Excavations on the Second Site of the Dominican Priory, Oxford*, Oxoniensia L: 131–208.

Lawson, Sarah (trans.) (1985) *Christine De Pisan: The Treasure of the City of Ladies or The Book of the Three Virtues*, Harmondsworth: Penguin.

Le Goff, Jacques (1984) *The Birth of Purgatory*, trans. A. Goldhammer, London: Scolar Press.

Leach, Arthur Francis (1898) *Memorials of Beverley Minster: The Chapter Act Book of the Collegiate Church of S. John of Beverley A.D. 1286–1347*, vol. I, Surtees Society 98.

Leach, Peter (ed.) (1984) *The Archaeology of Taunton Excavations and Fieldwork to 1980*, Western Archaeological Trust Excavation Monograph 8.

Leadman, I. S. and Baldwin, J. F. (1918) *Select Cases from the King's Council 1243–1482*, Selden Society 35.

Lewis, C. S. (1964) *The Discarded Image*, Cambridge: Cambridge University Press.

Lewis, N. B. (1937) 'The anniversary service for Blanche, Duchess of Lancaster, 12 September 1374', *The Bulletin of the John Ryland's Library* 21: 176–92.

Lilley, Jane M., Stroud, G., Brothwell, D. R. and Williamson M. H. (1994) *The Jewish Burial Ground at Jewbury, The Medieval Cemeteries: The Archaeology of York 12/3*, York: The Council for British Archaeology.

Litten, Julian (1991) *The English Way of Death*, London: Robert Hale.

Littlehales, Henry (ed.) (1895) *The Prymer or Lay Folks' Prayer Book*, Early English Text Society, Original Series 105.

—— (1905) *The Medieval Records of a London City Church (St Mary at Hill) A.D. 1420–1559*, Early English Text Society, Original Series 128.

Litzenberger, Caroline (1993) 'Local responses to changes in religious policy based on evidence from Gloucestershire wills (1540–1580)', *Continuity and Change* 8: 417–39.

Liversidge, H. M. (1994) 'Accuracy of age estimation from developing teeth of a population of known age (0–5.4 years)', *International Journal of Osteoarchaeology* 4 (1): 31–7.

Llewellyn, Nigel (1992) *The Art of Death*, London: The Victoria and Albert Museum.

Loades, David M. (1994) 'Rites of passage and the prayer books of 1549 and 1552', *Studies in Church History (Prophecy and Eschatology)* 10: 205–15.

Lockyer, Roger (ed.) (1962) *Thomas Wolsey, Late Cardinal, His Life and Death Written by George Cavendish His Gentleman-Usher,* London: The Folio Society.

Logan, F. Donald (1968) *Excommunication and the Secular Arm in Medieval England: A Study in Legal Procedure from the Thirteenth to the Sixteenth Century,* Toronto: Pontifical Institute of Mediaeval Studies.

Lomas, Richard (1989) 'The Black Death in county Durham', *Journal of Medieval History* 15: 127–40.

Lubin, Helen (1990) *The Worcester Pilgrim,* Worcester Cathedral Publications 1.

Lucy, Sam (1992) 'The significance of mortuary ritual in the political manipulation of the landscape', *Archaeological Review from Cambridge ('In the Midst of Life')* 11 (1): 93–105.

Luttrell, Anthony (1991) 'The two knights', in Siegrid Dill, Anthony Luttrell and Maurice Keen (eds) *Faithful unto Death: The Tomb Slab of Sir William Neville and Sir John Clanvowe, Constantinople 1391, Antiquaries Journal* 71: 174–90.

McCarthy, M. R. (1990) *A Roman, Anglian and Medieval Site at Blackfriar's Street, Carlisle: Excavations 1977–9,* Cumberland and Westmorland Antiquarian and Archaeological Society Research Series 4.

Maclure, Millar (1958) *The Paul's Cross Sermons, 1534–1642,* Toronto: Toronto University Press.

MacCraken, Henry Noble (1933) *The Minor Poems of John Lydate,* Part II: *Secular Poems,* Early English Text Society, Original Series CXCII.

McDannell, Colleen and Lang, Bernhard (1988) *Heaven: A History,* London: Yale University Press.

MacDonald, M. and Murphy, T. R. (1990) *Sleepless Souls: Suicide in Early Modern England,* Oxford: Oxford University Press.

McGuire, Brian Patrick (1989) 'Purgatory, the community of saints, and medieval change', *Viator* 20: 61–84.

McKinley, Jacqueline I. (1987) 'Burial 33', in Andrew Rogerson, Steven J. Ashley, Philip Williams and Andrew Harris (eds) *Three Norman Churches in Norfolk,* East Anglian Archaeology Report no. 32.

—— (1989) 'Spong Hill Anglo-Saxon cremation cemetery', in Charlotte A. Roberts, Frances Lee and John Bintliff (eds) *Burial Archaeology Current Research, Methods and Developments,* British Archaeological Reports British Series 211, 241–8.

McLaughlin, Megan (1991) 'Communion with the dead', *Journal of Medieval History* 17: 23–4.

Macquoid, Percy (1966) 'The home', in Sidney Lee and C. T. Onions (eds) *Shakespeare's England* II, Oxford: Clarendon Press.

McRee, Ben R. (1992) 'Religious gilds and civic order: the case of Norwich in the late Middle Ages', *Speculum* 67: 68–97.

Maddern, Philippa C. (1992) *Violence and Social Order, East Anglia 1422–1442,* Oxford: Oxford University Press.

—— (1995) 'Friends of the dead: executors, wills and family strategy in fifteenth-century Norfolk', in Rowen E. Archer and Simon Walker (eds) *Rulers and Ruled in Late Medieval England*, London: The Hambledon Press.

Madsen, Per Kristian (1994) 'Papal lead seals – an object of pious use in the Middle Ages', *Marsk og geest* 7: 15–25.

Magilton, John (1980) *The Church of St Helen-on-the-Walls, Aldwark, The Archaeology of York 10/1*, York: Council for British Archaeology.

—— and Lee, Frances (1989) 'The leper hospital of St James and St Mary Magdalene, Chichester', in Charlotte A. Roberts, Frances Lee and John Bintliff (eds) *Burial Archaeology Current Research, Methods and Developments*, British Archaeological Reports – British Series 211, 249–65.

Malory, Sir Thomas (1995) *The Death of King Arthur*, ed. J. Cowen, Harmondsworth: Penguin.

Marks, Richard (1984) 'The Howard Tombs at Thetford and Framlingham: new discoveries', *Archaeological Journal* 141: 252–68.

Marshall, Mary H. (1972) 'Aesthetic values of liturgical drama', in Jerome Taylor and Alan H. Nelson (eds) *Medieval English Drama Essays Critical and Contextual*, London: University of Chicago Press.

Martindale, Andrew (1992) 'Patrons and minders: the intrusion of the secular into sacred spaces in the late Middle Ages', *Studies in Church History (Christianity and the Arts)* 28: 143–79.

Mayor, K. (ed.) (1950) *Acta Stephani Langton . . . 1207–1228*, Canterbury and York Society 50.

Mayr-Harting, H. M. R. E. (1975) 'Functions of a twelfth-century recluse', *History* 60: 337–52.

Mays, Simon (1989) 'Human bone strontium analysis in the investigation of palaeodiets: a case study from a British Anglo-Saxon site', in Charlotte A. Roberts, Frances Lee and John Bintliff (eds) *Burial Archaeology Current Research, Methods and Developments*, British Archaeological Reports – British Series 211, 215–33.

—— (1995) 'Killing the unwanted child', *British Archaeology* 2: 8–9.

Meech, Sanford Brown and Allen, Hope Emily (1961 reprint) *the Book of Margery Kempe*, The Early English Text Society, 212.

Mellor, Jean E. and Pearce, T. (1981) *The Austin Friars, Leicester*, Council for British Archaeology Research Report 35.

Menache, Sophia (1990) *Vox Dei, Communication in the Middle Ages*, Oxford: Oxford University Press.

Merrifield, Ralph (1987) *The Archaeology of Ritual and Magic*, London: Book Club Associates.

Migne, J.-P. (ed.) (1853) 'Anselm: Admonitio Morienti', in *Patrologia Latina* 158: 686–7.

Minois, Georges (1989) *History of Old Age*, trans. Sarah Hanbury Tenison, Oxford: Polity Press.

Mizoguchi, Koji (1992) 'A historiography of a linear barrow cemetery: a structurationist's point of view', *Archaeological Review from Cambridge ('In the Midst of Life')* 11 (1): 39–50.

Moffat, Douglas (ed.) (1987) *The Soul's Address to the Body: The Worcester Fragments*, Medieval Texts and Studies 1.

Molleson, Theya and Cox, Margaret, with Waldron, H. A. and Whittaker

D. K. (1993) *The Spitalfields Project*, Volume 2: *The Anthropology: The Middling Sort*, Council for British Archaeology Research Report 86.

More, Thomas (1557) *Supplication of Souls*, London.

Morris, John (1980) *Nennius: British History and the Welsh Annals*, London: Phillimore.

Morris, Richard (1989) *Churches in the Landscape*, London: Dent.

—— (1994) 'Examine the dead gently', *British Archaeological News* 17: 9.

Musty, John (1995) 'Science diary', *Current Archaeology* 143: 433–5.

Muthesius, Anna Maria (1982) 'The silks from the tomb', in Neil Stratford, Pamela Tudor-Craig and Anna Maria Muthesius (eds) *Archbishop Hubert Walter's Tomb and Its Furnishings, Medieval Art and Architecture at Canterbury before 1220: British Archaeological Association Conference Transactions* V: 80–7.

Myers A. R. (1969) *English Historical Documents IV 1327–1485*, London: Eyre & Spottiswoode.

Mytum, Harold (1993) 'Kellington Church', *Current Archaeology* 133: 15–17.

—— (1994) 'Parish and people: excavations at Kellington Church', *Medieval Life* 1: 19–22.

Neale, John Mason and Webb, Benjamin (1843) *The Symbolism of Churches and Church Ornaments: A translation of the First Book of the Rationale Divinorum Officiorum, Written by William Durandus*, Leeds: T. W. Green.

Newman, Rachel (1989) 'Dacre', *Current Archaeology* 114: 233–5.

Niblett, Rosalind (1990) 'Verulamium', *Current Archaeology* 120: 410–17.

Nicolas, Harris (1972) *Privy Purse Expenses of Elizabeth of York: Wardrobe Accounts of Edward the Fourth* (Reprinted from the 1830 original), London: Muller.

Norris, Malcolm (1995) 'Later medieval monumental brasses: an urban funerary industry and its representation of death', in Steven Bassett (ed.) *Death in Towns: Urban Responses to the Dying and the Dead, 100–1600*, Leicester: Leicester University Press.

O'Connor, Mary Catherine (1966) *The Art of Dying Well: The Development of the Ars Moriendi*, New York: Columbia University Press.

O'Connor, Sonia (1994) 'Paved with good intentions', *Archaeology in York (York Archaeological Trust) Interim* 19 (3): 15–20.

O'Connor, T. P. (1993) 'The human skeletal material', in Warwick Rodwell and Kirsty Rodwell (eds) *Rivenhall: Investigations of a Roman Villa, Church and Village, 1950–77*, Council of British Archaeology Research Report 80: 96–102.

Olivier, Laurent (1992) 'The tomb of Hochdorf (Baden-Wurttemberg): some comments on the nature of archaeological funerary material', *'In the Midst of Life': Archaeological Review from Cambridge* 11 (1): 51–64.

Orme, Nicholas (1986) *Exeter Cathedral as It Was 1050–1550*, Exeter: Devon Books.

Ormrod, Mark and Lindley, Phillip (1996) *The Black Death in England*, Stamford: Paul Watkins.

Osmund, Rosalie (1990) *Mutual Accusation: Seventeenth-Century Body and Soul Dialogues in Their Literary and Theological Context*, London: University of Toronto Press.

Ottaway, Patrick (1982) 'A burial from the south aisle of Winchester Cathedral', *Archaeological Journal* 139: 124–37.

Owen, Dorothy M. (1971) *Church and Society in Medieval Lincolnshire,* History of Lincolnshire V.

—— (1984) *The Making of King's Lynn: A Documentary Survey,* British Academy Records of Social and Economic History 3.

Owst, G. R. (1926) *Preaching in Medieval England,* Cambridge: Cambridge University Press.

—— (1933) *Literature and Pulpit in Medieval England,* Cambridge: Cambridge University Press.

Page-Phillips, John (1970) *Children on Brasses,* London: George Allen & Unwin.

Palliser, David M. (1979) *Tudor York,* Oxford: Oxford University Press.

—— (1980) 'Location and history', in John R. Magilton (ed.) *The Church of St Helen-on-the-Walls, Aldwark,* York: Council for British Archaeology.

Panter, Ian (1994) 'Well-travelled coffins', *Archaeology in York Interim (York Archaeological Trust) Interim* 19 (3): 26–35.

Pavlac, B. A. (1991) 'Excommunication and territorial politics in high medieval Trier', *Church History* 60: 20–36.

Paxton, Frederick S. (1990) *Christianizing Death, The Creation of a Ritual Process in Early Medieval Europe,* London: Cornell University Press.

Payne, M. T. W. and Payne, J. E. (1994) 'The wall inscriptions of Gloucester Cathedral Chapter House and the De Chaworths of Kempsford', *Transactions of the Bristol and Gloucestershire Archaeological Society* CXII: 87–104.

Peacock, Edward (1902) *Instructions for Parish Priests, by John Myrc,* Early English Text Society, Original Series 31.

Phipps, Colin (1985) 'Romuald – model hermit: eremitical theory in Saint Peter Damian's *Vita Beati Romualdi* chapters 16–27', *Studies in Church History* 22: 65–78.

Platt, Colin (1978) *Medieval England, a Social History and Archaeology from the Conquest to AD 1600,* London: Routledge & Kegan Paul.

Platt, Colin (1996) *King Death: the Black Death and Its Aftermath in Late-Medieval England,* London: UCL Press.

Potter, Robert A. (1975) *The English Morality Play: Origins, History and Influence of a Dramatic Tradition,* London: Routledge & Kegan Paul.

—— (1984) '3. Morality plays and interludes: forgiveness as theatre (1975)' in Peter Happé (ed.) *Medieval English Drama: A Casebook,* London: Macmillan.

Powell, Susan and Fletcher, Alan J. (1981) ' "In Die Sepulture seu Trigintali": the late medieval funeral and memorial sermon', *Leeds Studies in English,* New Series XII: 195–228.

Powicke, F. M. and Cheney C. R. (eds) (1964) *Councils and Their Synods Relating to the English Church A.D. 1205–1313,* Oxford: Oxford University Press.

Prestwich, Michael (1985) 'The piety of Edward I', in W. M. Ormrod (ed.) *Symposium on England in the Thirteenth Century: Harlaxton Conference Proceedings,* Nottingham: University of Nottingham.

—— (1988) *Edward I,* London: Methuen.

Rahtz, Philip (1969) 'Upton, Glos 1964–1968', *Transactions of the Bristol and Gloucestershire Archaeological Society* 88: 74–126.

—— (1978) 'Grave orientation', *Archaeological Journal* 135: 1–14.

—— (1993) *Glastonbury*, London: Batsford.

—— and Watts, Lorna (eds) (1993) *The Trinitarian Order in England: Excavations at Thetford Priory*, British Archaeological Reports 226.

Raine, A. (1955) *Medieval York: A Topographical Survey Based on Original Sources*, London: John Murray.

Raine, James (1856) *The Obituary Roll of William Ebchester and John Burnby, Priors of Durham*, Surtees Society 31.

—— (ed.) (1863) *The Historians of the Church of York and Its Archbishops*, London: Longman.

Raine, James (ed.) (1879) *The Historians of the Church of York*, vol. 1, Rolls Series.

—— (ed.) (1884) *Testamenta Eboracensia: A Selection of Wills from the Registry at York V*, Surtees Society 79.

Ramm, Herman *et al.* (1971) 'The tombs of the Archbishops Walter de Grey (1216–1255) and Godfrey de Ludham (1258–65) in York Minster and their contents', *Archaeologia* 103: 101–48.

Rees, David (1985) *The Son of Prophecy: Henry Tudor's Road to Bosworth*, London: Black Raven Press.

Reinhard, J. (1941) 'Burning at the stake in medieval law and literature', *Speculum* 16 186–209.

Reyerson, Kathryn L. (1978) 'Changes in testamentary practice at Montpellier on the eve of the Black Death', *Church History* 47 (3), 253–69.

Richards, Julian D. (1992) *Viking Age England*, London: Batsford.

Richmond, Colin (1984) 'Religion and the fifteenth-century English gentleman', in Barrie Dobson (ed.) *The Church, Politics and Patronage in the Fifteenth Century*, Gloucester: Alan Sutton.

Riley, Athelstan (1908) *Pontifical Services*, vol. IV: *Illustrated from Woodcuts of the XVIth Century*, Alcuin Club Collections XII.

Riviere, Sue (1986) 'The excavation at Mitre Street', *Popular Archaeology* December 1985/January 1986: 37–41.

Robbins, Rossell Hope (1970) 'Signs of death in middle English', *Medieval Studies* XXXII: 282–98.

Robinson, John Martin (1982) *The Dukes of Norfolk: A Quincentennial History*, Oxford: Oxford University Press.

Rodwell, Warwick (1981) *The Archaeology of the English Church* London: Batsford.

—— and Rodwell, Kirsty (1977) *Historic Churches – A Wasting Asset*, Council for British Archaeology Research Report 19.

—— and (1993) *Rivenhall: Investigations of a Roman Villa, Church and Village, 1950–77*, Council of British Archaeology Research Report 80.

Rogers, Juliet (1984) 'Skeletons from the lay cemetery at Taunton Priory', in Peter Leach *et al.* (1984) *The Archaeology of Taunton Excavations and Fieldwork to 1980*, Western Archaeological Trust Excavation Monograph 8.

225

Rogers, Nicola (1993) *Anglian and Other Finds from Fishergate, The Archaeology of York 17/9*, York: Council for British Archaeology.

Rosenthal, Joel T. (1972) *The Purchase of Paradise*, London: Routledge & Kegan Paul.

Ross, John (1993) *The Register of John Kirkby I, Bishop of Carlisle*, Canterbury and York Society, 79.

Rosser, Gervase (1989) *Medieval Westminster 1200–1540*, Oxford: Clarendon Press.

—— (1991) 'Parochial conformity and voluntary religion in late-medieval England', *Transactions of the Royal Historical Society*, 6th Series, 1: 173–89.

Rowell, Geoffrey (1977) *The Liturgy of Christian Burial*, London: SPCK.

Rubin, M. (1987) *Charity and Community in Medieval Cambridge*, Cambridge: Cambridge University Press.

—— 1992 *Corpus Christi: The Eucharist in Late Medieval Culture*, Cambridge: Cambridge University Press.

Ryan, William Granger (ed. and trans.) (1993a) *Jacobus de Voragine: The Golden Legend, Readings on the Saints*, I Princeton: Princeton University Press.

—— (1993b) *Jacobus de Voragine, The Golden Legend, Readings on the Saints II*, Princeton: Princeton University Press.

Ryder, Peter (1991) *Medieval Cross Slab Grave Covers in West Yorkshire, West Yorkshire Archaeology Handbooks*, Wakefield: West Yorkshire Archaeology Service.

Rye, W. (1887–8) 'The order of funerals, ringings etc. at Norwich', *The East Anglian, or Notes and Queries*, New Series, 2: 389–92.

St John Hope, W. H. (1890) 'On the sculptured alabaster tablets called Saint John's Heads', *Archaeologia* 52: 703–8.

—— (1907) 'On the funeral effigies of the kings and queens of England', *Archaeologia* 60: 517–70.

—— (1915) 'The funeral monument, and Chantry Chapel of King Henry the Fifth', *Archaeologia* 65: 129–86.

Scott, Eleanor (1992) 'Images and contexts of infants and infant burials: some thoughts on some cross-cultural evidence', *Archaeological Review from Cambridge ('In the Midst of Life')* 11 (1): 77–92.

Scott, H. Von E. and Bland, C. C. Swinton (eds) (1929) *Caesarius of Heisterbach: The Dialogue of Miracles*, London: Routledge.

Scribner, Robert W. (1993) 'The Reformation, popular magic, and the "Disenchantment of the World"', *Journal of Interdisciplinary History* XXIII (3): 475–94.

Sekules, Veronica (1986) 'The Tomb of Christ at Lincoln and the development of the Sacrament Shrine: Easter Sepulchres reconsidered', *Medieval Art and Architecture of Lincoln Cathedral*, British Archaeological Association VIII, 118–31.

Shaw, M. (1984) *Joinville and Villehardouin: Chronicles of the Crusades*, Harmondsworth: Penguin.

Sheehan, Michael M. (1988) 'English wills and the records of the ecclesiastical and civil jurisdictions', *Journal of Medieval History* 14: 3–12.

Shoesmith, R. (1980), *Hereford City Excavations 1: Excavations at Castle Green*, Council for British Archaeology Research Report 36.

Simmons, T. F. (ed.) (1879) *The Lay Folk's Mass Book*, Early English Text Society, Original Series 71.

Smith, Toulmin (1870) *English Gilds*, Early English Text Society, Original Series 40.

Southern, Richard (1954) *The Making of the Middle Ages*, London: Hutchinson.

—— (1979) *The Life of St Anselm, Archbishop of Canterbury by Eadmer*, Oxford: Oxford University Press.

Spence, T. F. and Moore, W. J. (1969) 'The infant burial', in Philip Rahtz 'Upton, Glos 1964–8', *Transactions of the Bristol and Gloucestershire Archaeological Society* 88: 123–4.

Spenser, Brian (1980) *Medieval Pilgrim Badges from Norfolk*, Norwich: Norwich Museums Service.

Stanley, Arthur Penrhyn (1869) *Historical Memorials of Westminster Abbey*, London: Murray.

Stenton, Doris Mary (ed.) (1937) *Rolls of the Justices in Eyre . . . Yorkshire in 3 Henry III (1218–1219)*, Selden Society 56.

Stevenson, Joseph (1991 reprint) *William of Malmesbury: A History of the Norman Kings 1066–1125*, Llanerch: Llanerch Press.

Stirland, Ann (1985) 'The human bones', in Brian Ayres (ed.) *Excavations Within the North-East Bailey of Norwich Castle*, East Anglian Archaeology Report 28, 47–62.

—— (1989) 'Physical anthropology: the basic bones', in Charlotte A. Roberts, Frances Lee and John Bintliff (eds) *Burial Archaeology Current Research, Methods and Developments*, British Archaeological Reports – British Series 211, 51–76.

Stone, Brian (1977) *The Owl and the Nightingale, Cleanness, St Erkenwald*, Harmondsworth: Penguin.

Stratford, Neil (1982) 'Notes on the metalwork from the tomb', in Neil Stratford, Pamela Tudor-Craig and Anna Maria Muthesius (eds) *Archbishop Hubert Walter's Tomb and Its Furnishings*, Medieval Art and Architecture at Canterbury before 1220: British Archaeological Association Conference Transactions V: 71–93.

Strocchia, Sharon T. (1992) *Death and Ritual in Renaissance Florence*, London: The Johns Hopkins University Press.

Stroud, Gillian (1987) 'The human bones', in Andrew Rogerson, Steven J. Ashley, Philip Williams and Andrew Harris (eds) *Three Norman Churches in Norfolk*, East Anglian Archaeology Report no. 32.

—— and Kemp, Richard L. (1993) *Cemeteries of the Church and Priory of St Andrew, Fishergate, The Archaeology of York, The Medieval Cemeteries 12*, York: Council for British Archaeology.

Stuart-Macadam, Patty (1986) 'Health and disease in the monks of Stratford Langthorne Abbey', *Essex Journal* 21: 67–71.

Sumption, Jonathan (1975) *Pilgrimage: An Image of Mediaeval Religion*, London: Faber & Faber.

Tanner, J. R. (1948) *Tudor Constitutional Documents 1485–1603*, Cambridge: Cambridge University Press.

Tanner, Norman P. (1984) *The Church in Late Medieval Norwich 1370–1532*, Toronto Pontifical Institute of Medieval Studies and Texts 66.

Tarlow, Sarah (1992) 'Each slow dusk a drawing-down of blinds', *Archaeological Review from Cambridge ('In the Midst of Life')* 11 (1): 125–40.

Taylor, Lou (1983) *Mourning Dress: A Costume and Social History,* London: Allen & Unwin.

Thompson, A. Hamilton (ed.) (1915) *Visitations of Religious Houses in the Diocese of Lincoln*, vol. I: *Registers of Richard Flemyng and William Gray 1420–1436*, Canterbury and York Society 17.

—— (1966) *The English Clergy and Their Organisation in the Late Middle Ages: The Ford Lectures for 1933*, Oxford: Clarendon Press.

Trevisa (1938) 'Bartholomew', in G. G. Coulton (ed.) *Social Life in Britain from the Conquest to the Reformation*, Cambridge: Cambridge University Press.

Tristram, Philippa (1976) *Figures of Life and Death in Medieval English Literature*, London: Paul Elek.

—— (1983) 'Strange images of death', *Leeds Studies in English*, New Series XIV: 196–211.

Tweddle, D. (1986) *Finds from Parliament Street and Other Sites in the City Centre, The Archaeology of York, The Small Finds 17/4*, York: Council for British Archaeology.

Tymms, Samuel (1850) *Wills and Inventories from the Registers of the Commissary of Bury St Edmunds*, Cambden Society XLIX.

Vincent, Nicholas (1993) 'The early years of Keynsham Abbey' *Transactions of the Bristol and Gloucestershire Archaeological Society* CXI: 95–113.

Vitz, Evelyn Birge (1992) 'Review of Annette Garnier, *Mutations temporelles et cheminement spirituel: analyse et commentaire du "Miracle de l'Emperis" de Gautier de Coici.* (Essais 11). Paris 1988', *Speculum* 67: 988–9.

Volvelle, Michel (1976) 'Les attitudes devant la mort: problèmes de méthode, approches, et lectures differentes', *Annales E. S. C* 31: 120–32.

—— (1983) *La mort et l'Occident de 1300 á nos jours*, Paris: Gallimard.

Waldron, T. (1989) 'Some epidemiological problems in palaeopathology', in Charlotte A. Roberts, Frances Lee and John Bintliff (eds) *Burial Archaeology Current Research, Methods and Developments*, British Archaeological Reports – British Series 211, 290–1.

Walter, H. (ed.) (1848) *William Tyndale: The Obedience of a Christian Man*, The Parker Society.

Ward, S. W. (1990) *Excavations at Chester: The Lesser Medieval Religious Houses, Sites Investigated 1964–1983*, Grosvenor Museum Archaeological Excavation and Survey Reports 6.

Warren, F. (ed.) and White B. (intro.) (1931) *The Dance of Death*, Early English Text Society, Original Series 181.

Watts, Lorna and Rahtz, Philip (1985) *Mary-Le-Port Bristol, Excavations 1962/3*, City of Bristol Museum and Art Gallery Monograph 7.

Welander, David (1991) *The History, Art and Architecture of Gloucester Cathedral*, Stroud: Sutton.

Wells, Calvin (1967) 'A leper cemetery at South Acre, Norfolk', *Medieval Archaeology* XI: 242–8.

—— (1982) 'The Human Bones – Summary' in J. P. Roberts with Malcolm Atkin (eds) *St Benedict's Church (Site 157N): Excavations in Norwich 1971–1978 Part I*, East Anglian Archaeology Report 15: 25–7.

—— (1988) 'Appendix 3: an early medieval case of death in childbirth' in William J. White *Skeletal Remains from the Cemetery of St Nicholas Shambles, City of London*, London: London and Middlesex Archaeological Society.

Wemple, Suzanne F. and Kaiser, Denise A. (1986) 'Death's dance of women', *Journal of Medieval History* 12: 333–43.

Wenzel, Siegfried (1989) *Fasciculus Morum: A Fourteenth-Century Preacher's Handbook*, London: Pennsylvania State University Press.

Westlake, H. F. (1919) *The Parish Gilds of Medieval England*, London: SPCK.

White, William J. (1988) *Skeletal Remains from the Cemetery of St Nicholas Shambles, City of London*, London: London and Middlesex Archaeological Society.

Wickham, Glynne (1987) *The Medieval Theatre*, Cambridge: Cambridge University Press.

Williams, S. A., O'Sullivan, E. and Curzon M. E. J. (1989) 'Dental caries pattern in the primary dentition among English children living between the pre-Roman and late medieval periods', in Charlotte A. Roberts, Frances Lee and John Bintliff (eds) *Burial Archaeology Current Research, Methods and Developments*, British Archaeological Reports – British Series 211, 292

Wise, Philip (1991) 'Wasperton', *Current Archaeology* 126: 256–9.

Wood, A. C. (ed.) (1956) *The Register of Simon Langham*, Canterbury and York Society 53.

Wood-Legh, K. L. (1956) *A Small Household of the XVth Century*, Manchester: Manchester University Press.

—— (1965) *Perpetual Chantries in Britain*, Cambridge: Cambridge University Press.

Woodruff, C. Eveleigh (1917) 'Some early visitation rolls preserved at Canterbury I', *Archaeologia Cantiana: Transactions of the Kent Archaeological Society* XXXII: 143–80.

—— (1918) 'Some early visitation rolls preserved at Canterbury II', *Archaeologia Cantiana* XXXIII: 71–90.

Woolf, Rosemary (1968) *The English Religious Lyric in the Middle Ages*, Oxford: Clarendon Press.

Wordsworth, C. and Littlehales, H. (1910), *The Old Service-Books of the English Church*, London: Methuen.

Wunderli, Richard and Broce, Gerald (1989) 'The final moment before death in early Modern England', *Sixteenth Century Journal* XX (2): 259–75.

Ziegler, Philip (1982) *The Black Death*, Harmondsworth: Penguin.

SUBJECT INDEX

Abraham's bosom 10, 176, 198
Acts of Exeter Cathedral 113 (*see also* statutes)
alms-giving 1
angels 27, 28, 40
anniversary services 13, 16–17, 50
Aries (sign of the Zodiac) 27
Ars Moriendi 37–8, 40, 54
ashes 30, 31, 32
aumbry 10

baptism 127–8, 155
bedesman 33
bederoll 17–19; types 17–18; writing of 18–19
bellman 53
bells 31, 44, 42–3 (*see also* bedesman, bellman)
Beowulf 77
Black Death 133, 143, 175, 185, 189–95; impact of 190–2, 194, 195; statistics 190–1
board of the dead 32
body: age, determining of 129, 132–4, 141; autolysis, 120; boiled 87, 122; brains 121; burnt 107, 150, 183; cremation 106; decomposition (archaeological 119–21; decomposition (literary) 70–1, 82–3; diagenesis 121; DNA analysis 136–7; dismemberment 122–3; eaten (animals) 107, 108; entrails 92; ethnic affinity 135, 204–5;

embalming 44, 120, 122; environmental influence 134, 136; exhumation 88, 91, 94, 95, 103, 106, 150, 183; facial modelling 137; genetic influence 134, 136, 204;
heart 87, 92; height 134–5; incomplete 123; movement of (after burial) 93–4; obesity 139; position 180; putrefaction 120; rotted 120; sex, determining of 129–32; sin deforms 204; stature 141; stuffed 122; survival 119–21; transportation of 88, 89, 194; two 188; viewed 42, 65; worms 83; *see also* pathology, burial
Book of Common Prayer 199
Books of Hours 4, 195
burial: arm position 118; authorisation 88–89; conflict 90–2; of ecclesiastics 97–8, 169–171, 173; fees 58–60; functional 199; head on pole 120; head niche 180; interdict against 103; Jewish 203–4; mortuary fee 60; non-burial 120; oak 108–9; of poor 58–60; payments 91; pilgrim 166–8; pot 109; practices x; preservation 119–121; priests (*see* ecclesiastics); in prone position 118, 149; reburial 88, 184; refusal of 103–4; royalty

230

INDEX OF PEOPLE
AND PLACES